T0259521

PHYSICAL SECURITY SYSTEMS HANDBOOK
The Design and Implementation of Electronic Security Systems

PHYSICAL SECURITY SYSTEMS HANDBOOK

SYSTEMS HANDBOOK

The Design and Implementation of Electronic Security Systems

Michael Khairallah, PSP

ELSEVIER

AMSTERDAM • BOSTON • HEIDELBERG • LONDON
NEW YORK • OXFORD • PARIS • SAN DIEGO
SAN FRANCISCO • SINGAPORE • SYDNEY • TOKYO
Butterworth-Heinemann is an imprint of Elsevier

Elsevier Butterworth-Heinemann
30 Corporate Drive, Suite 400, Burlington, MA 01803, USA
Linacre House, Jordan Hill, Oxford OX2 8DP, UK

∞ Recognizing the importance of preserving what has been written, Elsevier prints its
books on acid-free paper whenever possible.

Library of Congress Cataloging-in-Publication Data
Application submitted.

British Library Cataloguing-in-Publication Data
A catalogue record for this book is available from the British Library.

ISBN 13: 978-0-7506-7850-6
ISBN 10: 0-7506-7850-X

For information on all Elsevier Butterworth–Heinemann publications
visit our Web site at www.books.elsevier.com

Printed and bound in the United Kingdom

Transferred to Digital Print 2011

Table of Contents

Acknowledgments

There are many people I want to thank for the opportunity to write this book. They encouraged me and helped provide the opportunity and motivation to bring these thoughts to print. The list of supporters goes beyond the months of research, writing, and editing back over 25 years of customers, clients, and coworkers throughout the security industry. In their own way, each of them contributed to my education, and I will always be grateful for their praise, their criticism, and their suggestions.

But no one deserves my appreciation more than my wife Gail. Her constant unwavering support allowed me to do much of the hard work needed to understand how to do business in this industry. Regardless of the outcome of a bid or project, she was there to encourage me, celebrate the good times with me, and when times were not so good, remind me that there is always tomorrow. Gail deserves credit for any success this work may enjoy.

I am especially grateful to the members of ASIS International, Chapter 29, in New Orleans. I have been a member of the chapter my entire security career. To every member who ever said to me, "You should write a book about that...," I say, here it is. To all my fellow ASIS members, thank you for your support.

High praise is also due the membership of IAPSC (The International Association of Professional Security Consultants). After finishing the first draft, I asked the association members for their help and guidance in doing a peer review of the book. Their response was overwhelming. Their comments and critiques helped focus and fine-tune the work in a way that could never be done from a single perspective. These men and women helped me see what I took for granted, and they offered many useful new ways of communicating the right path to successful installations.

Special credit goes to these security professionals for their support and guidance during the peer review:

- Michael Brady, CPP, ABCP
- Ken Braunstein, MA
- Jim Broader, CPP, CFE, FACFE
- William Crews, CPP
- Mary Lynn Garcia
- Robert A. Gardner, CPP
- Harold C. Gillens, PSP, CHS-III
- Brian Gurin, PSP
- Freddie Lee, CFE, MA, PhD
- Ronald S. Libengood, CPP
- Steve Meyer
- John Sullivant, CPP, CHS-III [CMSGT, USAF RET]

This list would not be complete without thanking the editors at Butterworth-Heinemann for the faith in me and the potential of this work. This was my first book and they were taking a chance on its success. They deserve credit for having the vision to see the benefits of this work to the industry.

It is my fondest wish that security professionals everywhere embrace these techniques and that this book helps to bring much needed consistency to our industry.

Michael Khairallah, PSP

Introduction

1

WHAT IS THIS BOOK ABOUT?

This book is a comprehensive guide to identifying the man-made threats to an organization, determining the vulnerabilities of the organization to those threats, specifying security products to mitigate the threats and acquiring and implementing the recommended solutions. It represents the culmination of 25 years of experience in the design, installation, and project management of security system solutions.

The techniques in this book will help the security professional conduct a physical security audit to identify ways to mitigate identified threats and then specify a new security system or system addition to improve security conditions. The book also describes methods used in evaluating the survey data, proposing the recommended systems to company management, preparing a system bid, and managing the bid process. The book concludes with a description of project implementation and how to follow up the implementation to verify proper use.

The depth of detail in the book assumes the reader is a security professional and has some experience and the technical skill necessary to create a basic security system design. The book organizes the process and provides an overall structure for best practices in specifying system components and managing the acquisition and implementation process.

The main emphasis of this book is to provide the security professional with a guide for doing the right things at the right time throughout all phases of a physical security audit. It is an aid to planning and documenting the studies necessary to establish needs, and it outlines the tasks for acquisitions and implementation of systems to deal with threats. Even the experienced professional will find this book helpful in organizing the approach to security audit projects.

WHEN IS THIS BOOK MOST USEFUL?

This book is most useful when company management has recognized the need for improved security and requires a physical security audit to identify and mitigate threats. A physical security audit is just one component of a complete Risk Assessment. A Risk Assessment includes several disciplines and examines all elements of risk to the company's operation. Some additional areas of concern that are not covered in this book are:

- Data security
- Industrial espionage
- Relationships with local law enforcement
- Security protocol evaluations
- Disaster protocol evaluations
- Personnel assessments
- Building design and reinforcement measures
- Threats from internal sources, employees and service crews
- Terrorist threats

The most important milestone in beginning the physical security audit process is company management's recognition that the company needs security improvements. The security professional must help build "institutional will" to proceed with system design and evaluation. Throughout the process, management agreement must be part of implementing the new security system to provide funding and foster acceptance of procedural changes.

This book will provide clear and meaningful guidelines for determining threats, assessing vulnerabilities, selecting system components to accomplish security goals, choosing the appropriate vendor to supply components, and implementing those components into a cohesive effective security system.

WHY IS THIS BOOK IMPORTANT TO YOU?

This is a guide to planning a security system audit to help avoid making expensive mistakes. Security system acquisition requires considerable planning of system details, coordinating vendor activity and comprehensive and adequate documentation. The security professional must clearly communicate system objectives for the implementation to be a success. In most security systems, but especially in access controls systems, an incorrect diagnosis of a problem or the failure to document those findings properly can result in costly errors. By using the techniques in this book, the security professional will avoid many of the common mistakes experienced in security system implementations.

This book will also help establish acceptance standards for getting the job done. These standards will be useful for the company and for the vendors hired to perform the work. By providing standards in all security system projects, the company will save money and the project team will save time. Standards are essential for measuring vendor performance. Without appropriate standards, performance quality is just guesswork.

WHO SHOULD USE THIS BOOK?

Security system project managers will find this book most useful when confronted by a major project for the first time. This book will be an excellent guide to developing the security audit plan and strategy, performing the audit and conducting all the steps necessary to implement the recommendations of the audit. Even if the security system project manager has years of experience, this book will be useful in organizing the necessary steps—from identification to implementation.

Security directors who are not project managers will find this book especially useful. It will provide a step-by-step process for identifying threats and vulnerabilities, designing the right system to mitigate threats and implementing the solutions.

Using this book is not a substitute for the skills of a qualified security systems' consultant. The reader may find that the level of expertise needed to conduct the required surveys may not be within their experience. In these cases, this book will serve as a guide to working with a professional security systems' expert.

A good indication that a consultant is a qualified expert is the certification of "PSP" following their name. The ASIS International Review Board grants the PSP or Physical Security Professional designation and defines a PSP as:

> The Physical Security Professional (PSP) designation is evidence that an individual is "Board Certified in Physical Security." It is awarded based upon experience and passage of an examination that provides objective measure of an individual's broad-based knowledge and competency in physical security. Ongoing professional development is required in order to maintain the credential. The PSP is administered by ASIS International, the preeminent international organization for security professionals, with more than 33,000 members worldwide.

Additional information on the PSP designation can be found on the ASIS International website at *www.asisonline.org*. To find a qualified consultant, the reader is encouraged to contact the International Association of Professional Security Consultants (IAPSC). Their website can be found at *www.iapsc.org*.

Further, membership in IAPSC provides assurance of high ethical standards. The IAPSC requires a code of conduct for its members and states:

> This Code of Conduct and Ethics signifies a voluntary assumption by members of the obligation of self-discipline above and beyond the requirements of the law. Thus, it notifies the public that members intend to maintain a high level of ethics and professional service, and proclaims that, in return for the faith that the public places in them, the members accept the obligation to conduct their practices in a way that will be beneficial to society.

This code of conduct is supported by these guidelines:

A. General
1. Members will view and handle as confidential all information concerning the affairs of the client.
2. Members will not take personal, financial, or any other advantage of inside information gained by virtue of the consulting relationship.
3. Members will inform clients and prospective clients of any special relationship or circumstances that could be considered a conflict of interest.
4. Members will never charge more than a reasonable fee; and, whenever possible, the consultant will agree with the client in advance on the fee or basis for the fee.
5. Members will neither accept nor pay fees or commissions for client referrals.
6. Members will not accept fees, commissions or other valuable considerations from any individual or organization whose equipment, supplies or services they might or do recommend in the course of providing professional consulting services.
7. Members will only accept assignments for and render expert opinions on matters they are eminently qualified in and for.

B. Professional
1. Members will strive to advance and protect the standards of the security consulting profession as represented in this code of ethics.
2. Members recognize their responsibility to our profession to share with their colleagues the knowledge, methods and strategies they find effective in serving their clients.
3. Members will not use or reveal other consultant's proprietary data, procedures or strategies without permission unless same has been released, as such, for public (or all consultants) use.
4. Members will not accept an assignment for a client while another consultant is serving that client unless assured that any conflict is recognized by and has the consent of the client.

5. Members will not review the work of another consultant who is still engaged with the client, without such consultant's knowledge.
6. Members will strive to avoid any improprieties or the appearance of improprieties.
7. Membership in the IAPSC is forfeited upon conviction of any felony or misdemeanor involving moral turpitude.
8. Members will never misrepresent their qualifications, experience or professional standing to clients or prospective clients.

C. Forensic
1. Members' fees will never be contingent upon the outcome of a case.
2. Members, when testifying, will carefully avoid taking the position of an advocate or appearing to take such a position; for justice requires the professional expert witness to be neutral with no personal interest in the outcome of the case.
3. If, after reviewing a case, it is apparent that the expert witness cannot provide testimony or assistance helpful to the case, the consultant will make this known to the client. If he withdraws from or his services are discontinued by the case, he will not testify for the opposing side unless compelled to by subpoena.
4. The consultant will not sign written opinions or affidavits prepared by clients. Testimony or report preparation, including the preparation of oral reports, will not occur until the consultant has performed a thorough evaluation of the circumstances, evidence, scene or other pertinent materials or places as he deems necessary to render a learned opinion.

D. Enforcement
1. Upon a formal complaint issued against any member of this Association or other person indicating a violation of any section of this Code of Conduct and Ethics, the Ethics Committee will investigate the allegations and make a recommendation to the Board of Directors regarding any disciplinary action to be taken against the accused member. Discipline may range from a formal reprimand and warning to a temporary or permanent suspension from the Association upon the discretion of the Board of Directors.

By knowing the steps involved in a professional security assessment and properly managed project, the company manager can work more closely with the professional to achieve superior results.

BEING A CONSULTANT

The security professional may be an employee of the company in need of a new physical security system or professional consultant. The security professional may also be an experienced security manager performing work for the first time as a consultant.

Regardless of the role the security professional, a fiduciary responsibility exists between the security professional and the company. That relationship requires that the security professional act in the best interest of the company and tempers those actions with consideration for all concerned. A good business deal is one where all parties feel that they have benefited from the transaction.

A security consultant's obligation is to help the company do business with the security marketplace. The primary mission is to identify needs, then provide physical security systems and procedures to the company that mitigate risks. Fairness and a sense of cooperation must prevail in all aspects of the project.

Remember that a security professional is a "business consultant" first and a specialist in the security industry second.

OVERVIEW OF THE SECURITY AUDIT PROCESS

It is important for all businesses to understand the risks that may affect current operations. Businesses need to understand what can threaten ongoing operations and how to mitigate those threats through protection of assets and insurance against loss. The goal is to minimize exposure to those situations that expose the business to loss.

A comprehensive Risk Analysis provides a way to better understand these risks and the steps taken to reduce and manage the risks more effectively. This approach employs a two step process; the probability of an event occurring and the likely loss should it occur.

One of the elements is an assessment of threats. These are events where systems fail or external forces attack the business system. Examples might include robbery of employees or theft. Threats are present in every system.

A second element is vulnerabilities. Vulnerabilities make a system more susceptible to attacks by a threat or make a successful attack more likely. For example, it would be more likely that a theft would occur if doors were not properly locked.

A third element in a Risk Analysis is controls. Controls are the countermeasures for vulnerabilities. There are four types:

1. Detecting controls—discover the attacks and trigger preventative or corrective measures.
2. Deterring controls—reduce the likelihood of a deliberate attack by presenting a more formidable target for the attacker.
3. Delaying controls—make an attack more difficult to achieve and permit more time to respond to the attack.
4. Response controls—reduce the effect of an attack by providing additional obstacles to the attacker.

Additional security requires an investment in capital equipment and manpower. Because this investment does not directly generate revenue, it should always be justified in terms of loss avoidance. The Risk Analysis process creates the justification for security recommendations in business decisions.

A Risk Analysis program enhances the productivity of the entire operation. By reviewing the existing security structure, it is possible to better utilize scarce resources. All departments in a business operation must be involved in a complete Risk Analysis. This would naturally include physical security, data security and human resource planning. Business management is responsible for decisions relating to the risk levels that the company is willing to accept. Risk Analysis should include appropriate information from each group and play a major proactive role in enhancing the safety and security of the entire operation.

Risk Analysis relates security directly to business issues. The Risk Assessment must be simple enough to enable the entire business staff to use it without special knowledge about security. In this way, security measures can involve more areas and enable security to become part of the entire business operation. This will permit management to ensure an adequate and appropriate level of security exists for all areas of the business.

This broad approach to Risk Analysis encourages more of the management staff to place security on their agenda and increase security awareness in the entire business. Security should be targeted, and related to potential impacts, threats and existing vulnerabilities. The Risk Analysis helps avoid excessive or unnecessary expenditure and promotes better operational decisions. Risk Analysis across multiple business systems allows quick identification of the areas of greatest risk to the business as a whole.

Risk Analysis brings a consistent and objective approach to all security reviews. Risk Analysis also aids communication and facilitates decision making across departmental boundaries. The Risk Analysis evaluates threats from different areas, such as intruders, criminals, disgruntled employees, terrorists, and natural disasters

This book focuses on physical security and concentrates efforts on man-made threats.

The diagram in Figure 1.6-1 illustrates the steps involved in a physical security audit.

CHAPTER 2, THE PHYSICAL THREAT ASSESSMENT

The review of any business operation begins with an examination of the threats to the operation. This is important because without knowledge of the potential for attack, physical security countermeasures

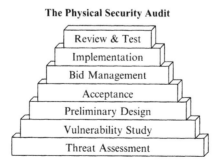

Figure 1.6-1 The steps involved in a physical security audit.

are just guesswork. The book provides guidance on conducting this assessment.

A Physical Threat Assessment examines and identifies the potential sources of man-made attacks. This examination includes a review of company records (usually in the security department) and extensive interviews with company personnel. The Physical Threat Assessment provides a careful assessment of the concerns of management and employees who work with the critical infrastructure of the business with the goal of identifying those company assets that are most critical to ongoing operations.

The process begins with a goal setting meeting. In this meeting, the security professional helps company management review and establish firm policies for acceptable levels of risk to the company's operation.

Following the goal setting meeting, the security professional conducts the Physical Threat Assessment to determine:

- Which employees are most susceptible to attack
- What equipment is most critical to the operation
- When are these assets most vulnerable
- Are there off premise assets that also require attention
- If there are other vulnerable assets
- Threats from damage to the assets of others

The process culminates in a report to company management that describes:

- What threats concern the company the most
- What threats "should" concern the company the most
- Which human assets are most threatened
- Which physical assets are most critical to continued business operations
- Liability exposure from the lack of adequate security measures

CHAPTER 3, THE VULNERABILITY STUDY

A Vulnerability Study is a comprehensive assessment of all current physical security measures and operational characteristics that affect the facility's ability to detect, deter, delay and respond to threats. It defines a protected perimeter and the nature of the perimeter barriers, then identifies all openings in the protected perimeter and establishes the optimum means to control and monitor those openings. This book instructs the reader on the methods used in conducting a Vulnerability Study and the techniques for recording the information gathered.

The Vulnerability Study begins with identifying critical assets of the operation then establishing a protected perimeter around those assets. This chapter discuses how to evaluate the material used to establish the perimeter and determine how well it can withstand attack from the perceived threats.

The Vulnerability Study identifies all openings in the perimeter then suggests monitoring and control measures for each opening. In some cases, access to or egress from the opening is denied while in other cases, electronic devices are suggested that grant access or egress based on user identification. The means for identification vary with each opening. A discussion of these variations is included in the chapter. It explains that the objective in a Vulnerability Study is to provide a way to detect, deter and delay attackers.

The Vulnerability Study reviews the current physical condition of the facility. It may suggest enhancements in existing lighting and improvements in the structural elements of the building or perimeter fencing.

After developing a plan for protecting the company's assets, Chapter 3 describes how to identify threats to Infrastructure Resources. These are services that are critical to ongoing operations and include electrical service, communications, water, sewage and other vital utilities. The company sometimes has a means to restore or supplement these resources if successfully attacked. The Vulnerability Study verifies these backup measures to confirm effectiveness, for example, whether emergency generators are available to supply power if the commercial power feed is lost.

After considering all protective measures to detect, deter, and delay physical threats, the Vulnerability Study examines the company's ability to respond to these threats. The chapter shows how to examine where security personnel duty posts are and the ways and means to communicate the presence of a threat to the response team. It also addresses procedures currently used to instruct the force on how to respond to detected threats and the manpower skill level and availability for threat response. The goal is to determine the skill level needed for response and the training requirements for the existing force.

The Vulnerability Study examines security force surveillance needs and capabilities. The chapter provides ways to observe the force's ability to view events in all areas of the facility and properly classify the event (threat or no threat). The reader will learn how to use closed circuit television equipment to expand the force's ability to quickly evaluate an event and provide a measured response.

After establishing the protective measures, the chapter describes how the Vulnerability Study determines if a Command Center exists and the ability of that center to gather, evaluate and disseminate information in a timely manner. There is a discussion of how to identify threat information resources and evaluate the protocols used to classify threats. The reader will understand how to determine the center's ability to communicate threat information to the force.

After addressing all the elements of detection, deterrence, delay, and response, the chapter shows how the Vulnerability Study identifies existing security equipment locations. These are areas throughout the facility where mission critical communications and power equipment for the security system equipment has been installed. The study evaluates the security of these rooms and their location relative to the protected perimeters.

The book shows how to record the findings using various documents. The documents are a detailed description of the existing system devices, how they are applied and, in many cases, the interconnection between devices. These documents are:

- The Door Detail Schedule
  This document describes the openings in the secured perimeters and details the following:
  - Access and egress control devices
  - Door locks
  - Door hardware
  - Door status switches
  - Space protection

- The Camera Detail Schedule
  This document describes the existing surveillance equipment in use. It includes:
  - Camera type
  - Lenses
  - Camera housings
  - Housing mounts
  - Special camera features
- Key Management
  Key Management studies and reports how the company issues standard metal keys and how these keys are controlled. It provides an indication of the how the non-electronic access control equipment is currently used.

After examining the company's asset vulnerabilities and documenting the areas of concern, the chapter instructs the reader to consider the consequences of loss. It provides an examination of asset value and the impact on the operation if the asset is lost. It also shows how the Vulnerability Study establishes the probability of loss to help company management make an informed decision on the value of security investments to offset losses. The chapter shows how the Vulnerability Study report describes:

- Human resource exposure
- Hard asset exposure
- Probability of loss
- Consequences of loss
- Recommended action

CHAPTER 4, THE PRELIMINARY SYSTEM DESIGN

The information from the Vulnerability Study forms the basis for system design. This chapter describes how to evaluate and document the data gathered during the Vulnerability Study to choose the right equipment to mitigate the threats uncovered. The chapter examines the best methods for recording a preliminary design and explains how these methods help to establish a well defined bid. Good bid definition is essential in finding the right product at competitive prices.

Effective system design begins with a complete understanding of the company's facility. This starts with interpreting the plans and blueprints of the structures on site and relating the elements of the existing plans to the observations documented during the Vulnerability Study.

The design establishes protected perimeters around critical assets using current floor plans and plot plans. This chapter describes how to mark asset locations on the plans, then how to establish protected perimeters. It shows how to form protected perimeters in concentric circles around the assets using existing or planned structures as perimeter boundaries. A discussion follows on how to identify openings in the perimeters and the best way to secure them.

The chapter also addresses selecting the proper type of alarm detection device for each opening and choosing the correct area sensor to use around protected assets to detect the presence of intruders.

Authorized employees (and in some cases, visitors) use some openings in the protected perimeter as routine access and egress points during business operations. In most cases, these openings require controls to ensure that unauthorized personnel do not enter the facility. The preliminary system design will assign control devices that validate the user's permission to pass through the opening. Card readers are the most prevalent form of control devices today. The chapter on system design reviews the various technologies and how they are applied.

This chapter also discusses the criteria a designer should use when selecting electric locks to control perimeter openings and life safety issues as they relate to locking doors electrically and meeting egress requirements.

The preliminary system design also includes the selection of video surveillance devices. The chapter examines what decisions are required for each camera location.

Chapter 4 discusses how to recommend facility modifications for optimizing the use of security equipment. Sometimes, small modifications in facility construction will provide substantial reductions in security equipment cost and make the environment easier to secure.

The chapter reviews Response Team Integration and the means for determining the effectiveness of alarm reporting and response. Proper alarm reporting and dissemination of alarm messages is essential to effective alarm response. The preliminary design must include adequate enunciation of intrusion alarms and features that enhance the response team's ability to quickly identify and classify each alarm. The preliminary design also provides a means for security management to instruct the response team during each alarm condition on the proper response.

CHAPTER 5, DOCUMENTING THE PRELIMINARY SYSTEM DESIGN

This chapter provides detailed instructions on completing the system design documentation. This documentation includes:

- The door detail schedule
- The camera detail schedule
- The concept drawing

Following the discussion on preliminary system design, Chapter 4 provides methods for preparing a cost analysis of the proposed system. It includes a discussion of the access control and alarm monitoring budget and addresses primary material costs and labor costs. Techniques for estimating cable runs are also provided with suggestions on estimating incidental costs.

There is also a discussion of the methods used to establish the video system budget and includes methods for estimating the primary material cost, estimating cable and estimating labor.

To complete the budget estimate, the chapter reviews how to forecast expense budgets for ongoing system maintenance and briefly discusses estimates for human resource requirements. These factors are assembled in a cost analysis to provide a meaningful investment forecast for management.

The chapter concludes with a review of legal issues that affect security system improvement projects and provides areas of caution for the system designer.

CHAPTER 6, PRESENTING THE SOLUTIONS

The chapter begins with a discussion of what company management wants to know to arrive at an informed decision. There is a review of the key questions to answer for management and directions for preparing the presentation. Those questions are:

- Why would I want to do this?
- What will happen if I do not do what is recommended?
- Who needs to be involved to implement and operate the system?
- When should I act?
- How long will it take to implement?
- How much will it cost?

The chapter discusses methods of presenting the recommendations and reminds the reader that companies sometimes reject good recommendations when the presentation does not adequately address the concerns of the audience. The chapter describes suggested presentation techniques and coaches the reader on effective ways to get the message across.

The chapter addresses the written presentation and discusses how an effective presentation report is organized. Each section of the written package is examined and includes:

- Section 1, Project objectives and scope of work
- Section 2, Threats and countermeasures
- Section 3, Benefits of the recommended solution
- Section 4, Recommendation
- Section 5, Investment required

The chapter also addresses the oral presentation and gives recommendations for assembling the right audience and scheduling the presentation meeting. It examines the ways in which an oral presentation is organized and the most effective ways to deliver the solutions' message to the audience.

This section also talks about "closing the deal" and what that means to the security professional and the company. Follow-up techniques are also discussed and how a security professional helps the company come to an informed decision.

CHAPTER 7, SYSTEM ACQUISITION–PART 1, TECHNICAL SPECIFICATIONS

The chapter begins with an introduction to the types of bids that are commonly used to acquire security system products. The chapter examines the merits of each bid type and the benefits and limitations encountered when using them. The bid types discussed are:

- The request for information (RFI)
- The request for quotation (RFQ)
- The request for proposal (RFP)

The chapter discusses the RFP bid type in detail with instructions on how to prepare an effective bid using this technique. There is an examination of two variations of the RFP:

- The single-step RFP
- The two-phase RFP

The chapter explains when to use each type of RFP and the benefits of one over the other in a given circumstance. The chapter selects the two-phase RFP for large complex installations and assumes that the security professional must prepare a bid for this type of situation. Instructions follow for constructing the two-phase RFP with examples for organizing the work. There is an examination of each part of phase 1 of the two-phase bid. It includes:

- Section 1, Invitation to Bid
  - Primary and secondary objectives
  - Scope of work
  - Anticipated future work
  - Design parameters
- Section 2, Bidder Qualifications
- Section 3, Performance Specifications
  - Door detail schedule and command center alarm and access control equipment list
  - Camera detail schedule and command center CCTV equipment list
  - Door elevation drawings
  - Camera elevation drawings

  ○ Network drawing
  ○ Command center drawing
  ○ Common equipment elevation drawings
  ○ Custom circuit drawings
  ○ Marked blueprints with equipment location
  ○ Split contracts
  • Section 4, Submittals

The chapter then addresses getting approval for the specifications from company management. It provides suggestions on assembling the right audience for the presentation and the best method for delivering the design concept.

It assumes that the company approves the specifications, then the chapter reviews the ways in which the security professional solicits bids for the project. It describes the ways to identify bidders and the best methods for notifying bidders that the project is available for bid.

There is an examination of the protocol for calling and conducting a pre-bid meeting and the relevant issues to discuss at the meeting. The chapter provides direction on how to conduct fair and open competition for the company's business and methods to ensure that all competitors receive an equal opportunity to win the contract.

There are also instructions for the bid acceptance and bid opening processes. The goal is to avoid any hint of favoritism in bid opportunities and to reassure the bidders and the company that all bidders have a fair and equal chance for success. The instructions provide a clear path for bid examination and, in cases of bids involving public funds, how to provide full disclosure and ensure universal acceptance of the process.

After discussion of the bid opening, the chapter addresses how to perform a technical evaluation on the systems offered. It refers to the methods used to create the bid specifications and how to use those methods to perform an effective, objective assessment of each offering.

The chapter assumes that certain bidders offered acceptable systems, and those systems must be analyzed in detail. There is a discussion on how to conduct bidder presentations and evaluate the reaction of company personnel to the systems presented.

The chapter concludes with the techniques used in making a final evaluation and how to bring together all elements of the evaluation process. It describes the ways to make effective recommendations for choosing the most responsive bidder.

CHAPTER 8, SYSTEM ACQUISITION—PART 2, THE BUSINESS PLAN

Chapter 8 begins with identifying participants for the phase 2 bid process. It reexamines the conclusions reached in the previous chapter and provides methods for selecting and notifying bidders of the opportunity to continue the participation process.

The chapter discusses the phase 2 bid process and provides instructions on constructing the "business plan" portion of the bidder selection. The chapter examines the phase 2 bid in detail and describes each section:

- Section 1, Invitation to bid
- Section 2, Additional bidder qualifications
- Section 3, Bid requirements
  - Basic definitions
  - Specific performance
  - Verifying conditions
  - Owner requirements
  - Life safety considerations
  - Prior approvals
  - Bid bond and performance bond
  - Insurance
- Section 4, Pricing requirements
  - Firm fixed price
  - Recommended spares
  - Projected cost for major system components
  - Annual hardware maintenance
  - Maintenance forecast
  - Annual software maintenance
  - System addition forecast
- Section 5, Execution of contract
  - Requirements after acceptance of bid
  - Equipment substitutions
  - Scheduling
  - Equipment storage
  - System staging
  - Job site rules and regulations for vendors
  - Supervision of work (project management)
  - Power quality and reliability
  - Cabling

- Cable labeling
- Component installation criteria
- Startup responsibility
- Card testing
- "As built" project drawings
- Test criteria
- System acceptance
- Change orders
- Default considerations
- Basis of payment
- Section 6, Post Installation Support
  - Personnel training
  - Warranty and service agreements
- Section 7, Submittals
  - Document submittals
  - Electronic submittal

As in phase 1, this chapter explains how to get approval for the specifications from company management. It reviews the techniques used by the security professional to present the concepts that are most informative to the audience.

The chapter assumes that the security professional receives approval for the phase 2 specifications and discusses the best way to release the bid to the bidders selected in phase 1. It addresses soliciting bidders and the pre-bid meeting. The chapter also provides guidance for bid acceptance and bid openings.

The chapter concludes with the Business Plan Evaluation and the final examination that brings together all of the evaluation elements to present a comprehensive report to company management. This is the final step in the bidder selection process.

CHAPTER 9, SYSTEM IMPLEMENTATION

Chapter 9 covers the implementation process for the acquired system. It begins with awarding the contract and the steps necessary to ensure that the awarded bidder has a complete understanding of the project requirements. The chapter also explains how to work with company purchasing so that the contract or purchase agreement reflects the project specifications.

There are distinct stages of system implementation identified as installation milestones. The chapter addresses each milestone and explains the follow up and tracking procedures. The project milestones are:

- Milestone Meeting 1—Cabling complete
- Milestone Meeting 2—Equipment staging complete
- Milestone Meeting 3—Equipment mounting complete
- Milestone Meeting 4—Final termination complete

When the installation process is finished, the security professional and bidder demonstrates the system's capabilities to the company. The chapter discusses the elements of the Final Test and Inspection and explains:

- Who should attend
- When the test should be conducted
- What should be covered
- Post installation submittals

The installation of the recommended security products is only one step in the overall solution. The chapter next addresses the administrative parts of system design. It begins with evaluating the security system personnel's ability to manage the new system and take advantage of all of the system features.

There is a discussion of job duties for the System Administrator and the techniques used by the security professional to help the company identify the most likely candidate for the position. There is also a discussion about the Help Desk in large, complex systems. Establishing a Help Desk makes system administration easier on all system users and provides users a greater level of understanding of system features and the programming required to take advantages of system features.

After defining job responsibilities, system user training is essential for proper implementation. The chapter provides for methods to establish a training agenda with the bidder and to evaluate the delivery of that training.

The chapter recommends that the security professional assist the System Administrator in making management decisions regarding system programming. The System Administrator needs the security professional's help in understanding the features available and how to take maximum advantage of all capabilities.

The chapter instructs the security professional in helping the System Administrator create user documentation for system management. The chapter explains the elements of system documentation and includes:

- Identifying the authorized population
- Organizing card reader data
- Delineating time zones
- Assigning access permissions
- Observing and recording video
- Responding to alarms
- Responding to alarm events
- System reporting
- Programming

In addition to system documentation, the company requires procedures for realigning employee performance to take advantage of the new capabilities. The chapter explains how the security professional can help the company develop system management procedures that defines employee conduct. The chapter covers:

- Procedures to issue credentials
- Procedures for lost or replaced security credentials
- Procedures for dismissed employees
- Procedures for changes in access permissions

After orientating users to the new system, the final step is System Turn On. The chapter describes how to bring together all of the implementation steps required for final system activation.

The security professional must evaluate the system after it is in service to confirm that the results meet the expectations. The chapter explains the techniques used in the evaluation process and how to determine if the company has realized the benefits expected from the system implementation. It also discusses the need for subsequent and ongoing training so that the company continues to receive full value for their investment.

The book concludes with comments about the goals and responsibilities of a security professional. It reaffirms the need for fair dealings in the marketplace and the requirement for high ethical conduct by practitioners.

The Physical Threat Assessment

INTRODUCTION

A Physical Threat Assessment is part of an overall Risk Analysis. The Physical Threat Assessment is a review of anticipated threats to personnel and property in the subject facility(s). The Physical Threat Assessment includes an internal assessment to discover threats perceived by company employees and threats described by law enforcement crime statistics in a community and national trends in similar operations.

If the company has been in operation for over 10 years and has a relatively effective security policy, a Physical Threat Assessment may be limited to the internal assessment and may be based entirely on anticipated threats by company management. Interviews with the company's employees may not be necessary in all cases nor would the security professional conduct a review of crime statistics and security concerns in similar operations in other companies. Company management will determine the depth of the detail needed to provide an acceptable level of evidence to assess

risk. Even an analysis with this limited scope may provide sufficient information for system design without the expense and time
associated with detailed research.

The Internal Threat Assessment begins with the concerns of
top management for the threats perceived to the overall operation.
That process continues down the layers of management examining
the perceptions at each administrative level then, if necessary, to the
frontline employees. Each level of employee may have a different
perspective on the possible threats to their portion of operational
responsibilities. Each successive level of interviews provides
greater comprehension in the overall assessment.

However, each successive step down the organizational chain
requires greater effort to conduct comprehensive reviews. These
greater levels of investigation result in higher costs for the assessment and a greater investment for the company.

Interviews at lower administrative levels will not always
reveal a substantially greater degree of information. There is a concept used by accountants and economists that describe this relationship, called "the point of diminishing returns." It is an
economic law, also called the law of diminishing marginal returns,
which expresses a relationship between input and output. It states
that adding units of any one input (labor, capital, etc.) to fixed
amounts of the others will yield successively smaller increments of
output. In common usage, the "point of diminishing returns" is a
supposed point at which additional effort or investment in a given
endeavor will not yield correspondingly greater results.

Simply put, the effort required to gather information from
every employee at a facility will substantially increase the cost of
the assessment but the value of that volume of information may not
be worth the price. Therefore, involve company management in
establishing the scope of work for the Physical Threat Assessment.
Discuss how much detail will provide an acceptable level of confidence in the assessment results.

Take the same approach with examining external threat data.
Some information, such as generalized local crime statistics, can be
obtained with relative ease from public records. However, industry
specific data may require a special report from a qualified firm, and
some of these reports can be costly. In addition, collecting industry
information from comparable business operations can be labor

intensive and expensive. Before committing to the collection and analysis of industry threat data or acquiring reports of industry specific crime statistics, discuss the cost/benefit relationship with company management. Determine the value of the additional information and allow company management to decide if these additional investments are worth the additional confidence they will add to conclusions about potential threats.

THE SCOPE OF WORK

Usually some event raises company awareness to the need for improved physical security in a facility or perhaps the general climate has become more threatening to company personnel or property. In any case, the company has determined that physical security needs modification to deal with the current level of potential risk.

The mission of the security professional is to help the company determine the ways in which improved physical security will protect the business operation, the security goals needed to achieve that protection and the means and methods to achieve those goals. Take charge and guide the process: however, remember that the management team makes the decisions. The security professional's role is to advise and recommend, then carry out the wishes of the company.

Begin by discussing the scope of work for the project. This establishes the boundaries for the studies and provides clear goals for the mission. Many of the elements of a Security Audit can vary in depth of detail. The variations establish a level of confidence in the results. For example, a Threat Assessment conducted only with top management personnel will produce a single perspective on the perceived threats to the organization. Additional interviews with mid-level managers may reveal concerns that would also concern top management, but because they are not exposed to the problems on a daily basis, top management may not be aware of these problems. For management to accept the security professional's recommendations, they must have confidence in the report. Therefore, it is important to establish an acceptable level of detail for the interviews.

Create a written Scope of Work that clearly describes the goals of the new physical security system and the level of authority and responsibility assigned to the security professional. One of the most useful documents to describe these goals and level of authority is the Work Breakdown Schedule. Figure 2.1 shows an example of a Work Breakdown Schedule.

POLICY REVIEW

The most important meeting in the Threat Assessment process is the initial goal-setting and policy review meeting. This is important because to efficiently evaluate risks, the security professional must know the level of acceptable risk the company will assume. Policy statements determine this risk level.

Obtain a copy of the company's current policy for security or acceptance risk. Review the statements to determine the level of risk associated with security concerns. The security professional may find that formal policy statements do not exist or the current policies do not adequately cover all the elements of risk. In these circumstances, prepare appropriate guidelines for the management team and be prepared to discuss the details of the security policy at the initial goal setting meeting. Some elements of risk are:

- Employee identification
  - Assigning credentials
  - Wearing credentials
  - Pictures on credentials
  - Biometrics identification on credentials
  - The need for other uses for credentials (copy machine)
- Visitor identification
  - Collecting visitor data
  - What visitor identify data to collect
    - Full name
    - Full address
    - Company name
    - Date of visit
    - Time arrived
    - Time departed
    - Purpose of visit
    - Person visited

Physical Security Audit, Work Breakdown Schedule

Stage	WBS	Task
Phase 1	1	**Goal Setting**
	1.1	Review of existing plot plans and related drawings
	1.2	Prepare for goal setting meeting, agenda and outline
	1.3	Initial goal setting meeting with management team
	1.4	Minutes of goal setting meeting and report on goals and objectives
	2	**Threat Assessment**
	2.1	Prepare for management interviews, introduction letters, questionnaire and discussion outline
	2.2	Interviews with management personnel
	2.3	Document interviews
	2.4	Obtain and review inside security reports, analyze and summarize
	2.5	Identify outside sources of threat data and request report
	2.6	Review reports of outside data and summarize
	2.7	Prepare Threat Assessment report for management team and create presentation
	2.8	Present Threat Assessment for management team
	2.9	Minutes of Threat Assessment meeting and report on Vulnerability Survey Plan
	3	**Vulnerability Study**
	3.1	Prepare survey plan
	3.2	Physical inspection of all access portals and entire secured perimeter
	3.3	Prepare documentation from Vulnerability Study
	3.4	Prepare Vulnerability Study report for management team and create presentation
	3.5	Present Vulnerability Study to Management Team
	3.6	Minutes of Vulnerability Study meeting and report on System Design
Phase 2	4	**System Design**
	4.1	Finalize Door Detail Schedules, Camera Detail Schedules and Key Management Schedule
	4.2	Prepare facility modification recommendations
	4.3	Preparation of conceptual drawings and top level system design
	4.4	Market review of all potential systems to meet conceptual design
	4.5	Prepare a System Acquisition Budget for Access Control, Alarm Monitoring and CCTV
	4.6	Prepare a Human Resources Budget
	4.7	Prepare report on System Design and presentation to management team
	4.8	Present System Design to management team
	4.9	Minutes of the System Design meeting
	5	**Performance Specifications**
	5.1	Prepare Performance Specifications initial draft and submit for review

Figure 2.1 Work breakdown structure.

Physical Security Audit, Work Breakdown Schedule

Stage	WBS	Task
	5.2	Follow up and discuss revisions with management team
	5.3	Revision to plans and specifications for final draft
	5.4	Prepare final draft of System Performance Specifications and presentation to management
	5.5	Present Performance Specifications to management team
	5.6	Minutes of the Performance Specifications meeting
	6	**Bid Management**
	6.1	Prepare Invitation to Bid
	6.2	Meetings with client purchasing to review ITB for conformity with purchasing policies
	6.3	Contact potential vendors for security products to ensure full participation
	6.4	Release bid and send special invitations
	6.5	Conduct pre-bid conference
	6.6	Respond to vendor questions following pre-bid
	6.7	Conduct bid opening
	6.8	Review and analysis of vendor offers
	6.9	Conduct vendor presentations
	6.10	Document analysis of vendor offers, prepare recommendation for most responsive vendor.
	6.11	Prepare presentation to management team for recommendation
	6.12	Present vendor bids and recommendation
	6.13	Minutes of the Vendor Recommendation meeting
Phase 3	7	**System Implementation**
	7.1	Prepare procurement recommendation
	7.2	Follow up and verify procurement
	7.3	Review vendor post award submittals and prepare responses
	7.4	Prepare and send Notice to Proceed
	7.5	Conduct Initial Walkdown meeting with vendor to review job requirements on-site
	7.6	Prepare report on Initial Walkdown for management team
	7.7	Site visits to verify progress
	7.8	Progress reports to management team
	7.9	Progress meetings with client
	7.10	Milestone meeting 1 Cabling Complete
	7.11	Report Milestone 1 to management team
	7.12	Milestone meeting 2 Equipment Staging Complete
	7.13	Report Milestone 2 to management team
	7.14	Milestone meeting 3 Equipment Mounting Complete
	7.15	Report Milestone 3 to management team
	7.16	Milestone meeting 4 Final Termination Complete
	7.17	Report Milestone 4 to management team
	7.18	Milestone meeting 5 Initial Test Complete
	7.19	Prepare final punch list

Figure 2.1 cont'd

Physical Security Audit, Work Breakdown Schedule

Stage	WBS	Task
	7.20	Report Milestone 5 to management team
	7.21	Inspect final punch list
	7.22	Final Inspection and Delivery with vendor and management team
	8	**Post Delivery Support**
	8.1	Confirmation of training arrangements and review of vendor training agenda
	8.2	Attend initial training class
	8.3	Assist client in preparation of security protocols
	8.4	Attend system turn on
	8.5	On-site spot check of training with system operators
	8.6	On-site spot check of protocol implementation with system operators
	8.7	Prepare report to management team on the success of system implementation

Figure 2.1 cont'd

- Identification credential verification (such as a driver's license)
- What are acceptable visitor credentials
- If visitor credentials should be held until departure
- If visitors should be photographed
- Will visitors require an escort
- Will the Response Team be required to search the visitor for restricted items
- Will the visitor be permitted to drive a vehicle on company property
- Will the Response Team be required to search visitor vehicles
- What are considered contraband items
  - Weapons (even registered firearms)
  - Cameras
  - Recorders
  - Cell phones
- Access and egress control requirements
  - For company grounds
  - For company buildings (all buildings or selected buildings)
  - For selected departments
  - The need to record access and egress by authorized individuals
- Perimeter controls for intruder alert
  - For company grounds
  - For company buildings (all buildings or selected buildings)
  - For selected departments (or areas within departments)

- Surveillance (to identify and classify incidents)
    - What are the critical areas of concern
    - The ability to do detailed observations
    - The ability for automatic event recognition by the video system
    - The length of time required to retain video recordings
- Response Team
    - The need for a centralized watch command
    - The need for roving patrols

The security professional assists the company in deciding the levels of acceptable risks or concern for each of these security topics. Write statements that describe the assigned risk levels. An example might be: "All employees are required to obtain and wear employee identification at all times while on company property." Another may be: "The identity of all visitors on company property must be verified by company security before a visitor is permitted to enter company facilities. Visitors must present a valid picture ID to the receptionist and the information on that credential must be recorded along with the time, date, and purpose of the visit."

These policy statements will set the stage for all the work to follow. The security professional will conduct the Threat Assessment with these policies in mind and can produce a more meaningful assessment of the current situation. These guidelines will be helpful for policy development.

A policy mandates standards for acceptable conduct. Policies generally contain the following elements:

- Statement of need or rationale
- Statement of purpose
- General principles
- Definitions
- Procedure
- Statement of relationship to existing policies

Policies translate the abstract business values of the operation's mission statement into practical terms to shape the behavior of personnel. The goal is for personnel performance to be consistent with the company's mission statement and values. Properly designed policies will:

- Decrease staff uncertainties about acceptable practices
- Reduce stress and conflict among employees
- Decrease ad hoc procedures and arbitrary decisions
- Increase the involvement of employees in decisions about the operations
- Improve the quality of business decision making within the company

A good security policy will:

- Promote the activities that safeguard the assets of the company
- Maintain compliance with applicable codes for the operation of the company
- Provide legal protection for company conduct

The usual steps in drafting policy include:

1. Examine institution's mission and values and determine how they apply to the policy
2. Agree on general principles by all top management
3. Obtain copies of policies from other institutions or organizations
4. Delegate the policy writing to a subcommittee or a standing committee on policy
5. Circulate the first draft for review
6. Meet with affected managers to discuss questions about the policy and obtain approval
7. Revise the policy based on manager input
8. Have legal counsel review and comment on the revised policy
9. Revise the draft again based on additional input
10. Follow the policy through organizational channels until approved
11. Conduct educational programs so that personnel understand and apply the policy
12. Evaluate the policy after it is in use and review and revise as needed

Policy development committees need to understand that a policy is never finished. Even though management approves the policy, it can be improved over time. New situations, new threats and methods of mitigation will necessitate policy revisions.

Some strategies for educating company staff about policies include:

- The affected staff members in the policy review and revision process
- Present cases in an educational format that highlight aspects of the policy
- Distribute summaries of the policy
- Include summaries of the policy in the company's newsletter
- Provide copies of the policy in areas where references are needed

GATHER PRELIMINARY DATA

If the security professional is not a direct employee, it will be important to learn about the company, the industry, and (if not a local resident) the community before the initial meeting. The security professional needs a general understanding of what the company does in their business environment and what some of the concerns are in their industry. Internet research and a review of past issues of the local newspaper will help establish familiarity with major security issues in the local community. Figure 2.2 provides a questionnaire for a company overview.

Before the goal-setting meeting, collect security data from the company's security manager including the initial reasons for interest in increasing physical security measures. Figure 2.3 illustrates a useful form for collecting this data.

Allow enough time for the respondents to reply to these requests for information and to analyze the data after receipt. Please note that the preliminary data, while important, is not an essential step. This data will be determined as the assessment progresses; however, gathering the information before conducting the interviews will make data collection easier and more meaningful. It will also start the respondents thinking about the mission and how they can best serve the process.

Threat Analysis Company Overview Questionnaire

Company Name: **Project:**   **Date of Survey:**

Buildings in Survey:

	Building Name	Floors	Hours of Operation (From-To)	Visitor Access Time (From-To)	Shipping/ Receiving Times (From-To)
1					
2					
3					
4					
5					

If this is a commercial building who are the other tenants?

	Company Name	Contact	Telephone
1			
2			
3			
4			
5			

Attach sheet for additional tenants

Primary Security Concerns:

1	
2	
3	
4	
5	

Attach sheet for additional concerns

Figure 2.2 Facility overview questionnaire.

Threat Analysis Existing Building Security

Company Name: **Project:**   **Date of Survey:**

Response Team

Manager of Security Function: Contract Security Response Team:

Name	Name of Security company:
Title	Prime Contact:
Telephone	Telephone:
E-mail	E-mail

Security Duties:

Staff   Contract

How many contract officers in the force?
How many watch sections per force in a 24 hour day?
How many officers stand watch in a section?

Where is the central command post (Building and Floor)?

Where are the post watchstations (Building and Floor)?

Employee Identification:

Are employees required to wear ID badges Yes / No?

If yes (please provide a sample badge):
Which department issues the ID badges?

What other functions do the ID badges serve?

Visitor Control

Where do visitors enter the facility (Building or Gate)?

Which buildings allow visitors?

1
2
3
4
5

What identity credentials are examined for admittance?

What information is collected from visitors?

Are department escorts required for visitors (yes / no)?

Existing Procedures

Do procedures exist for any of the following: (attached copy of procedures)

Key and Lock Control
Response for breach in security
Security Drills
Employee Awareness Program

Figure 2.3 Security management questionnaire.

THE GOAL SETTING AND POLICY REVIEW MEETING

Include the company's most senior management representatives in the initial goal-setting and Policy Review meeting. Institutional will is very important when launching the project, and full cooperation of all company employees is essential. The support of top management is vital in establishing this commitment on a company-wide basis.

Set the agenda for the initial meeting and call for all attendees. The security professional will act as a facilitator in this meeting and all future meetings regarding this project. That is why the security professional is there—to advise, guide, and recommend. This means that the security professional will take a leadership role in directing the meeting and helping the committee identify and reach the goals necessary to achieve a more secure environment. Figure 2.4 provides a sample meeting agenda.

The primary goal of improving security performance through the addition of electronic physical security systems is to protect the ongoing operation of the business. This meeting is to determine what the company is most concerned about with regard to threats to the operation.

The second step in the process is to determine what threats the company should be concerned about regarding ongoing operations. This is usually determined by researching the crime statistics of the area and the steps taken by similar organizations to counter the threats that cause them concern.

Upper management approval early in the process is essential to the success of the survey and any resulting recommendations. Obtaining upper management approval is not always easy. The historical view of security was a "cost" to the operation. It will come as no surprise to security professionals with experience in the industry that security is usually underfunded and undermanned. Company resources tended to flow toward elements of the business that created profit. One role of the security professional is to help the company see that profits and the long-term viability of the operation may be in jeopardy if the company does not take adequate security measures.

Moreover, employees and visitors must feel that the company has provided a safe and threat-free environment in which to conduct business. The presence of adequate security measures in

Meeting Agenda
Physical Security System Improvement Project

Date
Consultant Name and Title
Consulting Firm Name

Meeting:
Date / Time
Company
Building / Room

Invitees:
Name / Title (of each management member invited)

Subject: (Describe the purpose of the meeting and the expected outcome)
i.e.: The attendees will set the goals for company wide physical security system improvements and define the limits of change in company operations to meet those goals. Attendees will also form the system selection committee to evaluate the proposed systems.

Agenda
1. Introduction of all committee members
2. Roll of the security professional in the project
3. Roll of the Selection Committee in the project
4. Project Goals (why are improvements in security needed)
5. Security professional presentation
   - Threat Analysis
   - Vulnerability Study
   - The system specification process
   - Phase 1 technical bid process (Request for Proposal)
   - Phase 2 financial offer and corporate review process
   - Final selection and service evaluation process
   - System implementation
6. Committee Decisions
   - What are the concerns driving this change, set goals for improvement
   - What are the critical processes (assets) necessary to continue business operation
   - Open discussion for security system "Wish List" ("wants" instead of needs)
   - Threat Analysis options:
     - Independent study
     - Interviews with employees
7. Questions or suggestions from Committee for this process
8. Set the goals for the next meeting (what is to be discussed and what information is required)

END MEETING

Anticipated meeting time is approximately 3 hours

Figure 2.4 Initial meeting agenda.

today's threat-filled environment can become a true asset in attracting and retaining top quality employees.

Start the initial goal setting meeting by presenting the techniques used to identify the security needs of the company. Explain how the Selection Committee will set company security goals. This overview will orient the committee members to the design and selection process.

The key question in this meeting is: "What are the critical processes and assets needed to sustain business operations?" Encourage a free discuss in the committee to help learn what are the areas of concern. Identify each business operation and write it on an easel or white board so that all committee members can continuously review them. Foster a discussion about the solution to potential problems. Some of problems that the security professional may find are:

- Employees are entering sensitive areas without proper need or authorization.
- Visitors have been found in sensitive areas and cannot be controlled.
- Employees feel vulnerable or exposed to criminal elements.
- There are not enough security officers to view all areas of the facility.
- Emergency exit doors are used as normal passage doors.
- Valuable company assets are accessible by unauthorized personnel.

It would also be helpful to start a second list of "security solutions" identified by the committee. In today's "movie magic" security world, company employees who work with the security problems on a daily basis often learn about ideas or products that they feel would be ideal in their circumstance. Although some of these suggestions may be inappropriate, the "wish list" will help to elicit more information about the company's security problems. Remember that the security professional is there to guide, advise and recommend. Investigate all ideas for reasonable application and budget constraints. The company managers will make the final decision as to which of these options most closely meets their objectives based, in part, on the recommendation of the security professional.

When beginning a security improvement project, companies will frequently call for a vendor to perform their security survey before calling the security professional for assistance. There are pitfalls in this process that are usually not obvious to the company's management team. Security vendors are there to sell products, not perform an independent assessment. Product vendors will usually limit their recommendations to the products they sell and not provide a cohesive overall assessment of security needs.

Security system sales personnel will often portray themselves as "consultants," but their primary mission is to sell equipment. Many are quick to recommend expensive equipment solutions when threats or vulnerabilities are identified, but they fail to examine the consequences of inaction. For example, if doors to a particular area are unmonitored, an equipment salesperson may recommend the use of card readers and electric locks to secure the door. They may not consider the assets behind the door nor the frequency with which the door is used.

One of the key questions to answer when deciding to apply a card reader to a door is if there is something of value behind the door (people or property) and if the door is high traffic. If the door restricts access to a storage area that contains inexpensive cleaning supplies then a simple door status switch may be a better solution. If the door were opened only once a week during business hours, a standard lock with a metal key would be a more cost effective protection method. "Consequences of loss" is an important element of physical threat assessment. It is important to orient the employees attending the meeting to view the process as a mission of discovery for all possible threats and not just ones that can be solved using particular pieces of equipment.

To conclude the initial goal setting meeting, the security professional reiterates the problem areas identified, and helps the committee establish a priority or level of importance for each item listed. This list becomes the goals of the security improvement project. Some examples of identified goals, with respect to the problems identified earlier are:

- Control access to sensitive areas and require proper authorization for entry

- Establish corridors for visitor access and prevent unauthorized entry
- Prevent unauthorized personnel from entering specific employee areas
- Provide a means to expand and extend security officer presence to all areas of the facility
- Control the use of emergency exit doors and limit access and egress to emergency only
- Protect valuable company assets from unauthorized use and observation

End the discussion with a brief review of topics to be discussed at the next meeting and what information the security professional will provide the committee for their decisions.

Document the results of the initial meeting (and all meetings held with the company) to firmly establish what was discussed and what were the resulting decisions of the management team. A complete record of company decisions will help in defining why the security professional took the steps that followed the meeting. Figure 2.5 provides an example of meeting minutes.

In addition to the minutes of the meeting, request a letter of introduction to other company employees not included in the goal setting management meeting. It would be helpful to management if the security professional provided a sample letter to the top management person in the goal setting meeting and requested that the letter be reproduced on company letterhead with the top manager's signature. Transmit a copy of that letter to all interviewees before the scheduled interviews. See Figure 2.6 for a sample letter of introduction.

IDENTIFY ASSETS

The company's assets must be clearly defined so the security professional will know what to protect. After identifying assets the threats to those assets can be established. Threat identification leads to a recognition of vulnerability, and an estimate of potential loss comes from knowing the consequences of failing to mitigate those threats. This will establish the value of the solutions. Without this regimented approach, system component selection will be uncertain.

Minutes of Initial Meeting (Date)
Physical Security System Improvement Project

Date
Consultant Name and Title
Consulting Firm Name

The Physical Security Improvement Committee met for the first time on (date). The agenda for the meeting accompanies this report.

Those attending the meeting were:

Name	Dept / Company	Phone
(List each member)		

The committee convened and reviewed the process to be used in executing the physical security improvement project. The role of the consultant and committee was discussed and the purpose of this project was described as follows:

Develop specifications for a new physical security system to meet the following goals, then implement the most effective system found within budget to achieve these goals:

- Control access to sensitive areas and require proper authorization for entry
- Establish corridors for visitor access and prevent unauthorized entry
- Prevent unauthorized personnel from entering specific employee areas
- Provide a means to expand and extend security officer presence to all areas of the facility
- Control the use of emergency exit doors and limit access and egress to "emergency only"
- Protect valuable company assets from unauthorized use and observation

The project time line was discussed. It was noted that if all matters proceed as planned, the project will take approximately (number) months to complete, with completion being defined as an installed, working system.

The process for equipment specification and evaluation was then reviewed. That process included a two-phase approach, covering system features, the business plan offered by the vendors and the service capability of the vendors. The Committee was in agreement with the methodology presented by the consultant.

A Threat Analysis was discussed and it was decided by the committee that company managers were keenly aware of the threats to the organization and external research was not required in the threat analysis. An interview list of company personnel was established for the consultant to identify the personnel and hard assets to be protected.

Goals were set for the next committee meeting and included:

- Results of the management defined Threat Analysis
- An overview of the company's vulnerabilities as it relates to identified threats
- A budget for addressing these vulnerabilities
- A decision to proceed with system acquisition and implementation

END OF REPORT

Figure 2.5   Initial meeting minutes.

Date

LETTER OF INTRODUCTION

This is to introduce (Consultant) and members of the consulting firm of (Company Name). (Company Name) has been engaged to study the security systems and protocols used in our facility and report those findings to security management.

Please extend every courtesy to (Consultant) and his staff. They are authorized to review and copy incident reports, security logs, post orders, videotapes and other similar records maintained by our security staff during the course of their work for our company. The staff of (Company Name) may enter secure areas of the facility in the same manner as any of the company's employees. In areas where sensitive information is kept or critical systems are in use, (Company Name) has been informed that a company escort may be required.

The purpose of (Company Name) review is to help us better define our security needs and formulate a recommendation to improve our security systems, policies and procedures. Your full cooperation will be appreciated. Please advise my office of any concerns you have regarding this access to our facility and records.

Sincerely,

Security Manager

Figure 2.6 Sample introduction letter.

In the goal setting meeting, the assets that concerned the company the most were defined in "broad strokes." Before beginning interviews, make a list of these assets and prepare to expand on this list as the interview process unfolds.

Preparing an outline for interviews with company personnel. Figure 2.7 shows a sample data gathering form. The elements of this outline include:

- Which employees are most susceptible to attack?
- What equipment is most critical to the operation?
- When are these assets most vulnerable?
- Are there off-premise assets that also require attention?

As part of the preparation step, obtain copies of the facility building floor plans for review. Obtain an area plot plan if this is a large

Threat Analysis Department Questionnaire

Company Name:	Project:	Date of Survey:

Contact

Department Name:			Department Area:	
Manager's Name:			Building	Floor
Manager's Title:				
Phone Number:				
E-mail:				

Department Data:

Number of employees in this department:

Approximate area of department: Sq. Feet

Are visitors permitted in this area (yes / no):

Are deliveries received in this area (yes / no):

What critical operational personnel and assets are in this department:

Primary Security Concerns: Vulnerable times, off premise assets, threats from adjacent facilities

1
2
3
4
5

Figure 2.7 Department questionnaire.

campus with multiple buildings and the mission is to protect the entire facility.

Which Employees Are Most Susceptible to Attack?

When helping management determine which employees are most susceptible to attack, the advice of upper management is invaluable. All employees are valuable to a company but in most cases perpetrators are interested in those employees who represent high hostage value or are mission critical personnel. Company management can best direct attention to those employees who are the most obvious targets for hostile action.

As the security professional develops the physical security system, additional consideration should be given to the protection of employees who are most threatened. An example of this kind of employee is a key manager who is responsible for wage and disciplinary decisions. Reports in the news frequently describe cases where an employee returns to the place of employment with the intent to harm key managers after she or he was dismissed.

What Equipment Is Most Critical to the Operation?

To determine what equipment is most critical to the operation, it is best to discuss the operational process with production or operations' managers. Ask them what a perpetrator could do to effectively disable the operation. In most instances, the security professional needs to have a criminal mentality and try to imagine what the criminal would do, having insider knowledge, to disrupt the flow of business. The security professional can help the operations' managers establish an order of priority for those assets that are most critical to the business. This will help focus attention on those assets when designing the security system.

An example of such a situation would be an oil refinery with a production critical processor. The failure of this device will cause the entire plant to shut down even though other facilities on the plant are operational. This would be a top priority and deserve the most attention.

Given that same example, the loss of an engineering office or quality testing office in the plant might pose a disruption in the production process but would not instantly shut down the entire plant. This would be a less important priority and may deserve less attention. A third example would be an administrative office. Damage or disruption to this part of the facility may prove a serious inconvenience to the operation but may not stop production. In all cases, however, we are assuming that there is damage to the physical asset and not to personnel. Protection of personnel is always a top priority.

When Are These Assets Most Vulnerable?

Most businesses operate on cycles with critical timing elements. An example of this is a retail operation just before or during the Christmas shopping period. While business disruptions during any time of the year can create serious hardship for a business, retail operations make the majority of their earned revenues during the Christmas season.

Disruption to most retail operations is more severe during the Christmas shopping cycle. Additionally, certain times of the day render businesses more susceptible to crime. An example of this would be a law office with sensitive case files. While this office is vulnerable to attack 24 hours a day, surreptitious entry and the seizure of vital information would, in most cases, seem to be prevalent after normal working hours.

Most managers will consider the 24-hour day cycle but give little thought to the annual changes in business activity. It would be most helpful to remind facility managers when conducting these discussions to also think on this broader scale.

Are There Off-Premise Assets That Also Require Attention?

In addition to discussions with operations managers, some accounting personnel can provide information about off-premise assets. A comprehensive physical security plan must also consider these assets.

The Physical Threat Assessment will establish a list of all of assets that can by destroyed or damaged and result in significant business interruption. However, a comprehensive security plan will include provisions for damage due to natural threats such as hurricanes, floods, earthquakes, and similar catastrophes. We will not address other natural threats; the focus of this work is to assess manmade threats.

Begin with the assumption that there are perpetrators with deliberation and intent who seek to cause harm to the facility or to the individuals who work or visit the company. The security professional's objective in performing the physical security survey is to establish the means for detection, deterrence, delay, and response to manmade threats.

Other Vulnerable Assets

Determine what other assets or services are imperative to company operation. One example is public utilities such as communications, gas, water, and power. These are non-owned facilities but are essential to continued operation. What disruption can occur in the operations if these assets were successful attacked?

Threats from Damage to the Assets of Others

In addition to harm that would result from direct attacks on company assets, also consider consequential damage of attacks to the assets of others in the surrounding area. For example, if a chemical plant was located next to company property and a perpetrator successfully attacked the plant, assess the harm that could result to company assets from the damage or destruction of the neighboring facility. Toxic chemical spills and harmful vapors can be as deadly a threat as a direct attack on the company.

CONDUCT THE PHYSICAL THREAT ASSESSMENT

The security professional begins by scheduling meetings with the employees named by the system selection committee for the Physical Threat Assessment. Draft an outline for the interview before arrival. It is usually sufficient to draft a few bullet statements to trigger the conversation as the interview proceeds. In other cases, it may be more helpful to write out full and complete questions and read those questions aloud during the interview process. Each company is different; tailor each questionnaire to the company. However, the general outline of each interview guide should follow this process.

It is better to schedule meetings with top management well in advance of the planned meeting date. These managers usually have very busy schedules and requesting an appointment well in advance is a clear indication of respect for their time and priorities.

In these interviews, discuss the security needs of the company with those employees most concerned with company operation. The recommended physical security system will affect those individuals the most.

The objectives in this interview process are to determine the primary security concerns of the interviewee. Every employee in every corporation has a certain set of missions and goals. The protected resources are what they use to achieve these goals. Employees will usually know the vulnerable areas but a targeted investigation must follow any management interview. Do that investigation with a "criminal mind-set." Ask the employee what losses would jeopardize the company's operation but remember to examine all the ways that those losses can affect the company.

Ask if there are specific ideas or suggestions that the interviewee has for employing security devices in his or her area. Security has become a hot topic in the news and in fictional productions today. People see a variety of exotic devices and think that those devices would be ideal solutions for a problem they have. While the security professional must examine any recommendation shared by company employees, the security professional is not there to ask, "What do you want to buy?" Rather, employees' answers to the questions will reveal concerns they have about the security of the company assets and their charge. The security professional can then use those statements as a springboard to other lines of inquiry.

After interviews with upper management are finished, focus attention on the frontline managers overseeing areas that are of critical operational value to the company. Again, an outline for the interview and advanced appointments are essential to the success of the mission. Conduct the interviews using the same techniques used for upper management. Frontline managers are in day-to-day contact with the environment that is to be secured and are generally far more sensitive to the needs of their operational areas.

If the company has an existing security force, it is likely that the security force has a record of incidents in the forms or reports on file. The Threat Assessment should include a review of those reports. Inspect reports from all incidents that have occurred in the past three years on company property.

Verify the "top down" concerns of management through interviews with frontline personnel. After obtaining permission to discuss security concerns with staff workers, solicit comments from the workers who are involved with the day-to-day operation of the sensitive operational areas of the company. While these employees may not share the level of concern expressed by management, they are more keenly aware of the limitations and faults of the existing infrastructure and can be a substantial asset in identifying areas of weakness.

At the conclusion of the data gathering process, document the findings of the interview process for the management team. This is a report with a recommendation for the next step in the process.

3

Conducting the Vulnerability Study to Identify Physical Security Requirements

INTRODUCTION

In this chapter, we will review the techniques used to identify the facility's vulnerability in relation to the threats uncovered during the Physical Threat Assessment. This is called a Vulnerability Study. It is a thorough review of a facility to determine the likelihood that a perpetrator could successfully attack the assets of the company and details the means and methods recommended to mitigate the risks from those attacks. It defines a protected perimeter and the nature of the perimeter barriers, then identifies all openings in the protected perimeter and establishes the optimum means to control and monitor those openings.

A Vulnerability Study is also a comprehensive assessment of all current physical security measures and operational characteristics that affect the facility's ability to detect, deter, delay, and respond to threats. Included in the study is an examination of the physical systems and procedures used by the response team to manage the system and respond to identified threats. During the Vulnerability Study, the system's performance capabilities are tested to verify the life safety features of the systems.

For example, a company may have an existing access control system. There is usually an interface between the electric locking systems and the building fire alarm system to meet fire code requirements. These interfaces are tested during the Vulnerability Study to ensure proper operation.

PREPARE TO CONDUCT THE SURVEY

A Vulnerability Study begins with a review of the Physical Threat Assessment. The Threat Assessment identified the assets that require protection and the threats to those assets. To prepare for the Vulnerability Study and physical survey, develop a written plan to help keep the study on track. When conducting the study, there are many distractions. A written plan outlines the steps in the proper sequence to completion.

The Vulnerability Study plan should include at least the following:

- An inspection of all identified assets.
- Establishing a protected perimeter for each asset.
- An assessment of the physical barricades that comprise the protected perimeter.
- An identification of each opening that provides human access (of any kind) to the asset.
- A definition of the use of that opening (e.g., ordinary and usual access, emergency exit only, freight only, etc.).
- Means of control for each opening in each protected perimeter.
- Lighting conditions around the protected perimeters.
- An assessment of the means to affect the critical infrastructure that supports the asset (power, water, gas, etc.).

- A review of employee identification procedures.
- A review of visitor controls.
- An evaluation of the effectiveness of existing security systems in light of identified threats.
- A review of incident reporting procedures (if not done during the Physical Threat Assessment).
- A review of written security response procedures (if not done during the Physical Threat Assessment).
- A review of post instructions for the existing security force (if not done during the Physical Threat Assessment).

MEANS AND METHODS OF CONDUCTING A VULNERABILITY STUDY

A comprehensive Vulnerability Study includes all of the elements necessary to detect, deter, delay and respond to manmade physical security threats. The techniques used in making this determination are:

Inspecting Assets and Establishing a Perimeter

Using the floor plans and plot plans provided by the company, identify all of the assets in the protected areas. In many cases, the assets are simply the areas where work is taking place. A useful method of making these identifications is to highlight the asset in a meaningful way on the floor plans and plot plans.

Establish a security perimeter around each asset. The perimeters are usually walls or fence lines that encircle the asset. Please note that the term "circle" when used to define protected perimeters is a general term and not used to mean a "round" circle. The perimeter is simply the parts of the infrastructure that enclose the asset. Often these circles follow the contours of the surrounding structure and have a variety of shapes.

Physical security perimeters are concentric circles around each asset with each succeeding circle widening and having progressively lower levels of security. In that way, the most valuable resources receive the greatest focus of security system measures. Define the perimeters on the floor and plot plans by marking the walls and fence lines that encircle the assets.

When deciding on controls for these perimeters, a natural inclination is to rigorously provide insurmountable obstacles to threats at all possible levels. However, the practical application of this approach is expensive and can adversely affect the operation of the facility. It is more likely that a tailored approach would win greater acceptance from management.

Some typical elements of perimeter development include:

1. The facility's mission and objectives.
2. An assessment of the likelihood of intrusion by unauthorized personnel to areas of critical assets (people or property).
3. A determination of consequences of loss from perpetrators with deliberation and intent.
4. A review of existing countermeasures to threats, including emergency procedures and insurance reimbursement as a result of anticipated losses.

In many cases, the outer perimeter is the exterior wall of a building. However, it may also be necessary to control the grounds that surround the protected building or buildings. The type of threat mitigated will determine the need to protect the areas outside of buildings and the distance between a protected perimeter and the first occurrence of an asset within that perimeter. For instance, if the threat is intrusion by a perpetrator walking on company grounds, sufficient distance is required to detect the intruder and, using video surveillance, classify the threat. If the threat is an explosive device, greater distances will be required. There are a number of publications that already exist, which establish these recommended distances and there is no need to expand on these recommendations in this work.

Extend the dimensions of the perimeter beyond those recommended limits to allow for specific types of threats to highly sensitive assets. An example of such a circumstance is an oil refinery where the asset to be protected is a fuel storage tank. Management may have a high level of concern that a perpetrator with deliberation and intent will try to damage this fuel storage tank by use of incendiaries or explosives.

In such cases, where those tanks are located near the protective perimeter, extend the recommended protected area to a distance that mitigates the potential damage from such explosive or incendiary devices. This may include recommending that the company move or eliminate certain visitor parking areas or, in the case of large plants with public access roadways that are owned and controlled by the company, a rerouting of the roadway to avoid the sensitive asset.

Of course, there is a practical consideration in cases where the asset is located adjacent to or in close proximity to the company's property boundaries. In such cases, substantial barriers such as concrete walls may minimize the impact of an anticipated level of explosives discharged on the property perimeter. In such cases, the security professional may not have the expertise to evaluate the resiliency of a structure to withstand bomb blasts or other major catastrophes. Seek the advice of engineering experts in such matters.

There are also cases where it is impractical to erect such barriers, for instance, where the asset is located immediately adjacent to property boundaries. An example of this is the Oklahoma City bombing of the Federal building. In this case, it was impossible to extend the barrier beyond the limits of the anticipated force, and it would be either cosmetically unacceptable or simply impossible to erect blast walls to minimize the impact of an explosion. In these cases, emphasize other elements of the security survey to assist in the detection and deterrence of the anticipated threat. At this stage in the process, however, it is not important to establish the type of perimeter barricade used but rather to define the location of that barricade in light of the anticipated threat.

Assess the Resistance Value of the Perimeter Material

During the physical inspection, inspect the physical condition of the perimeter material. Some of this information is available in the company's drawings but physical conditions change over time. Fence lines and building walls can degrade and sometimes other material replaces these perimeter structures. In addition, wall configurations can change based on company needs and the floor and plot plans do not reflect these changes. Note the floor and plot plans with reminders to inspect these structures.

Identify and Control Openings in the Perimeters and Assess Resistance Value

All protected perimeters will have openings to permit routine business activity. In many cases, these openings are used infrequently or in special circumstances. An example of this is emergency exit doors in an office building. These doors are usually secured with mechanical locks. The Vulnerability Study includes the identification of mechanical locks as well as electric locks used in access control system. Include all openings, regardless of use, in the study.

Look for door status monitors on all doors in the protected perimeter. Doors secured with mechanical locks also need some form of detection to signal improper opening of the door. In addition to door openings, there are also windows and freight openings in the protected perimeter that likewise require some form of detection monitoring to determine the status of the opening.

Some openings in the protected perimeter are used extensively throughout the business day. In such cases, simple mechanical locks will usually not satisfy security objectives. In these cases, access control systems are used to require building occupants to present a credential to the system so that their authority to enter the premises may be verified. Upon verification, these access control systems release electrically controlled locks permitting access (and in some cases egress).

In addition to authorized entry by employees, visitors frequently enter controlled areas during the normal course of business. Under these circumstances, the survey must uncover and then recommend a way to identify these visitors and verify their authorization to access and remain on company premises. In today's business climate, businesses are paying more attention to visitor control. Concerns over industrial sabotage and espionage have increased substantially in recent years.

In addition to controlling the protected perimeter, the survey will include the means to identify perpetrators entering areas without authorization. Although the use of alarm monitoring equipment provides detection, it is recommended that closed circuit television (CCTV) equipment be used for event identification. The Vulnerability Study also includes the designated views needed to make appropriate observations.

Assess the resistance value of the barricades to each opening. Look at the doors and gates, and determine if the obstacles can be defeated by ordinary means. In some cases, doors may need to be replaced or repaired. There is a discussion later in the chapter on ways to evaluate these barricades.

Lighting

During the survey, determine if appropriate lighting sources are available around and within the protected perimeter. Ample lighting can be a significant deterrent to physical security threats and will be a consideration in selecting the type of CCTV equipment recommended. Review existing lighting sources around the protected asset and consider how it will deter the identified threat. Look for levels of illumination needed to observe perpetrators with the naked eye and using surveillance equipment.

The most common measurement of light output (or luminous flux) is the lumen. A lumen is a unit of light flow or luminous flux. The lumen rating of a lamp is a measure of the total light output of the lamp. Light sources are labeled with an output rating in lumens. For example, a R30 65-watt indoor flood lamp may have a rating of 750 lumens. Similarly, a light fixture's output can be expressed in lumens. As lamps and fixtures age and become dirty, their lumen output decreases, and lumen depreciation occurs.

Sufficient light must be available for CCTV equipment so that an observer can perceive and classify an event. Closed circuit television equipment cost is lower if ample light is available for standard grade cameras. Low light CCTV equipment can overcome low ambient light levels, but it is more expensive. Manufacturers of CCTV equipment provide lumen requirements for their equipment. It may be necessary to measure the available light using a light meter in some cases. Recommendations for additional lighting will provide illumination for CCTV equipment and provide deterrence in secured areas.

Inspect Infrastructure Resources

In most cases, infrastructure is not the primary target of malicious activity; it is the assets contained within the facility. However, the survey must consider the threat to the supporting infrastructure. If a perpetrator's intent is to exact revenge on the company for a wrong believed done to them, it may be just as useful to damage the utilities that provide critical services to the facility. Depending on the level of threat and the anticipated sophistication of the perpetrator, assess supporting utility sources for vulnerability.

In the case of public utilities, adding protective elements to such services would be a wasted investment since a perpetrator will simply attack the utility in an area not controlled by the company. It is recommended that the security professional recommend backup services to provide a replacement of lost power, communications or other utilities should the primary services suffer a successful attack.

Employee Identification

The Vulnerability Study will also consider how the company identifies employees in the facility. This includes a review of the means used to recognize employees, the methods for issuing and controlling the identity credentials and the challenges used by all employees.

In the Initial Goal Setting Meeting described in Chapter 2, we discussed the criteria for employee identification. The Vulnerability Study confirms that the process used meets the company's objectives to distinguish employees from other individuals on company grounds.

Visitor Control

Determine the criteria for admitting visitors to the facility. Most companies permit individuals who are not employees to conduct business on company grounds. An example might be sales representatives and customers. Establish where the visitors are permitted access and the verifications used to challenge the visitors to determine their intent on company grounds. Look for the records of visitor entry and note what information company personnel gathers from the visitor before granting access.

Also determine how that access is granted. Examine the access procedures to determine if the company requires an escort for the visitor or are they simply permitted to walk onto company premises after passing the first challenge.

Evaluate the Existing Security Systems

If the company has an existing physical security system, document where the components of those systems are located and the monitoring and display methods incorporated in the systems. If there are alarm monitoring systems, deliberately violate the protected doors (after first advising company security of your intent) and confirm that the alarms properly register with the response team.

If the company has access control equipment installed, obtain a void card (one that is not supposed to work) and a valid card (one that is supposed to work) and test each controlled door. The void card should be rejected and the valid card should be accepted. Also, verify the locking device used to secure the door. When the door is in a normal and locked condition, determine if it is possible to defeat the lock by ordinary means and gain access.

Also, if electric locking devices are used, plan a test of the life safety devices. This usually means triggering the fire alarm or fire suppression systems to confirm that these systems have the ability to unlock the controlled doors. Do these tests with the knowledge and consent of the facility managers and the response team. The maintenance personnel who service the detection systems can usually trigger these systems without sounding a general alarm and disrupting the company's staff.

Evaluate the Company's Ability to Respond

The primary goal of a physical security system is to detect, deter, delay, and respond to breaches in security. The element of "response" is important in the study because without a means to respond the other goals have limited value. A related objective in providing an enhanced physical security system is to provide the company's security force with information and control over the protected area.

As the security survey mission is communicated to management and the company staff, make clear that physical security systems are intended to aid and enhance the job of the security officer, not to eliminate the security force in favor of these new systems.

It is therefore to the benefit of the company to include the security force in discussions regarding the security survey. In some instances, security force management personnel may view the addition of new equipment as an effort to replace existing guard forces. Make every effort to counter this impression and emphasize the benefits of adding physical security measures as a tool for the guard force.

An effective physical security system will allow security force management to cover more area in less time and do a more comprehensive job of securing the facility without needing to increase the security staff. Further, an effectively designed physical security system will change the nature of the job done by the security force. Security officers will no longer stand in front of a door just to verify that authorized personnel enter. A security officer's work will focus more on response and less on deterrence, detection, and delay.

To achieve improvements in the area of response, review security procedures, watch post instructions, reporting methods, and other security force protocols that enable the company's security force to respond to threats. Without adequate response and reporting, much of the company's investment in these new security tools will be lost.

PREPARE FOR THE SURVEY

Begin by obtaining a copy of the blueprints for the company's facility. Usually, the physical plant or facilities' department maintains these documents. If the company is located in a very old building and there are no plans readily available, the first step is to sketch the physical layout of the grounds and buildings. Whether readymade drawings are used or sketches are developed for the facility, the same document types are needed. These documents are:

Plot Plan—The plot plan is an illustration of the property boundaries of the company and, usually, fencing or other perimeter barricades used to restrict access to company grounds. The plot plan will generally contain an outline of all buildings on the property although without any detail regarding the specific characteristics of the building. In many cases, plot plans have been used as a "base document" to establish a description of facility-wide services. Such services would include telecommunications, data communications and existing security measures. See Figure 3.1 for an example of a plot plan.

Floor Plan—A floor plan is an illustration of the walls and door locations of a building. It is essential to have a copy of the first floor of each building's floor plan, but it may not be necessary to obtain copies of the upper floors if security measures will be not be needed on those floors (see Figure 3.2).

Building plans are generally arranged in "sets." As a result, plan holders may ask you which set is needed. Request "floor plan only"—this is the most informative for Vulnerability Studies and the least cluttered. The electrical set is sometimes helpful but mechanical sets are usually not necessary.

IDENTIFY THE CONTROL PERIMETERS

Using the drawings described above to define the security perimeter. The security perimeter is always relevant to the protected assets. The Physical Threat Assessment identified those areas that are of most concern to the company. Establish the security perimeter based on the location of those assets.

There may be several perimeters within a facility. The perimeters are loosely defined as concentric circles around protected assets. During the Vulnerability Survey, it may be determined that there are insufficient barricades or too many openings in the protected perimeter to adequately secure the facility. The System Design recommendations may include additional walls, doors, or fence lines to create new perimeters.

Start with the exterior perimeter, usually the outer boundaries of the company's property line. Then establish the protected perimeters for each of the internal areas based on the location of the assets protected. For instance, if there are four buildings in the facility, each building is potentially another protected perimeter. Each inner layer will receive progressively higher grades of protection.

There are also circumstances, such as single facility office buildings where the outer perimeter is the building's outer walls and the internal perimeters are asset areas within the building. Each inner layer may have higher levels of security to protect highly sensitive assets. An example of such an arrangement would be to provide "building level" access control at the exterior perimeter and

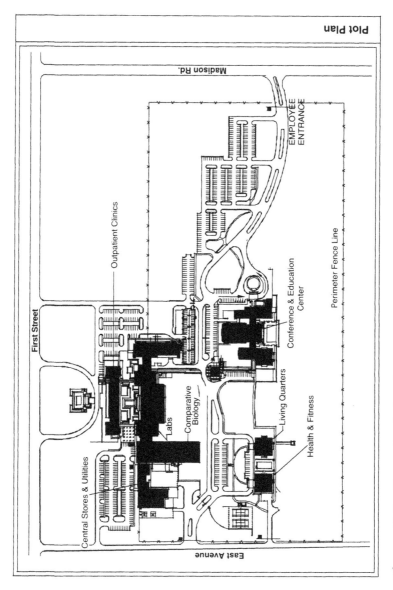

Figure 3.1   Example of plot plan.

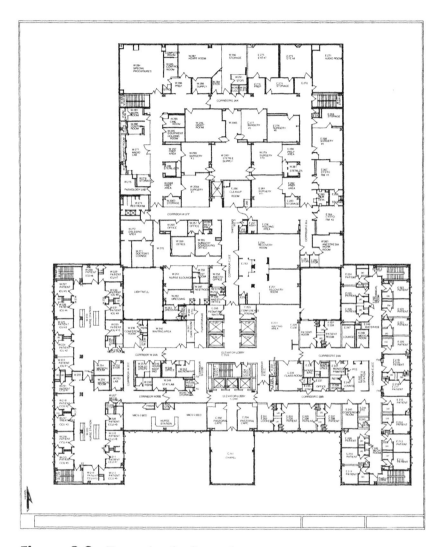

Figure 3.2 Example of a floor plan.

more restrictive access for a data processing center within the building. In the data center, there may be highly sensitive information. Access control to those areas will require greater protective measures such as biometric identification devices.

Each progressively smaller circle will provide higher levels of security to protect the more sensitive assets. When creating this design, it is only important to establish the perimeters and the level of security needed within each area. It is not necessary to establish controls for these openings at this time, but it is important to know the location of these openings. For example, in a fence line surrounding a protected perimeter, know where every opening exists in that fence line, even if the opening is seldom used. If the facility does not have a protected fence line, start with the outer walls that encompass the assets requiring protection. Be sure to include windows and other openings that may provide access to the facility. Do not assume that because an opening is rarely used, such as a fire exit, it does not need protection. Consider any break in the perimeter as an opening.

Perimeter Construction

After establishing the control perimeter, determine the types of material used to form these perimeters. Although the Vulnerability Study is primarily concerned with securing the openings to protected areas, it is important to consider the structures used to define perimeter controls. A part of the system recommendation may include "hardening" the perimeter structures to prevent forced entry. An example of this may be to use wall mesh to reinforce drywall construction or improvements to the perimeter fence lines. Verify information about the protected perimeter's material during the physical survey.

To determine if a perimeter must be hardened, consider the resistance value of the perimeter structure. Assess the degree of difficulty needed to breach the perimeter structure or defeat it in some meaningful way. For example, fence lines can be scaled or cut. If the perceived threat suggests a perpetrator with deliberation and intent may attempt to climb this fence line and, after so doing, pose an immediate threat to a protected asset, additional security measures are required.

Take an extreme view to defeat perceived threats when assets are highly vulnerable and located adjacent to perimeter fence lines. In those situations, a perpetrator with an explosive device may seek to damage the facility by placing that device near the protected asset, thereby causing the desired damage without actually having to defeat the perimeter line. In such cases, it will be necessary to harden that perimeter line with structural reinforcements to protect against those threats.

Consider the resistance value of the barricades used to control the openings. Sometimes it is impractical to reinforce an opening with sufficient resistance to prevent a deliberate attempt to access the perimeter. In addition to the physical security concerns, most businesses are also concerned about the cosmetic impact of security measures. An example of this would be the installation of "burglar bars" on windows. The company may consider this cosmetically unacceptable and, in most cases, it poses a violation to fire code egress rules.

Life safety issues are an important concern when securing a facility; pedestrians use openings to exit a facility as well as enter one. Hardened structures added to a security perimeter may prohibit egress from the facility in an emergency. Therefore, in lieu of hardening these access openings, it is often more acceptable to provide monitoring devices to detect and report specific threats when an unauthorized access to the facility is attempted.

Resistance Values of a Perimeter

When determining the resistance value of a perimeter the first consideration is saving lives. Protection of assets begins with protection of employees, then extends to the security of the physical assets of the facility. The term referred to in most blast resistance studies is the elastic region. The elastic region is the range within which the walls or other perimeter structures will withstand a blast force and then returned to the original shape. A wall with a higher elastic region value will not have permanent structural damage from a blast with a given force. However, a blast resistant design must assume that the structure needs to exceed the elastic region limits.

Proximity of the blast is a factor in blast elasticity. Therefore, an effective resistance to blast is standoff distance. Standoff distance is that distance at which a structure can safely withstand a blast of a given magnitude. In establishing protected outer perimeters, the standoff distance is usually the first consideration in the placement of the perimeter line.

To determine the blast resistance of the structure, first determine the threat a particular facility faces and whether or not blast threats are an important part of their security profile. This information should have been uncovered in the Physical Threat Assessment. Standoff distance is usually the best choice for resisting blast attacks. It is less expensive and easier to employ than attempting to harden the physical perimeter of structures. When in doubt, employ structural engineers to evaluate the integrity of a structure and determine its blast resistance value. Engage the services of a qualified engineering firm to assist in determining the blast elasticity of perimeter walls when the Threat Assessment suggests that blast damage is a threat.

Perimeter Controls

After identifying the protected perimeters, locate all of the openings on the perimeter line of each area. These are usually doors, gates and windows. Some openings may not be used frequently (such as emergency exits) but are a part of the system documentation and Vulnerability Study. During the physical survey, evaluate the types of physical barricades used at these openings. Pay special attention to the types of doors and doorframes used to seal the openings.

Door construction can vary with each facility. The challenge is to understand how that barricade may be threatened and if the barricade is substantial enough to resist that threat. An example of such a comparison is a hollow metal door as compared to a hollow wood door. If the Physical Threat Assessment indicates that the highest concern for security at an opening is ordinary passage by a pedestrian without tools or high motivation, a hollow wood door may be sufficient to deter access.

However, if perpetrators with deliberation and intent to gain access to the protected area threaten the facility and forced entry is expected, a hollow wood door would be of little deterrence. Metal doors with metal frames will provide greater deterrence and would delay the perpetrator longer, allowing early detection and response. In such cases, the system design recommendation will include replacement of doors to provide sufficient delay and deterrence to intruders.

SET THE VIDEO SYSTEM OBJECTIVES FOR THE SURVEY

After the security perimeter is established, assess the video systems needs. Assume a perpetrator has breached the protected perimeter or that attempts are being made to do so and detection has been made by other elements of the planned security system.

Evaluate the protection zone and determine which observation points would be most effective in observing the presence of the intruder and classifying their intent. Classification is important since an all out response may not be needed if the intruder is simply an employee who has inadvertently breached a controlled area. Pay special attention to the outer perimeters; these will afford the greatest response time for the security force.

Indicate the placement of a camera in the appropriate location that will afford the optimum view. Some of the elements to consider in camera placement are:

1. The range of view (left/right)
2. The angle of view (up/down)
3. The availability of lighting
4. The distance from the subject

Consider the physical mounting of the equipment and the availability of power. Judgment of the value of the view in relation to the cost of providing that view will determine the viability of the option. For example, a petrochemical plant with a large perimeter may require mounting poles and long power runs to provide the desired view. This may be financially unfeasible. Long lenses are used to offset long viewing distances but they will provide less useful images. Consider all aspects of camera placement in this step.

ESTABLISH THE COMMAND CENTER

Inspect the existing command center for the facility. If one does not exist, plan a command center for the facility in the recommendation. This establishes the centralized reporting location for alarms and the control point for openings throughout the system.

Usually, some type of security command posts exists in most organizations. This would be the most obvious place to locate the command center for any new security system. If the company does not have a security command center yet, there may be a control center for elevator and fire alarm reporting. The company's security manager can help to determine where the security command center should be located. Some elements to examine when reviewing a potential command center are:

- Located within the protected perimeter.
- Adequate lighting and ventilation.
- Easy access to the key areas of the facility.
- Sufficient room for equipment and security furniture.
- Available wall space for mounting equipment (CCTV).
- Ample access to commercial power.
- Cable pathways into the room.

Recommend enhancements to existing command centers to improve the effectiveness of the post and encourage heightened attention by the watch officers operating that post.

EQUIPMENT LOCATION

In addition to the command center, most large electronic security systems require the installation of control equipment to provide power and communications to end-point devices. It is sometimes necessary to have multiple equipment locations to minimize the impact of cable runs to each end point. There are several elements to examine when selecting equipment locations:

- Located within the protected perimeter.
- Controlled access to the space by means of secured walls and lockable doors.
- Adequate lighting and ventilation.
- Cable pathways into the room (a vital consideration).
- In multi-story buildings, cable pathways between floors.
- In multi-building complexes, access to network and inter-building communications.
- Sufficient wall space for mounting equipment control equipment.

• Ample access to commercial power and emergency power backup services.

Where these facilities are not available, recommend enhancements to the equipment location areas to make them suitable for equipment and cabling.

CONDUCT THE PHYSICAL SURVEY

Once the security perimeter is established, the access openings identified and the resistance value of the perimeter and openings evaluated, determine the valid access and egress requirements for the secured area. Do this with the help of the company employees during the physical survey.

Begin the physical survey by establishing a "walk through" schedule that includes a management representative of the operating department for that area and a representative of the physical plant or facilities' department. If the security professional's role in the company is not in security management, a company security manager should accompany the security professional on this physical survey. When starting the survey, write the names and titles of the parties participating in the survey and the date the survey was done for later reference.

Using the site plans and floor plans as a guide, start at the most active opening in the outer most perimeter then proceed to all perimeters identified in the physical survey plan. Identify the openings employees typically use. In some cases, employees use openings that management would prefer they not use. Plan a monitoring device for each opening.

Consider each opening in the protected perimeter and determine the following characteristics of the opening to decide if the opening requires an access control device:

1. Is there something behind the door of significant value to the company, either people or property?
2. Is there dangerous or hazardous material behind the opening that could be a liability to the company if accessed by unauthorized personnel?

3. Are there privacy issues regarding elements behind the opening?

   If the opening requires an access control device, then consider the following questions to decide how to handle the opening:

   1. When should this door be locked?
   2. When this door is locked are there times when access should be permitted?
   3. When this door is locked are there times when egress should be permitted?
   4. Does management plan to monitor access or egress (or both) at this door by means of a security officer? If not, will the company need a record of entry or exit at this opening?
   5. Is this a primary exit door? In most buildings, an "Exit" sign above the door identifies a primary exit door. Fire code requirements in most states call for primary exit doors to be clearly marked and available for egress at all times.
   6. Does this door lead to other doors that are considered primary exits and are there other avenues of escape to that exit without passing through the subject door?
   7. Are there select individuals (as opposed to all company employees) who are permitted to use this door?

   It is generally best to begin the survey at the main or front entrance. That term does not always apply but it means the opening in the protected perimeter that has the highest level of traffic. Then walk the full length of the exterior perimeter, examine each opening in the perimeter and make a determination on how best to secure that opening. The Operations personnel attending the walk through can explain how a particular opening is used. Appearances can be deceiving. A door that appears to be secured and infrequently opened may in fact be a high traffic door but simply lacks the evidence of the traffic. Operational personnel from the department will know best how an opening is used.

   During the walk through, examine the structure of the perimeter barricades to confirm the information gathered in the planning step. Confirm that the barricade is substantial enough to withstand the anticipated threats and that it is in good repair.

DOCUMENT THE FINDINGS

The level of detail in gathering this information can be overwhelming for most systems. Documenting the findings is an essential part of the job. To aid in this process, are the Door Detail Schedule and the Camera Detail Schedule.

The Door Detail Schedule (DDS)

During this physical survey, the security professional will record the information obtained about the openings on the Door Detail Schedule (see Figure 3.3). Write the name of the area where conducting this part of the physical survey on the DDS. Include floor numbers where applicable.

To fill in the DDS, determine the "common name" given to each opening or alarm point in the protected area. The common name is the one given to that location by company personnel and used on a day-to-day basis. The "formal name" for the opening is usually provided on the floor plan or plot plan. This will be the primary identifier when discussing openings with company employees in future meetings and will serve as the primary reference for communicating equipment locations to vendors during the bid and installation process.

The formal name is usually more exact and reflects the relative location in the building. The architect of the building usually generated these names during the design phase (e.g., corridor 12, door 15). However, these designations frequently give way to a common description recognized by employees in everyday situations (e.g., lab door). It would be useful to record both.

Using the security level assignments made during the preparation step, assess each opening in the protected perimeter. Show the means of access, egress, locking, and alarm (see Chapter 6 for a complete description) on the Door Detail Schedule. Continue in a like manner for the entire outer perimeter, then move to each inner perimeter, assessing each opening in each perimeter. The primary

Door Detail Schedule

By: (Consultant Name)
Revision: 0
Date: (Date)

Client: (Company)
Work Location: (Area)
Project: (Project Description)

Door Description	Location Ref on Drwg	Access	Access Special	Lock	Lock Special	Egress	Egress Special	Fire Alarm Interface	Number of DSS Alarms	Number of PIR Monitor	Number of Panic Alarms	Drawing Ref	Remarks	Distance to Panel	Feet of Conduit

Figure 3.3   The door detail schedule.

mission is to establish the traffic patterns throughout the facility. This will be a guide in the application of electronic access control devices and, to a certain extent, the application of CCTV equipment. Specific technical details are not important at this step but a review of the type of equipment assigned would be of value. A discussion of some of these elements follows.

Access and Egress Control Devices An access/egress control device is a card reader, PIN pad, biometric measuring device, or other identification device that uses a characteristic of an individual or the properties of a credential the individual possesses to identify the person requesting access or egress. At this point, it is only important to note that some form of identity recognition is needed for access or egress at controlled openings.

Exit Button After locating access control devices, and if egress control devices are used, specify the placement of egress buttons. There are a variety of regulations concerning the placement, use, and operation of egress buttons. Refer to the National Fire Protection Association (NFPA) Life Safety Handbook for guidance on the current recommended handling of egress devices. These are life safety issues and carry moral, ethical and legal responsibilities. The state and local fire marshal enforce these regulations and failure to follow them can result in the fire marshal closing the company's facility until the violations are corrected.

In addition to egress buttons, the code requires a variety of other means of egress from a protected area. When specifying any form of security system that restrains egress from a protected space, complete familiarity with the entire section of NFPA Means of Egress requirements is imperative.

Door Locks The appropriate lock is vital to the proper operation of any access control system that controls an opening. Electronic access control systems are designed to make a decision on admitting an individual through an access opening but what restrains the individual from entering the opening is the door and lock. It is important to choose the appropriate lock for a given door. A well-designed properly installed access control system can be easily defeated if the appropriate locking mechanism is not properly selected and installed.

Door locks fall into two broad categories: locks that work with the existing door hardware and locks that are not dependent on the existing door hardware. No single choice is best in all circumstances. An example of a locking device that works with door hardware is an electric strike. The electric strike replaces the "strike plate" on the doorframe. The strike plate is what permits the existing door hardware to hold the door closed.

Other locks are completely independent of the existing door hardware such as power bolts and power magnets. These devices usually have one component installed on the doorframe and another component installed on the door. The relation between these two devices is such that the application (or release) of power will permit the door to open. These products generally hold an opening closed by a mechanical or magnetic means and act independently of any other mechanism on the door. Again, a complete examination of these devices is not necessary at this point; only the designation of a lock and lock type. Each door characteristic has an impact on the lock chosen for the door. Gather as much information as possible about the subject door before deciding on the locking mechanism to use. Consider the following when selecting the lock type for an opening:

1. The nature and construction of the door.
2. The door swing (inward swing or outward swing).
3. The height of the door. (Do not use locks that are installed at the door header on very tall doors. This causes the door to warp.)
4. The material the door is made of (in judging the application of electric latches).
5. The ability to bring low voltage electrical power to various points on the doorframe.
6. The type of control devices that will be used on the door. (Egress controls are sometimes necessary in certain application and will dictate the use of special hardware or locks that do not work with existing door hardware.)
7. The applicable fire codes that govern the use of the door.

Door Hardware When choosing an electric strike for a door, information is also required about the existing door hardware.

Electric strikes are designed to replace door strike plates and not all electric strikes are compatible with all strike plate cutouts. Further, not all electric strikes are compatible with all door handle hardware.

The most appropriate means for determining compatibility between strike and strike plate is to use a cross-reference document published by the electric strike manufacturers. However, the exact make and model of door hardware is not always easy to determine by simply examining the outer surface of the door hardware. Perform a tracing of the strike plate that will be replaced by the new electric strike. This will save considerable time in the system design step.

Using a piece of ordinary paper, title the paper with the name and location of the door. Place the paper over the strike plate, aligning the edge of the paper with the edge of the door jam. Note the side of the paper where the jam is located. Trace the outer edges of the entire strike plate and the inner edges of the cutouts—holes in the plate that accept the door handle hardware (keeper and bolt). Be sure to indicate on the tracing the location, size and center of the mounting screw holes. This will also be an essential part of making the appropriate electric strike selection. A lock hardware supplier can use this tracing to match an electric strike to the existing strike plate. Share these documents with vendors when releasing the bid. It will assist them in preparing their cost proposals.

Door Status Switches (DSS) Plan to monitor all security perimeter openings. Door status switches, sometimes called door contacts or alarm contacts, are used to monitoring openings. Door status switches are simple mechanical sensors that detect the status of an opening. Although the name implies a DSS is for door installations, these switches are also for windows and other types of openings.

In general, a DSS consists of two components: a magnet attached to the door leaf and a reed switch that detects the presence of that magnet. Simply put, when the door is closed the alarm contact is in close proximity to the reed switch and holds it closed. When the door is open, the magnet is away from the reed switch and the switch opens. This provides a signal to an electronic security system that indicates the door is open. During the physical survey, indicate where a DSS is needed at an opening and the number of DSS required.

Space Protection If a room, a passageway, or some open area requires protection, use a space protection device. These detectors register the presence of individuals in the protected area. Similar to locks and door status switches, there is a wide variety of such devices available in the market. It is not important to decide on which device to use during the physical survey, it is only important to note the need for such a device.

The Camera Detail Schedule (CDS)

Inspect the areas that require video observations. Record information about the location of each camera and the view each camera will have. During this physical survey, record the information obtained about the video views on the Camera Detail Schedule (CDS).

Begin by writing the name of the area where this part of the physical survey is being conducted on the CDS. Include floor numbers where applicable (see Figure 3.4). List the name and view of each camera location on the CDS and the equipment criteria. Similar to the DDS, this will be the primary identifier when discussing camera views with company employees in future meetings and will serve as the primary reference for communicating equipment locations to vendors during the bid and installation process. A discussion of the sections of the CDS follows:

Camera Type Consider the light level and the view required. It may be required to also view the location at night to determine the amount of available light. In most cases, a standard camera will permit adequate viewing for most well illuminated areas. However, the Physical Threat Assessment may indicate that the area in question is in close proximity to a vulnerable asset or is highly susceptible to intrusion. In these cases, a low light level camera may be needed for night viewing. At this point, it is not important to specify the exact model of camera. Instead, determine the type of camera needed based on the anticipated available light throughout the observation period.

Camera Detail Schedule

Client: (Company)
Work Location: (Area)
Project: (Project Description)

By: (Consultant Name)
Revision: 0
Date: (Date)

Camera View	Location Ref on Drwg	Camera: Standard / Low Light	Lens: Zoom / Fixed= 2, 3, 4, 8, Z	Iris: Auto / Manual	Housing Indoor / Outdoor With Fan / Wiper	Special: Hood (H)	Mount: Ceiling / Wall / Pedmt / Post	Mount Duty: Heavy / Medium / Light	Pan / Tilt Control (1)	Alarm Input (1)	Auxiliary Lights (1)	Drawing Ref	Remarks	Distance to Monitor	Feet of Conduit

Figure 3.4 Camera detail schedule.

Lenses The lens decision provides the "angle of view." The width of the scene viewed and the distance of the camera from the subject area determine this. There are formulas to help the security professional make this determination; however, suppliers provide a handy tool for making this decision. It is a handheld lens that assumes a certain size for the camera pickup element, then allows the user to view what the scene would look like for a given lens size. Select the appropriate size lens and record that on the CDS.

In some cases, a single focal length lens may not be adequate for obtaining the views needed to make proper identifications in the subject area. In these cases, a zoom lens is the correct choice. Again, use the lens tool to determine the minimum and maximum focal lengths for the correct lens.

Auto Versus Manual Iris Lenses The lens iris controls the amount of light that enters the lens. In most applications, an auto iris is usually selected because it automatically adjusts to changing light conditions. Exercise caution when placing an auto iris lens on an outdoor camera with a wide range of views.

If the view requires a pan and tilt drive, and the device is set to "auto pan" (the camera pans left and right automatically), the security professional must consider the light levels of the background throughout the entire pan cycle during a 24-hour period. If the background light shifts significantly, the auto iris will be in constant operation and damage will eventually occur due to excessive use.

Camera Housings Cameras require housings to prevent tampering and to provide protection from the elements. Determine if the camera needs an indoor or outdoor housing and if special devices are needed to counter the effects of weather. An example of such devices would be a sun shield in hot climates or wipers in rainy environments.

Housing Mounts Housings are attached to structures by means of mounts. A variety of fixed position mounts are available. Record the surface style needed for the subject installation on the CDS. The choices are wall, pedestal, parapet, or post mounts. There are also movable mounts called pan and tilt drives. Each type of mount is usually associated with a housing type to provide a complete and working system. Use a general description to establish the basis for system design.

Special Camera Features   For some views with pan tilt zoom features, it may be necessary to auto program the camera to home in on a particular angle of view with a predefined zoom. In these cases, note the need for an alarm input to trigger the auto functions of the camera system and what event will evoke the trigger on the CDS.

KEY MANAGEMENT

Electronic security controls are not always required for every facility door. In many cases, door status switches are the only security devices needed. The door status switch will indicate to the system operators when improper door openings occur but will not control the door.

Use mechanical locks to control doors in these cases. Prepare a key management schedule for these locks. This can be an arduous task. One of the reasons electronic security systems are required in a facility is because key management is out of control. Duplicate keys for sensitive areas are frequently given to occupants who do not have an essential need for access.

As part of an overall security plan, recommend that all existing mechanical locks be re-keyed so that the existing metal keys will no longer work. Create a new set of metal keys for the re-keyed doors and recommend proper distribution. Once again, documenting the possession of these metal keys will be an essential part of the overall security plan. Use a matrix to document key management. The matrix indicates which doors are keyed and who has possession of those keys (see Figure 3.5). Start the with the names of the doors in the left hand column and groups holding keys for these doors are indicated across the top row. Use a symbol such as an "X" to indicate a group has access to and holds a key for a particular door.

Other reference sources are available that discuss the ways and means of using master and sub-master keying plans. It is not the intent of this work to address those issues but merely to remind the security professional that such plans exist and need to be

Key Management

Client: (Company)
Work Location: (Area)
Project: (Project Description)

Floor	Door Lock	Adminis-tration	Maintenance	Clinic Managers	Pharmacy
Basement:	amphitheater	X		X	
	tunnel to laundry	X	X		
	fire exit, west side front	X	X	X	X
First Floor:	medical records admin	X		X	X
	family doctor	X		X	
	loading dock	X	X		
Third Floor Psyc Ward:	east front fire exit	X	X	X	X
	ward desk	X		X	
	central desk	X		X	
Fifth Floor:	East fire exit	X	X	X	X
	West fire exit	X	X	X	X
Sixth Floor Pharmacy:	pharmacy dispensing	X			X
	fire exit 1	X	X	X	X
	fire exit 2	X	X	X	X
Seventh Floor Neurology:	fire exit 1	X	X	X	X
	fire exit 2	X	X	X	X

Figure 3.5   Key management matrix.

studied carefully before a re-keying effort is made. Usually, the implementation of an electronic security system signals the re-evaluation of all security measures in a facility. Instruct the company to issue only a minimum number of keys under any re-keying process.

CONSEQUENCES OF LOSS

After gathering data on the facility's security perimeters and assessing the vulnerabilities, consider the consequences of loss. Further interviews with the operations and financial employees of the company may be required to establish this analysis. The goal is to determine the impact of a violation of the security perimeter on the ongoing operation of the company.

Make a list of the critical assets of the company and then identify the ways in which a perpetrator could successfully defeat the existing security measures. Next, examine what impact that attack would have on the operation and seek the assistance of company personnel in establishing a cost of that impact. Remember that the cost is not just the loss of the asset but also includes the loss of revenue in removing the asset from service. The conclusions from this analysis will help justify the investment in security equipment and provide additional motivation to act.

CONCLUDING THE SURVEY

At the conclusion of the survey, document all findings and prepare a report for the management team. Base the conclusions of the report on the data gathered then formulate a recommendation on how best to proceed. A valid recommendation may be to do nothing at all. If the company's existing security measures and the facility's configuration are adequate to protect it from the expected threats, the security professional's report can be used as a basis for the company's decision to use resources for other operational requirements. The mission of the Vulnerability Study is to determine the company's readiness to counter expected threats.

The report should detail the existing assets, the protected perimeters, the openings in the perimeters and the current methods of controlling those openings. The report should also provide the results of the tests conducted on the effectiveness of existing security systems and the life safety tests. Conclude the report with an explanation of the consequences of loss and a recommendation for improvements or changes needed to meet the company's security goals as defined in their policy statement. This concludes the Needs Assessment or Phase 1 of the Security Audit.

4

Creating the Preliminary System Design

INTRODUCTION

In this chapter, we will discuss how to evaluate the data gathered during the Vulnerability Study to choose equipment that will accomplish the goals stated during the Initial Goal Setting Meeting. This book is not a substitute for the services of a trained professional. The book may be used as a guide for security professionals who do not engage in system design on a regular basis. If the project is large or complex, a professional security consultant should be included in the design team. This book will help the security director or project manager understand the requirements of system design and work more effectively with the security consultant.

A good indication that a consultant is a qualified expert is the certification of PSP following their name. The ASIS International Review Board grants the PSP or Physical Security Professional designation. To find a qualified consultant, the reader is encouraged to contact the International Association of Professional Security Consultants (IAPSC). Their website can be found at *www.iapsc.org*.

If it is not possible to engage a qualified professional consultant, the reader is encouraged to include other publications in her or his project reading list. Some of those publications are:

- Design and Evaluation of Physical Protection Systems (Mary Lynn Garcia, 2001)
- Effective Physical Security (Lawrence J. Fennelly, 1997)

Both books are available from Butterworth Heinemann.

In this work, the focus is on the commercial aspects of describing the specified system. The techniques recommended here are intended to help the security professional provide enough detail concerning the desired system so that it will be clearly communicated to the vendors and will result in informative and useful responses to the competitive bid opportunity.

In this chapter, we will identify the system components needed to achieve the security goals. In the next chapter, we will perform a cost analysis of the proposed system to determine if our ideas meet the "rule of reason." The "rule of reason" refers to a value judgment that the management team will make regarding the proposed solutions. If we are attempting to protect $50,000 worth of assets with $75,000 worth of systems and services, it is unlikely that the company will accept the recommendation. In providing this recommendation, one must also consider the probability of loss. How likely is it that the assumed risks will occur? Even if the costs of the recommended security systems are reasonable, if the probably of occurrence is very low, the value of the security solution is diminished.

We will also consider the operational value of the asset. The value of an asset may be high and the cost of securing it may be low but if the asset has little operational value, then the lack of operational value diminishes the effectiveness of the security solution recommendation. It is best to disclose the comparisons to the management team and allow them to make the cost/benefit decision. The job of the security professional is to evaluate, analyze, and recommend the most effective physical security system. The company is responsible for making the decision to invest in security assets.

The results of a Vulnerability Study determine system design. System designs are also based on other client specific requirements. Company requirements may include but are not limited to the application of specific credential technologies (i.e., smart cards), control point devices for unique circumstances (biometric and card reader design), network configurations (the use of on-site Local Area Networks or LAN) and control and display methods (using existing workstations to manage access control and CCTV systems). Consider all factors when creating a preliminary system design. This chapter will help guide the design process.

PRELIMINARY SYSTEM DESIGN

The Vulnerability Study identifies the areas of the facility that required additional security measures to meet the company's security goals. The security professional identifies the security products and procedures to satisfy those needs. Design documentation starts with marking the floor plans and plot plans obtained during the Vulnerability Study.

Interpret Facility Plans

Start by orienting the mission to the existing facility plans. There is a set of symbols on most facility plans to aid this interpretation. Most plans follow a standard format so that building craftsmen can more easily interpret how to construct the building project. Locate the "symbol key" developed by the author of the drawing for that set of drawings. This key will indicate symbols for convenience outlets, smoke detectors, fire alarm signal switches, and other important building features. When in doubt, seek the advice of those who prepared the drawings.

The most useful format for these plans is CAD (computer assisted drawings). Where possible, obtain drawings in CAD format and provide the security recommendation markings on a "separate layer" of the drawing. Use CAD to produce drawings in reduced size to facilitate easy communications with the company and the vendors. Skilled computer users can reproduce the drawings in PDF files using a common software tool called Adobe

Acrobat. The Acrobat reader software is available at no charge on the Internet but one must purchase the software that produces the PDF document. Creating drawings in Acrobat format will allow the drawings to be reproduced and transmitted electronically and viewed more easily and viewed more easily.

Document the Protected Perimeter

Confirm the location of the protected assets on the plans and mark the location of each asset and all sensitive areas that will require additional security measures. Keep in mind that an asset can sometimes be an entire building.

Confirm the protected perimeter established during the Vulnerability Study by marking the walls, fence lines or other perimeter boundaries that make up the perimeter. If the plans used are in paper form, it is useful to mark over the existing perimeters with a red pencil so that the perimeter is clearly established. Use the same techniques for CAD except that the markings will be electronic and applied in a separate layer.

Identify each opening in the perimeter by "breaking the line" and, if necessary for clarity, circle the opening area. Mark the plan with name of the opening established during the Vulnerability Study on the Door Detail Schedule (DDS). This would also be a good time to cross match the common name for the opening given by the company employees with the proper name provided on the plans. If those names differ, add the plan name to the DDS and the common name on the DDS to the plans.

Establish the proposed command center and the equipment locations identified during the Vulnerability Study on the plan. In addition to endpoint devices, establish other material locations necessary for a complete and working system. Specifically, locate an appropriate area for access control panels, lock power supplies and camera power supplies. It is best to place this control equipment within the controlled perimeter. The most common choice for equipment placement is telephone closets or electrical closets inside a protected building. Always look for sources of commercial power and cable trays or other cable routing pre-designed to the building when selecting an equipment location. This will aid in the installation of security systems and helps to reduce the overall cost of the project.

Because of the sensitive nature of this equipment, the space chosen for the equipment must have limited access and monitoring is required on all openings to that space. This usually means placing a door status switch on the access doors to the area and providing space sensors within the controlled area to ensure that unauthorized individuals do not access the equipment.

In some cases, individuals who are not a part of the security team may need to access the same space where the equipment is located. An example of this might be a telephone closet for maintenance or installation of telephone system components. In those cases, specify lockable housings for the access control equipment and power supplies for CCTV equipment and place door status switches on the doors to these equipment boxes so that unauthorized access or tampering with the mechanisms may be detected. Refer to these plans as the "marked plans." The management team and vendors will use them to interpret the system design.

Select the Alarm Detection Devices

Designate the most appropriate sensing device for all openings in the protected perimeter and all sensitive security areas. For example, openings that permit access to the facility require status switches or similar detection devices to monitor their condition.

A status switch may also be referred to as a door status switch, DSS, (also known as door contacts and alarm contacts). These devices monitor the status of a movable barricade or door and are also used on window openings, fence openings and other structures that restrict access to an opening. See Figure 4.1 for an example.

DSS are made in many sizes, shapes, and styles and the appropriate door status switch for a particular opening is relative to the style of door or window being protected. For instance, in cases where cosmetics are an issue for a controlled door, "button contacts" are generally used.

A button contact consists of two components, a small magnet inserted in a window leaf or door and a corresponding sensor inserted in a window or door frame. The sensor is wired to the alarm monitoring panel and provides a signal when the window is opened. When the door or window is closed, the magnet is in close proximity to the sensor and holds a "reed switch" closed. When the

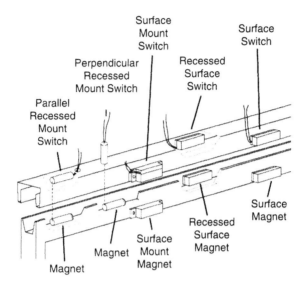

Figure 4.1   Door status switch.

door or window is open, the magnet is away from the sensor and the reed switch opens. It is this action of an opened/closed switch that provides the door status signal.

In some cases, DSS are normally opened while in other cases these contacts are normally closed. The type of alarm system used will determine the selection of normally opened versus normally closed door status switches. The manufacturer of the alarm monitoring system will define which type of contact is appropriate for the system. In most cases, normally closed contacts are required.

In surface mounted DSS applications, the door status switch consists of two components and a cable connects the DSS on the doorframe to the alarm system. These devices are usually mounted to the inside surface of the door in close proximity to one another. When planning the use of surface mounted DSS, it is best to place the contact as far away from the door hinge as possible. This will mean the DSS will be more perceptive to small movement in the door and is less likely to be defeated. Almost all DSS employ the use of some type of reed switch and magnet. Use the application manuals from the door status switch manufacturers to select the most appropriate contact. The astute security professional will have a thorough understanding of which contacts are most appropriate in which circumstances and will select the proper contact for the opening.

In addition to perimeter protection, certain areas of the facility will require the use of space protectors. A space protector is a device that monitors an area rather than a perimeter opening. An example is a drug locker in a pharmacy. It may be possible to breach a protected perimeter without using an established opening. A determined perpetrator can cut walls or access an area through the ceiling. The function of a space protection device is to sense the presence of an intruder in a protected area and signal that presence to an alarm monitoring system.

Select the Deterrence Devices

Begin by assessing which openings in the system require routine access and egress control and then decide on the appropriate access control device. Access control devices come in a variety of styles and types to meet specific applications. The following is a list of some of the more common types of devices available today.

It is not the intent of this work to list all available styles of all available devices in the market today. That list is dynamic and would be outdated in very short order. Instead, this list provides a broad grouping of devices and their more common applications. The informed security professional will frequently review the products from manufacturers to know what features are available for system design.

Card Readers A card reader is an electronic device that registers the presence of a security credential and transmits the identity information on that credential to an electronic physical security system. Card readers require that the authorized population carry a credential to provide identification. That credential is usually a credit card size encoded card (see section below on card technologies). This is the most common form of access control identification today. Card reader systems rely on the possession of a credential to identify a member of the authorized population. A limit of this technology is that credentials can be stolen or lost and the identity of the individual possessing the credential cannot be ascertained without additional identification criteria such as keypads or biometric measuring devices. However, card reader systems are frequently used in security applications because of their relatively modest cost and because they generally provide a secure environment if the authorized population is sensitive to the need for securing the card.

Card Technologies Since card readers are the most prevalent technology in the marketplace, some consideration should be given to the benefits and limitations of various card technologies. A brief history of card technology will provide the reader with some insight as to how the industry evolved and some of the benefits and limitations of these technologies.

The earliest card technology employed in security systems is the Hollerith card. The Hollerith card was a credit card sized credential with small holes punched in the card. The card was inserted in a reader and various sensing devices in the reader read the pattern of punched holes. If the pattern matched, access was granted. However, this card was easy to duplicate and the number of patterns encoded on the card was limited to the physical size of the card. This card is still in use today.

From the Hollerith card, a new technology was born called barium ferrite insert. A barium ferrite insert card used a magnetic material called barium ferrite to encode magnetic spots on the card. The most common type of barium ferrite encoded card had 36 magnetic spots arrayed in a matrix and these spots could vary by polarity and gauss level. Polarity could be plus or minus and there were up to five gauss levels for each spot.

When this card was presented to a card reader, it read the encoded magnetic matrix and, if the appropriate code was presented, the access was granted. It is easy to understand how this card was superior to the Hollerith card in that it was very difficult to duplicate, and the number of encodeable values at each spot was ten times greater than the standard Hollerith card. This card is rarely used in current applications although some older systems can still be found.

During the use of these two products, magnetic stripe cards were also being developed for security applications. Magnetic stripe cards provided an encoded bit pattern on a magnetic strip attached to the back of the card. These cards are used today for credit card identification and other forms of unique credentials.

Eventually, the magnetic stripe card gained wide acceptance in the security industry and, for a time, was widely used as an inexpensive, relatively secure credential. Magnetic stripe cards are still in wide use today, see Figure 4.2.

One of the limitations of a magnetic stripe card is that it can be duplicated through ordinary means. Manufacturers have taken steps to prevent this duplication process and have been relatively successful at preventing card duplication.

However, the magnetic stripe card has another limitation that cannot be overcome. When a user presents a magnetic stripe card to a card reader, the card must pass through a slot that causes the magnetic stripe card to rub on a card read head. This physical contact causes residue (body oils, dust, and airborne particles) to accumulate on the read head. In cases of long-term use or highly contaminated environments, this residue causes scarring on the magnetic strip, thereby rendering it unreadable. The chief advantage of magnetic stripe cards is that they are inexpensive.

In the late 1980s, a new card technology achieved a high degree of popularity. This has come to be known as the "Wiegand card." The Wiegand card used small pieces of bi-alloy wire embedded in the card that had certain magnetic properties. When this wire passed through a magnetic field at the proper orientation, the bi-alloy wire would create variations in the field commonly described as a "magnetic pop." Depending on how the wires are arranged, a readable signal was produced that could be interpreted by an access control panel as a binary bit stream. This signal could then be translated into 0s and 1s, the language of computer systems (see Figure 4.3).

Figure 4.2   Magnetic stripe reader.

Figure 4.3 Wiegand reader.

This card technology had the benefit of relatively low cost with a high number of possible combinations and did not share the limitations of contact residue found in magnetic stripe cards. As a result, it became a highly effective technology and the makers of that technology provided a standardized interface to connect this card to a variety of access control panels from different manufacturers. Although this technology is still in use, other more popular technologies have reduced the number of systems that use it.

It is the rapid rise in popularity of the Wiegand card that prompted the interface standardization between the card readers and access control panels. As a result, when subsequent card technologies were developed, it became useful and practical to build those technologies using the standard Wiegand interface. Hence, there is universal compatibility of card readers today with a variety of manufacturer's access control panels.

Competing with these technologies in the early years of access control was proximity cards. The earlier proximity cards required a battery to be installed in the card, and the card was commonly referred to as an "active" proximity card. These active proximity cards constantly generated a signal read by card readers. The reader acted like a receiving antenna for the access control system. If the card transmitted the proper code, the antenna would read that card and the system would grant access.

However, one of the limitations of this card was the installed battery. These proximity cards came with a warranty that was generally associated with the life of the installed battery. These batteries could not be changed easily and when a battery wore out, the card became useless. Over the life of the card, the battery would wear down and the "read range" or ability for the card reader to see the card diminished. Eventually, the read range became "contact" thereby reducing the effectiveness of the proximity value of the card.

This card technology is no longer used but the application gave rise to the most popular card technology in today's market. Current versions of proximity cards are termed "passive" and do not require batteries in the card (see Figure 4.4).

Passive proximity cards have a computer chip and antenna embedded in the card. When the card is within close proximity to a passive proximity card reader, the reader transmits a signal read by the chip in the card. This transmitted signal energizes the chip causing it to transmit a coded pulse read by the reader and, if the appropriate code is on the chip, the access control system will grant access. This form of proximity card has gained wide acceptance throughout the security industry. Most new proximity card reader applications use this technology.

Keypads A keypad is a button matrix that usually provides numeric keys so that the authorized population can signal their identity using a remembered authorization code. One concern regarding the application of keypads is that unauthorized individuals may obtain authorization codes and credentials are not required to gain access to the protected area. As a result, the authorization code can be replicated an unlimited number of times and individuals who would not otherwise have access to the facility can

Figure 4.4 Proximity card reader.

defeat the system. This concern is overcome by a strict enforcement of security procedures and proper employee orientation.

A second concern is that someone may observe an authorized user enter his or her code and simply repeat the button pattern. Some keypads use a scramble technology that reorients the number key pattern each time the keypad is used. The application of such devices will usually eliminate this limitation. This type of keypad is commonly referred to as a scramble keypad.

Biometric Measuring Devices   The most secure form of access control to ensure that the individual requesting access is the person to whom access permission is granted is biometrics. A biometric measuring device records a unique characteristic of an individual and grants access based on this identity. However, these devices are (for the most part) expensive when compared to the credential based technologies and keypads.

Consider all aspects of the decision when choosing a technology for granting authorized access. This means that costs should be a part of the decision. Biometrics is the most appropriate choice when the identity of the individual receiving access to the controlled area is of prime importance or if the area being protected is mission critical and a high degree of confidence is needed that the person to whom access is granted is the same person for whom access permission was intended.

There are also indirect costs to consider when selecting biometrics as the access control device such as the difficulty in conducting the enrollment process and maintaining the network necessary to manage the enrollment database. Each biometric technology has additional considerations as presented below.

1. Eye Scan—Retina
    Eye scan devices are highly sophisticated biometric measuring devices that require that the user's eye information be entered in the system through an enrollment process. This process differs from manufacturer to manufacturer but essentially the eye scan reader records the retina pattern of an individual in the authorized population and stores that pattern for later comparison. The eye scan unit is then set to read those patterns when an appropriate identification

(usually a key pad entry) is given to the eye scan device. The eye scan reader then compares the enrolled scan with the current scan and, if they match, access is granted.

2. Eye Scan—Iris
    The iris eye scan reader works in a similar fashion to the retina scan reader but reads a different part of the user's eye. In an iris reader, the iris pattern is recorded and used for later comparison.

3. Hand Scan
    Hand-scan readers measure hand characteristics of individuals in the authorized population. It is presumed that characteristics such as length between knuckles and other hand size features are unique in each individual. Like eye scan devices, hand scanners require an enrollment process and then compares the enrolled data to subsequent readings when an individual authorized population requests access to the controlled area.

4. Finger Matrix
    A finger matrix fingerprint reader uses fingerprint images to distinguish individuals. An enrollment process is required that records a fingerprint pattern of an authorized individual. During a request for access, the pattern presented by the requester is compared to the pattern on file. If they match, access is granted.

5. Voice Recognition
    Voice recognition systems require that an individual in the authorized population speak a series of words for the enrollment process into an enrollment reader. When requesting access at a controlled door, the user is given a set of word(s) to repeat and if a voice pattern match exists, access is granted. Voice recognition has waned in popularity in recent years but such systems are still in use today.

To complete this part of the preliminary design process, select the most appropriate identification device for each door and document that device on the DDS. Be sure to consider egress control as well as access control.

Egress control provides the benefit of knowing when a user exits the facility. It is most useful when employing a feature called "anti-passback." Anti-passback allows a security system to measure the entries and exits of an authorized user. It forces the user to badge in and out by automatically restricting some from re-entering if they failed to badge out. This is especially useful in high security applications such as computer rooms and server farms where it is important to know who was in an area at some point in time.

Select the Delay Devices

After deciding on the access and egress control methods, determine the means of locking these openings. Use the data gathered during the Vulnerability Study to decide on the locking methods for each door in the system.

In the case of doors where access is usually not required, a simple metal key and locking device is acceptable for the application. Moreover, mechanical locks are far less expensive than electric locks and less prone to service problems. An example of such a door can be a fire exit used only in cases of emergency. In most cases, existing locking hardware is satisfactory for the job; however, the keys that provide access to this lock are to be restricted. In some cases, it may be necessary to re-key these doors to ensure that unauthorized access is not possible (see Chapter 3, Key Management). In the case of existing lock hardware, test the lock to verify operation.

Electric locks are required for access control systems. Electric lock selection is door hardware dependent. This is because lock selection also affects an individual's ability to access or egress a facility.

Locks come in a variety of styles as listed below:

1. Electric panic hardware
2. Electric strikes
3. Power magnets
4. Power bolts
5. Power door latches

Each of these lock types has special characteristics and the lock selection must be based on the door being controlled, the egress features of the lock and the power control type needed in the application.

1. **Electric panic hardware** employs a solenoid embedded in a panic device (see Figure 4.5) that will retract a latch bolt when energized (or de-energized).

   Electric panic hardware is generally used on outer perimeter doors and frequently in fire exit applications. Electric panic hardware employs both electrical and mechanical means for retracting a door latch.

   When exiting a building, a user need only push on the panic hardware device to retract the latch bolt and open the door. These types of locks are usually considered very safe and reliable and should be employed whenever possible. However, these locking devices are difficult to install and generally more expensive than other types of locking devices.

   In some models, the panic hardware comes equipped with built-in door status switches that determine the condition of the latching device. However, knowing the condition of the lock is not the same as knowing the condition of the door. A door may be left ajar while the lock latch is fully extended, thereby providing the system monitors with an indication that the door is locked when in fact it is not.

   In addition to the installation of the electric panic hardware it is necessary to specify the installation of an "electric hinge" on all doors where such hardware is installed. Electric hinges replace the standard hinge on the door with built-in circuitry that allows electricity to pass through the hinge, thereby entering the edge of the door where the hinge is installed. Usually, the door is "cored" to permit passage of wire from the electric hinge to the location where the electric panic hardware is installed. This installation is not simple and if not done properly, can result

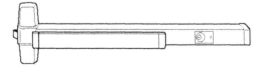

Figure 4.5   Electronic panic hardware.

in permanent damage to the door, rendering it useless. In such circumstances, it may be necessary to replace the door. Electric panic hardware is generally recommended for new construction when doors can be specially ordered to accommodate electric hinges and electric panic hardware.

2. **Electric strikes** replace that part of the door known as the strike plate (see Figure 4.6).

    The strike plate is the flat metal piece mounted on the doorframe adjacent to the doorknob. When a door is closed, the latch bolt or strike extends from the door handle mechanism into the doorframe. The latch bolt or strike lines up with the strike plate mounted on the doorframe and provides a hardened surface to prevent the door from opening.

    The installation of an electric strike requires the removal of the strike plate and the matching electric strike installed in its place. It is also necessary to option the door handle to prevent turning the handle from the protected side of the door. There is a hinge in the electric

Figure 4.6 Electronic strike.

strike on the portion that restricts the latch bolt or strike. A solenoid-controlled pin keeps the hinged part in place and acts like a standard strike plate. When power is applied or removed from the solenoid (depending on the style of lock, fail safe, or fail secure, see below), the pin retracts, thereby removing strike plate resistance from the door latch. When released, a user may open the door by pushing (or pulling) on the door without turning the door handle. On a door with an electric strike, turning the handle and pushing the door open provides egress as with a standard strike plate. This retracts the latch bolt and provides unrestricted egress from the protected area.

Electric strikes come in a variety of sizes and styles. These locks are not generally interchangeable. Specify electric door strikes based on the existing door hardware installed, and use a tracing of the strike plate to identify the proper lock for the door (see Chapter 3).

The application of an electric strike should be limited to those circumstances where controlled access is required but users need unrestricted egress. In some applications where electric strikes are used, door status switches are not used. This is because the access device used to gain access to a secured door can signal the alarm monitoring system that an authorized door opening is taking place but egress does not signal the access control system.

As a result, the alarm monitoring system does not know an authorized individual is opening the door for egress and will signal a security breach. When this happens repeatedly, it becomes a "cry wolf" syndrome and eventually the alarm is ignored, causing security personnel to not respond appropriately when a genuine security breach is in progress.

If it is essential to use an electric strike for life safety reasons, also provide an egress sensor that detects the presence of an authorized user exiting the protected area. Use the egress sensor to signal the alarm monitoring system that the door is about to open legitimately and program the system to shunt (turn off) the alarm. This arrangement will reduce the false alarm signals and allow monitoring of the door when in a secured condition.

3. **Power magnets** have become very popular as the lock of choice by most security installation companies. This is because power magnets are generally very easy to install and are fail safe (see below). Power magnets as shown in Figure 4.7 usually consist of two components: a strike plate and a magnetic lock.

    The strike plate is a piece of flat metal installed at the top of the door at a point farthest from the door hinge. That plate is aligned with an electromagnet that is mounted on the doorframe. These locks are generally installed on the protected side of the door to prevent vandalism and sabotage.

    Once mounted, there are wires from the magnet to a power source controlled by the access control system. When power is on, the lock locks and when power is off the lock is unlocked. When installed properly, these locks have a resistance force, depending of the model of the lock, from 650 pounds to 1500 pounds of force. That is to say, 1500 pounds of force against the subject door would be required to defeat the magnet. In most cases, that much force would generally result in pulling the door away from its hinges.

    However, door resistance values vary. Select a lock based on the resistance value of the door. It does little good

Figure 4.7   Power magnet locks.

to have a door lock that will resist 1500 pounds of force when the door itself can only resist 500 pounds of force.

When selecting power magnet locks, pay close attention to local fire code ordinances. Under current NFPA guidelines, primary exit doors must be operable in a single motion. If power magnet locks are installed and an exit button is used to provide lock release (as is commonly done), doors with door handle hardware will require a two-step process for egress. The two steps are defined as first pushing the egress button and second turning the door handle to open the door. In most instances, prevailing fire codes will not permit this use.

Power magnet locks can be defeated by a variety of means. One of the most common methods of defeating power magnet locks is to tape a small piece of metal or similar object across the face of the lock or the strike plate thereby lowering the contact value between the two components. When this occurs, the lock will seem to be locked and will offer resistance to minimal force when the door is being tested. However, when stronger force is applied, though less than the stated holding value of the lock, the lock will yield and the door will open.

To overcome this limitation, specify a power magnet lock with a "bond sense" feature. Bond sense is a lock status feature that measures the holding force of the lock and can signal an alarm if the lock is defeated in the manner described above.

Although the installation of these locks is relatively inexpensive and easy, it is inappropriate to apply this type of lock indiscriminately. Choose the most suitable lock for the application based on the guidelines presented in this chapter.

4. **Power bolts** are generally installed in much the same way as power magnets; however, power bolts require that the door be aligned so that an eyelet attached to the door aligns with the latch bolt (see Figure 4.8).

    It is this alignment requirement that places the greatest restriction on the application of power bolts.

    Power bolts generally have some type of sensor mechanism that tells the lock when the door is properly

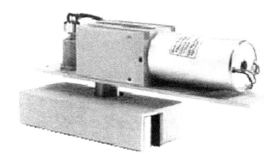

Figure 4.8 Power bolt.

aligned with the doorframe so the bolt can be released. If the bolt is released too soon, it will not line up with the corresponding eyelet and, although the door lock will signal that the bolt is thrown and the door is in a locked condition, the door will not be secured.

Additionally, power bolts are often installed inside the door header and not surface mounted like the power magnet. This usually requires considerable installation effort and these locks are therefore limited to new construction installations. Some versions of these locks are surface mounted and may be employed in a retrofit installation but these types of installations have diminished because of the popularity of power magnets. Recommend power bolts in applications where concealment is a consideration.

5. **Power latches** are door handle hardware mechanisms that restrict the use of the door handles, thereby preventing an individual from gaining access to a protected area. The power latch prevents a user from turning the door handle when outside the protected area. Generally, egress is unrestricted since the door handle always operates on the unprotected side of the door. This lock is installed by embedding the entire mechanism in the door and includes a solenoid and pin device that prevents the door handle from turning.

A limitation of this type of lock is wiring to the mechanism and the necessity to core the door to accept the power latch. As in the case of electric panic hardware, an electric hinge is required and the door must be cored to allow the passage of the electric cable through the door.

Therefore, the same risk for door damage applies as it did in the case of electric panic hardware.

The advantages of this type of lock are that it is unobtrusive and usually meets with all fire code requirements. However, this lock is difficult and expensive to install, and it is usually recommended only in cases of new door construction.

Failsafe and Fail Secure and Normally Open and Normally Closed The preceding lock descriptions used several terms that require additional definition. Those terms are normally opened and normally closed (NO/NC) and fail safe and fail secure. To help understand these terms please refer to Figure 4.9. These terms are frequently used in security applications to define the way locks and signaling devices work when associated with access control and alarm monitoring systems.

Normally opened and normally closed refer to the condition of a circuit connected to a door status switch or lock. When manufacturers create these devices, an assumption is made about the circuits that connect the device to the control or monitoring equipment.

Normally opened means that in a nominal state there is no continuity in a circuit; current cannot pass between the two wires connected to the monitoring point of the access control or alarm monitoring device. Normally closed is just the opposite, it means

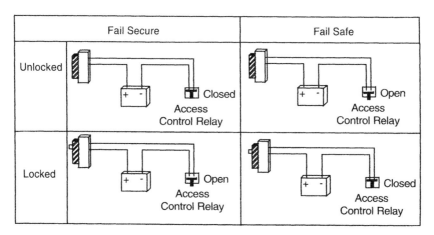

Figure 4.9 NO/NC and Fail Safe/Fail Secure.

that there is continuity across these two circuit wires and current can flow through it.

When locks are employed, the terms fail safe and fail secure refer to the nominal condition of the lock. A fail safe lock is one that unlocks when power is removed and requires power in order to remain locked. Fail secure refers to a lock that remains locked until power is applied to it to unlock it.

In most cases, fire code requires that locks be fail safe, thereby permitting unrestricted egress from the facility when a fire occurs, and the fire has damaged the power supply in the facility. Do not assume that fail safe locks are the best choice in every circumstance.

In some cases, fail secure locks are the most appropriate lock selection. For instance, in cases where fire exit stairwell doors require the application of electric locks for controlled access to a protected area, fail secure locks are chosen when an electric strike is needed.

A fail secure electric strike will permit unrestricted egress into the stairwell to exit the building because egress is obtained by simply turning the door handle. If power is removed from the lock it does not restrict egress. Further, the fail secure electric strike will continue to restrict access when power has been disabled. In emergency situations access is generally not required (certain exceptions exist in the case of re-entry doors, see the NFPA Handbook for an explanation of re-entry doors).

If the door has a fail safe electric strike installed and power is removed from the lock, it would be in a constant unlocked state. This also means that there would be nothing to restrain the door from opening. During a fire, there may be an explosion (or the simple force of the burning material) that would exert a force against the door. In this case, the door would open since there is no strike plate to restrict the door.

Occupants of a high rise building who were attempting to exit the building through an emergency stairwell would find themselves confronted by an open door that could not be held closed by the door hardware since the electric strike is in an opened condition. This would expose the occupants of the stairwell to the hazard on the floor where the incident was taking place. In such cases, fire codes will not permit the installation of a fail safe lock on this type of door. The term used to describe a condition where the door is always held closed by the door hardware is "positive latch."

Fire Alarm Interface   The fire alarm interface referred to in the DDS is a connection between the Underwriters Laboratories Inc. (UL) approved building fire alarm panel and the power supply used to power the electric locks. This is always a normally closed fail safe circuit. It permits the fire alarm panel to signal the lock power device to remove power from electric locks in emergencies. Conditions vary from manufacturer to manufacturer of fire alarm panels but generally this circuit is rated at a maximum of 24 volt, 2 amps. The lock power devices available today usually conform to these criteria, and a circuit with these limits provides adequate current carrying capacity to apply or remove power from nearly all the locking devices currently used.

Rarely is the fire alarm interface an option—in almost every case it is a requirement. When planning the fire alarm interface, request that the fire alarm panel service company or in-house personnel responsible for the fire alarm system make the required connections to the panel. In some locales, the local fire inspectors have established specific forms that must be completed and submitted for approval to the State Fire Marshal's Office before making such fire alarm panel connections.

To complete this section of the system design, choose the appropriate lock for the application and record that selection on the DDS.

Other Life Safety Considerations   In addition to life safety requirements the Americans with Disabilities Act (ADA) describes certain limitations on the use of card readers and other control devices as they relate to individuals with mobility impairments. One of the most frequently overlooked ADA requirements refers to the location of access control devices. A rule of thumb is to require the placement of all devices used for gaining access to a controlled area be placed no higher than door handle height to comply with ADA regulations. Review all ADA requirements to ensure that system design meets these guidelines.

In healthcare institutions, there are other requirements that stipulate how certain assets should be protected. A complete listing of these requirements can be found in publications from the Joint Commission on Accreditation of Healthcare Organizations (JCAHO). JCAHO provides a variety of resources as reference tools on securing healthcare information and the responsibilities for healthcare providers in serving patients and staff.

Other regulations for healthcare institutions can be found in the Health Insurance Portability and Accountability Act (HIPAA). Although this act tends to focus more on information security, there are applications for physical security requirements that provide control measures to data terminals, system hardware, and other information-related assets. When working in a healthcare environment include a review of these regulations in the system design step.

Network and Command Center Equipment After selecting the end-point control devices, determine which equipment location can best serve the end-point devices. The configuration of network devices will vary from manufacturer to manufacturer but some commonalities exist.

For planning purposes, assume that each network panel has a capacity for 8 card readers and 32 alarm points. (This is not a given, these capacities differ for each system manufacturer.) However, making such assumptions will permit the security professional to create a Concept Drawing that shows the relationship between the system components and that serves to more clearly communicate what is to be accomplished to the management team and the vendors. Adjust variations in the final capacity count after choosing the system. Assess the number of network panels needed based on the number of end-points defined and record these devices on a list entitled "Command Center Alarm and Access Control Equipment."

Next, determine the number of display monitors and printers needed to display alarm and control information and provide the user with access to the control capabilities of the system. This would also be the most appropriate time to locate these devices on the facility plans. To complete this step, mark the equipment and display locations on the facility plans and the Command Center Alarm and Access Control Equipment list.

Select the Video Devices

Video devices have become the fastest developing products in the industry. Video systems are used for identifying and classifying conditions from a remote location. To accomplish this, the system must provide a useful view of the secured area at the monitoring location. Although there are rapid changes in the technology, there are some general guidelines when selecting the appropriate video devices. These guidelines are listed below by equipment type.

Lenses The CCTV lens gathers and focuses the available light from the target scene on the camera pickup device (see camera description below). There are three important characteristics of a camera lens, focal length, iris and F value (otherwise know as foot candle value).

The focal length of a lens describes the ratio of the size of the image at a given distance from the lens to the size of the image projected on the camera pickup device. This can be expressed as a formula where the size of the image divided by the size of the object is equal to the image distance divided by the object distance.

There are mathematical formulas that exactly specify this relationship but for security design purposes, there are simpler ways to achieve the desired results. There are handy tools from CCTV manufacturers that provide a quick and easy way to specify the required lenses. These tools are essentially sighting tubes that provide a representation of the view offered by different size lenses for a given camera pickup. Using these tools can make the job simpler and easier.

The iris in a lens is used to help make exposure control possible. The iris controls light volume entering the lens to match the shutter speed of the camera and reduces or removes residual aberrations. The iris also improves depth of field or the zone of sharpness in the view of the lens. The iris is usually a diaphragm designed in a circular fashion and opened to provide the appropriate amount of light for the best possible picture.

There are three types of lens' irises in common use: the manual lens, the motorized lens and the auto iris lens. Manual lenses require the installer to set the iris during installation. These types of irises are usually used in situations where the ambient light is fixed, such as indoor scenes where the room lighting is constant.

Motorized iris lenses permit the user to remotely control the iris setting from the viewing console. These are usually used in circumstances where there are modest light changes or camera placement results in significant changes in back lighting.

Auto iris lenses are connected to the camera. The camera has circuitry that controls the iris setting based on the light hitting the camera pickup surface. These are the most common irises used today. They adjust automatically to changing light conditions and are used in situations where the available light varies.

F value, or foot candles, is measurement of the intensity of light on a white surface one foot square illuminated by a standard candle placed one foot from the surface. In photography terms, it is the measurement of the maximum amount of light a lens will pass from the scene to the camera pickup at the largest iris opening. This value is usually expressed as the F value of the lens.

Review the views required for remote monitoring and select the most appropriate lens for the application. Record the selection on the Camera Detail Schedule.

Cameras   There are many types of cameras available today and the technology is constantly improving. Creating a comprehensive list of all available types would be difficult and any such list would soon be obsolete. Focus attention on the performance requirements of the camera to determine which type is most suitable for the installation. If the application is properly described, the vendors will be able to determine which camera provides the best fit from the current technology given the requirements specified. The job of the security professional is, in part, to confirm that the camera offered meets the required specifications. Some considerations are:

- Requirements for color versus black and white
- The range of ambient light and backlight compensation
- Light to dark ratio
- Motion in the viewing scene
- Resolution of the image at a defined distance (level of detail in the image)
- Viewing in all weather conditions

Base the selection of cameras jointly on the lenses chosen for the application and the considerations described above. Choose the most appropriate camera characteristics and record that selection on the Camera Detail Schedule.

Housings, Mounts and Auxiliary Equipment   Camera system manufacturers provide a wide assortment of ancillary devices used with CCTV cameras. Creating a comprehensive list of all possible features would quickly become obsolete in this fast paced technological environment. Additionally, the combination of camera, housing and mount are usually manufactured as a "set" and choosing a set of products can provide a better compatibility between the components that selecting individual products.

However, there are some general aspects of auxiliary camera equipment to consider. The specifications need to provide enough detail for the vendors to offer the best possible combination of equipment to meet the needs of the company. Some of these considerations are:

- The surface orientation when mounting the camera (wall, ceiling, post, etc.)
- Indoors versus outdoors
- Long exposure to direct overhead sunlight
- High humidity and rain
- Requirements for pan and tilt drives
- The need for auxiliary lighting after dark

To complete the auxiliary equipment selection, choose the most appropriate characteristics and record the selection on the Camera Detail Schedule. Finish the process by indicating on the facility plans the location of the camera equipment and the areas (usually indicated by hash lines) viewed by these cameras.

Monitors   Captured video images must be displayed in a useful way. The primary goal in using video equipment is to observe, identify and classify activity or situations in the observed area.

As with most other CCTV devices, the speed of technological development in the industry makes the creation of a comprehensive list of monitor features difficult. Some basic guidelines are shown below in preparing a recommendation:

- Color versus black and white—The color choice is usually a function of the cameras selected. If there are any color cameras in the system, the monitors must also be color.

- Monitor size—The monitor size recommended depends on the distance the view is from the monitor. Generally, the farther the distance, the larger the monitor. The sample scale in Figure 4.10 provides a rough guide to this measurement:

Consider the images viewed. If quad or other multiple image devices are used with the selected monitor, the corresponding images will fill only a small portion of the screen (in the case of quad devices, 1/4 of the screen). Larger monitors may be required to provide a useful image.

However, also remember that the installer will place the monitor in the security command center. These rooms are frequently small and space is at a premium. Consider the overall size or footprint of the monitor when making a selection. It will be difficult to use the equipment effectively if the screen is large enough to view the images but the monitors are too large to fit conveniently in the space provided.

Resolution—A CCTV monitor represents an image by projecting lines on an image screen. This is usually referred to as lines of resolution. The resolution of color monitors is less than monochrome. This is because three dots are needed to make each image point: red, green, and blue.

Monitors can only produce the resolution available from cameras and control equipment. Hence, specifying a high-resolution monitor with a standard resolution camera will not necessarily produce significantly better results. The most useful approach is to remember that the resulting image resolution is no better than the lowest resolution of any component in the system (from camera

Distance from monitor (feet)	Monitor Size
0.5 – 1.0 foot	9"
1.0 – 1.5 feet	12"
1.5 – 2.0 feet	15"
2.0 – 3.0 feet	17"

Figure 4.10 Table: Distance from monitor.

through all devices to the monitor). The most cost effective approach to selecting a monitor is to choose one that matches the overall resolution of the system.

To complete the monitor selection, choose the most appropriate monitor features and prepare a list titled Command Center CCTV Equipment. This list will become a part of the preliminary system design. Indicate the equipment location on the facility plans.

Video Controls and Signal Processing   If motorized lenses or mounts are required for adequate viewing, add controls to allow the user to adjust these motorized devices for the best possible image. Motorized control devices are specified where applicable and must be compatible with the motorized CCTV end-point devices. Add these features or capabilities to the Command Center CCTV Equipment list.

If certain circumstances require the CCTV images to be continuously monitored to detect specific conditions in the scene, the use of signal processing equipment may be required. An example of this equipment is a video motion detector.

A video motion detector provides the ability for a user to designate an area of view that will be continuously measured by the signal processor. When the system observes an unexpected condition, it alerts the command post that this condition has occurred, usually by means of visual and audible alarms. An example would be a scene where no activity is supposed to take place. The camera will monitor an unchanging condition. When someone enters the camera's field of view, the signal processing equipment detects this change in the image and signals an alarm.

Other features in this array include the ability to detect changes over time. If a parked vehicle in a garage is expected to move within an eight hour period and does not, signal processing equipment is available that will alarm the lack of activity and signal the command center by imposing a circle over the image.

The list of CCTV software features is growing daily. It is not the intent of this work to describe all of these features in detail. An astute security professional will constantly monitor the developments of such features in the marketplace and be prepared to choose the features that are right for the application.

Select the control and signal processing features and add them to the Command Center CCTV Equipment list to complete this portion of the preliminary system design.

Video Recorders Video recorders are likewise undergoing a rapid evolution. Listed below are some items to consider when specifying digital video recorders (DVR).

- Recorded image resolution, lines of resolution recorded
- Frame rate, number of images captured (usually measured in frames per second)
- Maximum internal storage capacity
- Multiple views for recording and playback
- Alarm inputs (for switching between time lapse and real time recording)
- Optional audio recording
- The ability to output to a standard VHS format

Select the capabilities that are best suited for the application and add those features to the Command Center CCTV Equipment list.

Facility Modifications

The security system can only perform as well as the weakest area of the existing (or planned) facility structure. This includes walls, doors, and windows that provide the protected perimeter. Based on the evaluation of the resistance value of the perimeter structures, document recommendations for additional walls, doors, fences, and hardening devices to resist the anticipated threats.

In some cases, the security professional may suspect a problem but not be able to define the correct solution for that problem (as in the case of hardened walls to resist bomb blasts). Direct the company's management team to seek the services of a qualified engineer in the system recommendation. Use the additional services to determine what is needed to properly protect the area. Specify the expected threats, the probable vulnerabilities, and the expected outcome from the suggested modifications. Provide as much detail as possible to clearly define the area in question and the benefits expected from the recommended solution.

Response Team Integration

Thus far, the preliminary system design has only considered the products necessary for detection, deterrence and delay. Security response is an integral portion of the security solution. Establish a command post to centrally display alarm signals and dispatch response officers. Competent, trained officers are required to staff the post.

Help to establish criteria for the officers who will respond to the anticipated threats when they occur. This would include brief job descriptions and an outline of recommended procedures to follow when an event occurs. Document these recommendations and add this description to the overall preliminary system design.

Documenting the
Preliminary System
Design

5

INTRODUCTION

In this chapter, we will complete documenting the preliminary system design and estimate the cost for the equipment selected to accomplish the security system goals. The techniques recommended here will help the security professional describe the recommendation to the management team and bidders and then provide the capital budget for the project.

We will test our plan using the "rule of reason" defined in Chapter 4. We will also consider the operational value of the asset, the probability of loss and the consequences of loss. It is important to repeat that the job of the security professional is to evaluate, analyze, and recommend the most effective physical security system. Company management will decide if the value of mitigating the identified risks is worth the investment in security assets.

COMPLETE THE SYSTEM DESIGN DOCUMENTATION

To arrive at a clear definition of the required system and to prepare a budget for management consideration, the security professional must now finalize the system documentation. This will provide the detail needed to communicate the system plan to company management and provide enough information to establish a budget for the project. The Door Detail Schedule (DDS) and the Camera Detail Schedule (CDS) are the fundamental documents in this process. All other documents are related to and are dependent on these schedules.

Door Detail Schedule

The DDS is a matrix that describes all of the door equipment needed to make the system operational. This document can be prepared in written form and copied to make the work easier. If the security professional is also familiar with spreadsheet software, building the DDS using a spreadsheet product such as Microsoft Excel will be significantly easier. Figure 5.1 shows an example of a DDS.

Begin this matrix by listing the "Door Name" in the left hand column. Frequently, facilities do not use formal names for individual doors. It would be helpful to use the original plans to determine the formal designation for each opening.

If facility plans are not available or do not contain formal door names, employees usually have a "common name" for the opening. Facility occupants will generally recognize that name when repeated to them. Match the marking of the formal designation on the plan with the common name given to the opening by the employees. Ensure that both names are shown on the DDS and the marked plans.

If a floor plan is available with formal door names, show those names in the next column called "Location Reference on Drawing." The security professional must establish a reference for all openings so that all parties working on the project will have a clear, unambiguous key to the opening in question.

The title of the next column is "Location Reference"; it is a numbering plan. Start the numbering plan with the floor number followed by a dash then a number selected for that opening. Start

Client: (Company)
Work Location: (Area)
Project: (Project Name)

By: (Consultant Name)
Revision: 0
Date: (Date)

Door Detail Schedule

Door Description	Location Ref on Drwg	Access	Access Special	Lock	Lock Special	Egress	Egress Special	Fire Alarm Interface	Number of DSS Alarms	Number of PIR Monitor	Number of Panic Alarms	Drawing Ref	Remarks
Basement:													
amphitheater	B-1			PM-D				FAI	1			DD1DY	
tunnel	B-3								2			DD2NY	
tunnel to laundry	B-4	CR		2PM		B		FAI	2			DD2PY	Client must replace or modify door
fire exit, west side front	B-8								1			DD1NY	
First Floor:													
old pediatrics	1-1	CR		PM		B		FAI	1			DD1PY	
old pediatrics	1-1					PIR						NA	add exit detector to manual button exit
Lasalle entrance	1-5		Auto Door						2			MCL-CC1	Door will be manned or locked manually always
front entrance	1-7										2	NA	
west entrance	1-8					PIR			2			MCL-CC2	Door manually locked EGRESS ONLY. Alarmed
admitting	1-9										8	NA	
medical records admin	1-11										1	NA	
walk-in clinic	1-14.1										1	NA	
walk-in clinic	1-14.2										1	NA	
family doctor	1-15										4	NA	
walk-in clinic 2	1-16										1	NA	
east entrance	1-17	CR		2PM		B		FAI	2			DD2PY	
west entrance	1-18	CR		2PM		B		FAI	2			DD2PY	
fire stair	1-21								1			DD1NY	
walkway	1-22	CR		2PM		B		FAI	2			DD2PY	Remove door edge seals during installation
psyc triage	1-24										1	NA	
west rear stair	1-25	CR		2PM		B		FAI	2			DD2PY	Client will repair door before installation.
loading dock	1-26	CR	Auto Door		Auto Door		Auto Door	FAI	2			AUTODR2	Auto door vendor to provide door lock
ER Admit	1-27										4	NA	
Triage Station	1-28										3	NA	
Admitting	1-30.1										1	NA	
Admitting	1-30.2										1	NA	
loading dock freight elevator	1-31	CR	Elevator Control	Elevator Control		B	Elevator Control					MCL-CC3	connect to elevator floor control buttons
loading dock passenger elevator	1-32	CR	Elevator Control	Elevator Control		B	Elevator Control					MCL-CC3	connect to elevator floor control buttons

Figure 5.1 Door detail schedule.

with number one and proceed through the number series until all openings have a designation. When changing floors, restart the numbering plan so that the first door identified on the second floor will be designated 2-1 and on the third floor 3-1 and so forth. This numbering plan is not rigid; any numbering system may be used. However, consistency in the numbering plan is essential to make it easier for other professionals in the project to understand the reference notations. This additional designation for the opening will provide a more concise reference when transferring opening identity information to other documents.

Additionally, by using this reference method, there will be certain advantages in unusual situations. For instance, main entryways of office buildings frequently have multiple door leafs. To help remember that all door status switches associated with each door leaf are associated with the same door input on an access control or alarm monitoring panel, a decimal can indicate multiple leafs. For instance, if the main door to a building has four door leafs and the door designation is 1-1, they can be described as 1-1.1, 1-1.2 and so forth.

The next column is "Access." Under this column, indicate the methods used to gain access through that opening. If a card reader controls the opening, use the symbol CR. A suggested list of these symbols is in Figure 5.2.

The next column in the matrix is "Access Special." Use this designation for other devices installed in conjunction with the primary access control device. For instance, it may be necessary to place a key switch on an entry opening in addition to the card reader to permit facility managers to enter the building if the access control system fails. This key switch can be used to disable one or more locks in the building system for emergency access. Use such auxiliary means of access sparingly.

The next column in the matrix is "Lock." Indicate how that opening will be locked in this column. Refer to Figure 5.2 for a recommended list of symbols to indicate door locks. It would be helpful to the other professionals involved in the project to indicate the lock by brand and model. However, during the general system design and budget estimate, an exact lock specification is not essential. The symbols shown in Figure 5.2 only designate the type of lock to use. This is an important characteristic of the door since the

Door Detail Schedule Symbols

Material Code	Symbol
Card Reader	CR
Key Pad	KY
Biometric Device	BM
Power Magnet	PM
2 Power Magnets	2PM
Electric Strike	S
Delay Power Magnet	PM-D
Fire Alarm Interface	FAI
Exit Thumb Button	B
Exit Palm Button	PB
Emergency Release	ER
Existing Door Hardware	HDWR
Exit Sensor	ES
Touch Sense Bar	TS
Door Status Switches	DSS
Space Sensor	PIR
Panic Alarms	PANIC

Figure 5.2   Recommended list of access/egress symbols.

locking type helps determine the egress method used and the manner in which to secure the door.

The next column in the matrix is "Lock Special." Use this column for additional features of the locking device such as reverse brackets for power magnets and special alarm sensors needed to provide ample security for the opening.

The next column in the matrix is "Egress." The egress features of an opening establish the means to exit the facility. In most applications, egress is unobstructed to comply with life safety codes. However, in some cases egress control is also required. An example of such situations is when the "anti-passback" feature is desired. In those circumstances, it is important to know when a user has left the facility. Use the same symbols from Figure 5.2 that apply to access control devices to indicate egress control.

The next column in the matrix is "Egress Special." Like the other specialized columns, this one is used to indicate devices that will be applied in alternate use circumstances. For instance, the NFPA Life Safety Handbook specifies that egress criteria for power magnet locks include a passive infrared detector (PIR) to provide unimpeded egress from the facility. Indicate the use of a PIR in this column.

The next column in the matrix is "Fire Alarm Interface." This column is only applicable if the subject door will be locked by a mechanism that does not permit unrestricted mechanical egress. An example of unrestricted mechanical egress is the application of an electric strike with a free passage exit handle. In those cases, there are no constraints to an individual wishing to exit a controlled area and simply turning the door handle will allow egress. Another example of such unrestricted egress is the use of panic hardware. Like the electric strike, panic hardware provides unrestricted egress by simply pushing on the panic device on the door.

In other cases where the locking device is a power magnet or power bolt, it is an essential life safety feature to connect the lock on the subject door to the fire alarm panel. Connect the power supply of the locking device to the fire alarm panel to accomplish this. Arrange the connections so that if the panel goes into an alarm state, power will disconnect from the lock providing unrestricted egress (see Fire Alarm Interface). Indicate "yes" under this column for all door locks that require interface to the fire alarm panel.

The next column in the matrix is "Number of Door Status Switch Alarms" normally abbreviated as DSS alarms. In the case of a single leaf door, this number is always one; however, some doors have more than one leaf. For instance, in cases where there are two door leafs; the number of DSS alarms is two. This will indicate to others on the project that two door status switches are required for this door so that both leafs may be monitored. It would also be helpful to remind the vendors in the Remarks column that the contacts are to be wired in series.

The next column in the matrix is "Number of PIR Monitors." This is simply a shorthand way to indicate an area and not necessarily a door. Use this when area monitoring is required. This alarm point will be included in the overall security plan. In these cases, the door description is actually a room description. Show the number of PIR detectors to protect this space under this column.

Note: The term PIR is used here generically to mean all forms of space sensors. There are devices other than PIR detectors used to monitor areas. Do not assume that this nomenclature means it applies only to PIR detectors.

The next column in the matrix is "Number of Panic Buttons." Again, like space detectors, panic buttons do not relate to particular doors but are included in the overall security plan as indicated here. Panic buttons are generally alarm-signaling devices used by occupants of a facility to indicate that they are in distress. Like the space sensor, list panic alarms in the door description as a point and with the name of the location for the alarm. These points are not associated with a particular door.

The next column in the matrix is "Drawing Reference." A drawing reference is nomenclature that identifies a particular elevation drawing used in association with the devices shown on the rest of the schedule for that door. Elevation drawings will indicate placement of devices so that there can be no misunderstanding as to where to mount the device. Build a library of elevation drawings to use as standard references when compiling a security system implementation plan.

The next column in the matrix is "Remarks." In this column, indicate any special considerations for this door not fully described in the other columns. It is always better to over-document than under-document. Remarks may include such items as a requirement to change door hardware or supply special features to the door that are needed to make the security equipment proposed for that door work properly.

The next two columns in the matrix are "Distance to Panel" and "Feet of Conduit." Neither of these columns is an essential part of system design and may be omitted if specific cable estimates are not required in the budget that will be established for the security system. As the names imply, they are an indication of wiring and conduit needed to perform the installation. Often, however, such budgetary information is an essential part of the cost mix. By providing these elements in the DDS when preparing the system design, it will be easier to estimate these costs later. It is usually not necessary to display cabling and conduit descriptions to the management team. Collect this data for budget purposes.

Camera Detail Schedule

The CDS, like the DDS, documents the end-point devices on the project and aids in understanding the design of the proposed camera system. It is also used to establish the budget for the project. Like the DDS, the CDS is a matrix that can be more easily develop using a spreadsheet program. An example of the CDS is shown in Figure 5.3.

The first column in the CDS is "Camera View." The camera view or camera location indicates what this camera is looking at or where the camera is located. Often this designation is "rooftop—northeast corner" or "rear hall door." Much like the DDS, use names for camera views easily recognized by company employees. Establish this nomenclature when doing the site survey with the help of the security manager and security staff.

The second column in the CDS is "Location Reference on Drawing." As in the case of DDS, a facility plan is an essential part of communicating where these devices are to be located. It is unlikely that there will be preexisting designations for these camera locations so the security professional must again use a numbering plan to provide a clear and unambiguous reference for the camera. This is important for discussing camera location and features and associating the camera with other equipment. Also, similar to the DDS, that numbering plan starts with a floor designation followed by a dash then followed by a numbering system that identifies specific locations.

The next column in the CDS is "Camera." There are two options for camera type: standard and low light. This does not necessarily mean these are the only two types of cameras available. There are specialized cameras used in special applications. However it is not wise to develop a preconceived list of exact camera models without a detailed examination of all products on the market. This would artificially limit the choices and competitive aspects of the bid. In the initial steps of system design and budget preparation, that level of detail is not required. Therefore, simply indicating a top-level camera type would be preferable. To aid in the application of the symbols, there is a table in Figure 5.4 that provides a recommended set.

The next column in the CDS is "Lenses." Again, at this stage in system development it is essential only to indicate if the lens is a fixed or zoom lens and the appropriate magnification required for either type. In the case of zoom lenses, indicate the lowest and highest number that the lens will zoom and, in the case of fixed lenses,

Camera Detail Schedule

Client:(Company)
Work Location:(Area)
Project:(Project Description)

By:(Consultant Name)
Revision:0
Date:(Date)

Camera View	Location Ref on Drwg	Camera: Standard / Low Light	Lens: Zoom-Fixed- 2,3,4,8,Z	Iris: Auto / Manual	Housing Indoor / Outdoor With Fan / Wiper	Special: Hood (H)	Mount: Ceiling / Wall / Pedmt / Post	Mount Duty: Heavy / Medium / Light	Pan / Tilt Control (1)	Alarm Input (1)	Auxiliary Lights (1)	Drawing Ref	Remarks	Distance to Monitor	Feet of Conduit
Main Entrance	E-1	S	F-4	A	O		C	L				CD1		250	25
Freight Dock	E-2	S	F-4	A	O		C	L			1	CD1		275	25
Roof E	E-3	L	Z 75-200	A	OF/W	H	PED	H	1			CD2		375	150
Roof W	E-4	L	Z 75-200	A	OF/W	H	PED	H	1			CD2		375	150
Roof N	E-5	L	Z 75-200	A	OF/W	H	PED	H	1			CD2		375	150
Roof S	E-6	L	Z 75-200	A	OF/W	H	PED	H	1			CD2		375	150
Water Tower	E-7	L	Z 75-200	A	OF/W	H	PED	M	1			CD2		375	150
Parking Lot 1	E-8	S	F-2.3	A	O		POST	M				CD3		450	75
Parking Lot 2	E-9	S	F-2.3	A	O		POST	M				CD3		450	75
Parking Lot 3	E-10	S	F-2.3	A	O		POST	M				CD3		450	75
Lot Entrance	E-11	S	F-4	A	O		POST	L				CD3		450	75
Lot Exit	E-12	S	F-4	A	O		POST	L				CD3		450	75
Floor 1															
Hall 127	1-1	S	F-8	A	-		W	L				CD4		150	25
Science Lab	1-2	S	F-8	A	-		W	L				CD4		150	25
Fire Exit A	1-3	S	F-8	A	-		W	L		1		CD4		150	25
Fire Exit B	1-4	S	F-8	A	-		W	L		1		CD4		150	25
Fire Exit C	1-5	S	F-8	A	-		W	L		1		CD4		150	25
Fire Exit D	1-6	S	F-8	A	-		W	L				CD4		150	25
Floor 2															
Hall 2323	2-1	S	F-8	A	-		W	L				CD4		200	25
Elevator Lobby	2-2	S	F-8	A	-		W	L				CD4		200	25
Hall 2456	2-3	S	F-8	A	-		W	L				CD4		200	25
Floor 3															
Hall 3323	3-1	S	F-8	A	-		W	L				CD4		250	25
Elevator Lobby	3-2	S	F-8	A	-		W	L				CD4		250	25
Hall 3456	3-3	S	F-8	A	-		W	L				CD4		250	25
Floor 4															
Hall 4323	4-1	S	F-8	A	-		W	L				CD4		300	25
Elevator Lobby	4-2	S	F-8	A	-		W	L				CD4		300	25
Hall 4456	4-3	S	F-8	A	-		W	L				CD4		300	25

Figure 5.3 Camera detail schedule.

Surveillance System Designations

Material Code	Symbol
Standard Cameras	S
Low Light Cameras	L
Lenses	
Fixed 2.3 / Auto	2.3/A
Fixed 4 / Auto	4/A
Fixed 8 / Auto	8/A
Zoom /Auto	Z/A
Fixed 2.3/Manual	2.3/M
Fixed 4 / Manual	4/M
Fixed 8 / Manual	8/M
Zoom / Manual	Z/M
Housing	
Indoor	I
Outdoor	O
Outdoor / Fan	OF
Outdoor / Wiper	OW
Outdoor Fan / Wiper	OFW
Outdoor Hood	H
Mounts	
Ceiling / Light Duty	CL
Ceiling / Medium Duty	CM
Ceiling / Heavy Duty	CH
Wall / Light Duty	WL
Wall / Medium Duty	WM
Wall / Heavy Duty	WH
Pediment / Light Duty	PL
Pediment / Medium Duty	PM
Pediment / Heavy Duty	PH
Post / Light Duty	POL
Post / Medium Duty	POM
Post / Heavy Duty	POH
Pan and Tilt Motor Drive	1
Control Receivers	RT
Specials	
Alarm Input	1
Auxiliary Lights	1

Figure 5.4 Recommended list of CCTV system designations.

indicate the fixed focal length desired for that lens. Camera manufacturers often provide handy tools that will illustrate the appropriate lens size for a given measurement of distance and field of view. By using such tools, you may select the measured distance between the camera and the object you wish to view and the vertical and horizontal field to be included in that view. These shortcut tools will then provide you with the appropriate lens size.

The next column in the CDS is "Iris." There are three designations for iris: automatic, motorized manual, and manual. Use an automatic iris in outdoor applications to automatically adjust for varying light conditions. Motorized manual lenses allow the user to remotely change the iris setting based on the desired light level needed for a quality image. Use manual lenses for indoor applications where the light source is predictable and fixed. These irises are adjusted during installation and remain at that setting.

The next column in the CDS is "Housing." Housings may be indoor or outdoor and may have a variety of special features. Some of these features are fans for hot environments and wipers for clearing rain from the outer surface of the housing window to permit a clearer view. Make the appropriate decision for which housing you wish to place at this location and indicate so in this column.

The next column in the CDS is "Special." This column indicates those features usually associated with a camera housing, but it is a separate component for the camera location. An example of such a device is a sun hood. A sun hood is a device used to mount above camera housing to keep sunlight from shining directly on a housing, thereby reducing the amount of heat buildup inside the housing and extending the life of the CCTV camera.

The next column in the CDS is "Mount." There is a variety of mounts available for cameras and within each category, there is a variety of types of mounts. Again, other professionals on the job will need a specific indication of the type of mount needed for this camera installation. However, as previously stated, it may be impractical to take the specification to this level of detail at this point in system design. Therefore, only indicate if this is a ceiling mount, wall mount, pedestal mount, or post mount. This will be very helpful in determining the budget for the project.

The next column in the CDS is "Mount Duty." Most manufacturers make several styles of mounts depending on the type of housing used for the camera and the application of the housing. Manufacturers designate these as heavy duty, medium duty, and light duty. Again, for the purposes of system design and budget estimates, indicating the strength of the mount should be sufficient to establish pricing.

The next column in the CDS is "Pan/Tilt Control." Use a pan/tilt control motor drive for all applications where a zoom lens is used. Attempting to use zoom lenses without pan/tilt control can frequently lead to zooming in on an object and not being able to see the most significant part of that object.

The next column in the CDS is "Alarm Input." Although this does not apply in every case, some manufacturers provide control devices for pan/tilt zoom control operations that have alarm input connections that can signal the CCTV system of a potential security violation. Indicate when alarm inputs are be used in this column. If alarm inputs are used, add alarm detection devices such as a door status switch to the system.

The next column in the CDS is "Auxiliary Lights." Use auxiliary lights in situations where additional illumination is required for the camera to properly view an area. Like alarm input, some manufacturers provide control output relays that can switch lights on under circumstances where additional illumination is needed. In other cases, auxiliary lights are used at any time the light level of the subject area falls below the required illumination for the camera to view the area properly.

The next column in the CDS is "Drawing Reference." Drawing reference for camera detail serves the same function as drawing reference for door detail. These are elevation drawings and indicate the placement of equipment.

The next column in the CDS is "Remarks." Use the remarks column in the same manner as in the DDS. Indicate any special considerations or special alterations that are required to the camera installation site that must be performed before or coincident with the installation of the security equipment.

The next two columns in the CDS are "Distance to Monitor" and "Feet of Conduit." The same rules apply here as applied in the DDS. These are not required fields at this stage of system development; however, the security professional will find it most helpful if they indicate an estimate of cable feet in these columns for each camera to prepare budgets quickly and easily. As with door detail, it is not necessary to share the information in these columns with the management team, because the data will only be used to establish a budget.

Concept Drawing

In addition to equipment schedules, it is helpful to graphically illustrate the project design to the company's management team. A concept drawing can best accomplish this. Such a drawing will convey the interconnection between the devices described in the DDS, CDS, Command Center CCTV Equipment and Command Center Alarm and Access Control Equipment lists. This is a top level illustration and is usually a block diagram showing all the major elements of the system (see Figure 5.5 for an example).

PREPARE A COST ESTIMATE OF THE ACCESS CONTROL AND ALARM MONITORING SYSTEMS

System design and documentation is only one step in the decision making process in developing a security plan for a facility. If the cost to implement the plan is prohibitive, the management team will not accept the recommendation. However, the initial budget submitted by the security professional must contain the best overall recommendation without regard to cost cutting efforts.

The reason for this is simple. If the security professional designs a system that considers cost first and does not place the security needs of the organization ahead of cost containment, there can be justifiable criticism if the system fails to perform as expected. Establish the initial budget based on the optimum security solution without regard to cost containment.

If there is an established budget and the security professional has been asked to work within that budget, a second proposal may be generated that meets the cost objectives set by the company.

This alternate plan includes all of the essential items of the system but makes it clear that this alternate recommendation lacks certain features needed to provide all of the risk reduction elements to secure the facility.

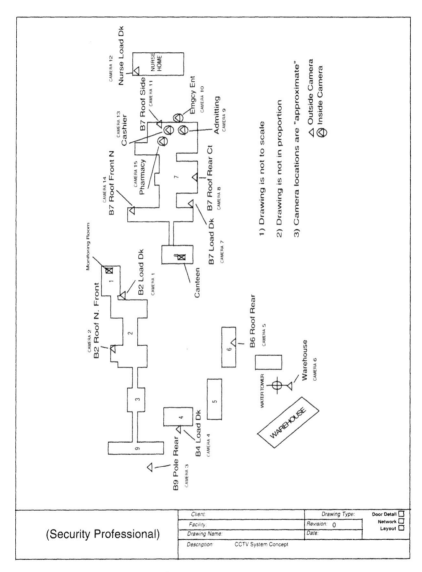

Figure 5.5 System concept drawing.

Another alternative is to use a phased approach to system implementation. However, priorities change with prevailing business conditions. Good intentions and long range security plans will sometimes give way to seemingly more important or urgent business priorities. As a result, Phase 1 may be the only step actually implemented. It is therefore important that the essential elements are included in the first step and progressively less important parts of the system are implemented during the succeeding steps. A guiding principle is to design each phase as though the following phases will not take place. In that way, the most urgent and critical elements of the system are implemented first.

Present all proposals simultaneously to ensure that the optimum recommendation is clear. Highlight the limitations of each choice so the management team can make informed cost decisions. Remember to consider the indirect costs such as system maintenance, additions, and replacements.

The Access Control and Alarm Monitoring Budget

Before the days of personal computers, it was common to prepare financial models using columned workbooks calculated manually. It is not the author's intent to compel the security professional to become a computer expert; however, detailed cost estimates generally result in extensive arithmetic and can lead to unintentional errors resulting in wrong conclusions.

The most useful general application software tool available today for such detailed analysis is an electronic spreadsheet. The most common electronic spreadsheet tool in use today is from Microsoft called Excel. If the security professional has a working knowledge of Microsoft Excel and can employ this tool effectively in preparing cost estimations, it will save considerable time and effort. This is not a recommendation or endorsement of a particular software product and should be viewed only as a convenient common point of reference when discussing the methods and techniques for doing a cost estimate.

Pricing in a competitive market is highly fluid and can sometimes vary by as much as 20%. At this stage of the process, the security professional is merely establishing a budget for the management team review. The firm fixed price of the system will be determined by competitive bidding. However, budget amounts are necessary to properly fund the project. If a doubt exists about the price of a particular item—overestimate. It is always easier to say to management that the project cost less than it is to say the project cost more.

The security professional must also have marketplace experience and access to vendors that can share approximate prices for security system components. Oftentimes, vendors are encouraged to share such information since they feel it will give them a competitive advantage when the project is released for bid. Product prices are also available from manufacturers' websites in some cases. If budget information is not readily available, budget prices can sometimes be obtained by calling manufacturers. For instance, door status switch manufacturers and locking system manufacturers will frequently divulge list price upon request. Recognize that these are not the best prices, but rather base prices for establishing an overall security system budget.

Primary Material Costs

Begin the cost assessment with the DDS. This document was prepared earlier and provides a detailed list of all the end-point components needed in a security system. Count the number of devices listed on the schedules by type. The result will be a specific number of card readers, keypads, cameras, locks, etc. Do the same for the equipment shown on the Command Center Alarm and Access Control Equipment list.

In the sample budget (Figure 5.6), the first section is for material used in the project.

Group the DDS and Command Center Alarm and Access Control @Text:Equipment into the following categories:

- Electronic controls
- Locking systems
- Exit devices
- Alarm monitoring equipment
  Also shown are:
- Network and control material
- Cabling
- Conduit

Access Control Security System Budget

Client:	Client Name	By	: (Consultant)
Work Location:	Department	Revision: 0	
Project:	(Project Description)	Date	: (Date)

This is a budget estimate for the above captioned project. The amounts shown should be within 10% of the final price of this system, providing the scope of work is not changed. The entire project will be managed by (Consultant) including system acquisition and project management

Material

Door Devices		Qty	Cost	Subtotals
	Card Reader	1	$308	
	Subtotal Door Devices			$308
Systemwide Devices		Qty	Cost	
	Network Panels	4	7200	
	Subtotal Systemwide Devices			7200
Locking Systems		Qty	Cost	
	Power Magnet	1	750	
	Subtotal Lockig Systems			750
Exit Devices		Qty	Cost	
	Exit Thumb Button	1	90	
	Subtotal Exit Devices			90
Alarm Monitoring Equipment		Qty	Cost	
	Door Status Switches	20	200	
	Space Sensor	5	550	
	Subtotal Alarm Monitoring Equipment			750
Network and Control Equipment		Qty	Cost	
	Lock Power with FAI	1	800	
	Subtotal Network Control Equipment			800
Cabling			Cost	4201
			Total Material Cost	$14,099

Labour	Cost	
Design & Project Management Services	2787	
Equipment Delivery & Installation	10,780	
Final Hook Up for All Devices	$2,475	
System Testing	Included	
User Training	Not Required	
Total Labor Cost		$16,042

Summary:
Thank you for allowing (Consultant) to help develop this budget for your new security project. We estimate your project cost to be:

	Material	$ 14,099
	Labor	16,042
	Project Grand Total	$ 30,142

For Budget Purpose Only
Please contact (Consultant) if you have questions about this estimate.

Figure 5.6 The access control and alarm budget.

Show the unit price and extended price for each line item of material. Use caution when establishing the unit price for individual components and because this is a budget estimate, if in doubt, use a higher price to ensure that adequate funding is available for these devices. Multiply the component count by the unit price to obtain the extended price. This is where the cabling estimate on the DDS is most useful.

Labor Costs

The next section shown in the sample budget is for Labor. Base the costs on an anticipated number of hours needed to install each device. The hourly estimate was derived from a table developed for this purpose and is based on historical experience from several sources. The security professional may want to establish a library to compile local historical data based on projects complete. However, the estimates provided in the table in Figure 5.7 are a general guide for approximating the amount of time needed to install a specific component.

What is probably unknown at this point is the installation rate charged for the hours required. It is usually advisable to obtain the standard market rate for electricians in the local community. If this information is not available, R. H. Means publishes a list of estimated construction costs that provides an hourly rate for electricians. Use this rate to establish the installation cost based on the number of hours anticipated for a given device.

The Final Hookup Cost is also a part of the labor estimate. Final hookup is the work operations reserved for vendor technicians. The easiest way to define the distinction between installation and final hookup is to view installation as all cable pulls and mounting work up to but excluding the connection of the cable to the end device.

Generally, vendors prefer their employees to terminate all electronic devices to ensure that the person making those connections has been properly trained by the manufacturer and is supervised by the company responsible for the equipment warranty. The estimated number of final hookup hours for most of the commonly used equipment is in Figure 5.7 and is a good rule of thumb in estimating Final Hookup Cost.

Access Control and Alarm Monitoring
Installation Estimate of Hours

	Symbol	Hrs to Install	Hrs for FHU
Electronics Controls			
Card Reader	CR	1.00	1.00
Key Pad	KY	1.00	1.00
Biometric Device	BM	1.00	2.00
Locking Systems			
Power Magnet	PM	3.00	0.25
2 Power Magnets	2PM	6.00	0.25
Electric Strike	S	4.00	0.25
Delay Power Magnet	PM-D	8.00	0.25
Exit Devices			
Exit Thumb Button	B	0.50	0.25
Exit Palm Button	PB	0.50	0.25
Emergency Release	ER	0.75	0.25
Existing Door Hardware	HDWR	0.00	0.00
Exit Sensor	ES	2.00	0.25
Touch Sense Bar	TS	4.00	0.25
Alarm Monitoring Equipment			
Door Status Switches	DSS	1.00	0.25
Space Sensor	PIR	1.00	0.25
Panic Alarms	PANIC	1.00	0.25
Network & Control Material			
Lock Power with Fire Alarm Interface		1.00	1.00
Network APM Panels		1.00	4.00
PCs (inc display, kybd etc.)		2.00	
Access Control Software			8.00
Cable Estimate		Feet / Hour	
Reader Cable		100	
Control Cable		100	
Communications Cable		150	
Conduit		NA	

Figure 5.7   Table of installation hours for access control.

Determine the hourly rate used to calculate the resulting cost of this final hookup by contact with the local security system vendors. Polling three or more vendors should provide a good average hourly rate. Most vendors in a defined geographic market usually have very similar costs.

Estimate Cable

One of the most difficult items to assess in this cost analysis is the cable estimate. These estimates are difficult to develop because cabling is rarely pulled in a straight line. A variety of impediments and limitations to cable paths are usually found in ceilings and walls and require alternate cable routes.

A rule of thumb to follow when establishing cable estimates is to pace off the distance between the end-point device and the access control panel, adding an additional 20 feet for each end of the cable to allow for passage from the ceiling down to the appropriate device. Multiply that estimate by 1.3 to allow for errors in your calculations and the unavoidable scrap of unusable cable. Again using the electricians' labor rate and the "feet per hour" amounts shown in Figure 5.7 will provide a guideline to calculate an approximate cost for cable installation.

Cable material costs can vary considerably. There are several factors used to establish cable cost. Cable type is the first to consider. The simplest way to determine cable types is to select a system that appears to be appropriate for the application at hand. Most manufacturers publish their cable requirements on their websites and provide requirements at no charge. Cable requirements are usually expressed in Belden wire number.

The Belden wire cable company is widely recognized as a high quality manufacturer of communication and control cable. As a result, many manufacturers use Belden wire descriptions as the standard for specifying their cable requirements. Other cable manufacturers will provide what are termed Belden equivalents for the cables they manufacture. The security professional may obtain prices for Belden cable from a variety of sources. This is usually quoted in a cost per foot and sold in lots of 500 and 1000 feet.

It is important to know if "plenum rated" cable is required in the facility where the system is being proposed. In the 1970s, manufacturers developed plenum cable to reduce the potential for human injury from burning cable insulation in building fires. It is currently a fire code requirement. One case in particular resulted in deaths due to noxious fumes from burned cable insulation and not a direct result of the fire. That incident prompted the code change.

To understand the need for plenum rated cable one must first know that in modern buildings HVAC systems provide conditioned air to occupied spaces and that air must be returned to the HVAC system for re-heating or re-cooling. The return air "plenum" or airway in these buildings is simply the space between the ceiling tiles and the floor above. This is also the space where installers generally place cables for most retrofit installations.

Plenum rated cable is required if the facility in which the system being proposed has these types of return air ceilings. This cable is also referred to as Teflon jacketed cable. The jacket was designed to burn at much higher temperatures than ordinary PVC insulation. The cost difference between plenum rated cable and PVC cable can be as much as three times. In older buildings, this problem usually does not exist because the return air was provided through ductwork.

Consult with the local facility manager or maintenance engineer to determine if the cable needed in the buildings should be plenum rated. They will usually know the answer.

The plenum jacket requirement applies if standard copper cable is used or if fiber optic cables are used. Long runs not associated with a LAN drop or cable runs that have the potential for signal degradation will sometimes require the use of fiber optics. Although there are cost differences between the application of copper and fiber, using a copper cost for the budget estimate will usually prove adequate. The final decision regarding choice of fiber or copper cabling will be made as part of the bid process. The participation of the providers can be most helpful in making the final cabling decision.

The use of existing LAN services may significantly affect cable costs. Most of the more sophisticated systems today can make use of these existing facilities. However, using a company LAN creates other issues such as drop availability, protocol compatibility, and bandwidth requirements. Before choosing this option, discuss these requirements with the company's IT or communications group. In either case (use LAN or do not use LAN), some cabling is always required between the access control system network device (sometimes referred to as the Access Point Manager or APM) and the end-point devices such as locks, door status switches, and egress buttons.

Estimate Incidental Costs

In addition to the direct expenses described above, there are other indirect expenses associated with any project installation. Those indirect expenses are travel, training and project management.

Travel cost estimates are required if the facility is located in areas where local vendors are not available and inter-city travel is anticipated. Make an allowance for the travel costs from the installation and final hookup crews. Estimate travel and per diem cost using the Government Services Administration (GSA) standard cost estimates available on the worldwide web. These cost tables may also be obtained by contacting the government services administration directly.

Calculate Training cost by counting the number of individuals who will administer the system (be sure to consider multiple shifts for security officers). Assume that a single training class will have no more than ten people. In cases when more intense training may be required, reduce the estimated class size to only five individuals. Allow three full business days for each training session at approximately six hours per day. Multiply that by the hourly rate established for final hookup services from vendor technicians. This will be the estimated training cost. If manufacturer training is expected as part of the system specification package, (as opposed to local vendor personnel) also add the travel and per diem cost necessary to bring this vendor to the facility.

Project management tends to be one of the most difficult elements of the labor cost estimation to assess. This is because the demands on the project manager vary with the experience level of the vendors and other support personnel from the client's facility involved in the process. A number of factors affect how project management is assessed and these calculations can become difficult and tedious. Since this is a budget estimate, the most appropriate shorthand rule to follow is simply to assess project management based on the overall cost of the project. A rule of thumb used for project management in construction with regard to architects and other professionals is 7% to 10% of the total cost of the project.

PREPARE A COST ESTIMATE FOR THE SURVEILLANCE SYSTEM

Use the same rationale in preparing the video system budget as used in preparing the access control system budget. The CDS and Command Center CCTV Equipment list provides the component count for the CCTV budget. Figure 5.8 provides an example of a video system budget.

Primary Material Cost

The first element of the budget is material. Within material, the first subcategory is a combined cost for cameras, lenses, housings, and mounts. Group all of these items as a single line item. In Figure 5.8, each item is broken out individually. Use this method if the management team wants to examine equipment at a detailed level.

The set of costs in the sample budget is auxiliary equipment. Auxiliary equipment includes alarm input modules, auxiliary lights and similar devices. Auxiliary equipment usually refers to devices installed at the control points or perimeter observation points.

The next group in the sample video budget is monitoring and recording equipment. Once again, if management does not prefer a substantial level of detail, the security professional may group all of these components into a single line item budget. However, the first step in the roll up is to group all the monitoring equipment into a single line item, then group the recording equipment into a separate line item. In Figure 5.8, all of these items are separated into even lower groups defined as switchers, monitors, recording equipment, lenses, and position control equipment. This format assumes that the management team would be interested in that level of detail.

Estimate Cable

The last item in the material estimate is cabling and conduit. Take cable lengths for this estimate directly from the CDS that was prepared

Closed Circuit Television System Budget

Client:	Client Name	By	: (Consultant)
Work Location:	Department	Revision: 0	
Project:	(Project Description)	Date	: (Date)

This is a budget estimate for the above captioned project. The amounts shown should be within 10% of the final price of this system, providing the scope of work is not changed. The entire project will be managed by (Consultant) including system acquisition and project management

Material

Cameras, Lens, Housings and Mounts	Qty	Cost	**Subtotals**
Cameras	4	$1,400	
Lenses	4	400	
Housings	4	900	
Mounts	4	475	
Subtotal Cameras, Lenses, Housings and Mounts			**$ 3,175**
Auxiliary Equipment	Qty	Cost	
Auxiliary Lights	3	1875	
Subtotal Auxiliary Equipment			**1875**
Monitoring and Recording Equipment	Qty	Cost	
Monitors	2	750	
Recording Equipment	2	2300	
Subtotal Monitoring and Recording Equipment			**3050**
Cabling		Cost	**293**
Total Material Cost			**$ 8,393**

Labor	Cost	
Design & Project Management Services	$ 1,500	
Final Hook Up for All Devices	300	
System Testing	Included	
User Training for 2 Users	Not Required	
Equipment Delivery & Installation	$ 1,459	
Total Labor Cost		**$ 3,259**

Special Contract Cost Items	Cost	
Intercom system	$ 350	
Total Special Contract Cost		**$ 350**

Summary:
Thank you for allowing (Consultant) to help develop this budget for your new security project. We estimate your project cost to be:

Material	$ 8,393	
Labor	3,259	
Special	350	
Project Grand Total	**$ 12,002**	

For Budget Purpose Only

Please contact (Consultant) if you have questions about this estimate.

Figure 5.8 Sample CCTV budget.

during the system design survey or estimated in the same fashion used for access control cable estimates. This cabling estimate will include at minimum, low voltage video cable, power, and control cable (along with connections to commercial power supplies) and conduit. A discussion of cable and conduit estimating is in the section on preparing an access control budget.

Estimate Labor

After estimating material, estimate the labor. Figure 5.9 is a similar table as the one described for access control equipment. It provides a recommended breakdown of the labor cost line items.

As in access control, equipment delivery and installation represents that portion of the work involving cable, conduit, camera mounts, and housings installation. Generally, this is a basic estimate of man-hours at a given rate expected from a security installation company.

Likewise, final hookup for all devices is an estimate of hours for a technician from a local vendor at the vendor's anticipated rate (see the access control budget for a discussion of establishing these rates).

System testing and user training are both generally a part of the vendor's responsibility and again, these were addressed in the access control budget estimate. Please refer to that section for discussion of estimating these costs. Also refer to the access control budget discussion for design and project management services.

Special contract cost items are a result of unique circumstances in an installation that requires the material and labor from specialized companies. An example of this in a CCTV installation environment might be the installation of cameras, mounts and other system components in a location that requires special lift equipment. Add the cost of equipment rental for the lift equipment and operator to the CCTV budget.

FORECAST EXPENSE BUDGETS

The above calculations establish only the capital investment required to institute the proposed system; there are other costs involved. In addition to the capital budget, provide an expense

Surveillance System Installation
Estimate of Hours

	Symbol	Hrs to Install	Hrs for FHU
Cameras			
Standard Cameras	S	1.00	1.00
Low Light Cameras	L	1.00	1.00
Lenses			
Fixed 2.3 / Auto	2.3/A	0.25	1.00
Fixed 4 / Auto	4/A	0.25	1.00
Fixed 8 / Auto	8/A	0.25	1.00
Zoom / Auto	Z/A	0.25	4.00
Fixed 2.3 / Manual	2.3/M	0.25	0.25
Fixed 4 / Manual	4/M	0.25	0.25
Fixed 8 / Manual	8/M	0.25	0.25
Zoom / Manual	Z/M	0.25	4.00
Housings			
Indoor	I	0.50	0.25
Outdoor	O	1.00	0.25
Outdoor / Fan	OF	1.00	0.25
Outdoor / Wiper	OW	1.00	0.25
Outdoor Fan / Wiper	OFW	1.00	0.25
Outdoor Hood	H	1.00	0.25
Camera Mounts			
Ceiling / Light Duty	CL	3.00	0.25
Ceiling / Medium Duty	CM	3.00	0.25
Ceiling / Heavy Duty	CH	4.00	0.25
Wall / Light Duty	WL	2.00	0.25
Wall / Medium Duty	WM	2.00	0.25
Wall / Heavy Duty	WH	3.00	0.25
Pediment / Light Duty	PL	3.00	0.25
Pediment / Medium Duty	PM	3.00	0.25
Pediment / Heavy Duty	PH	4.00	0.25
Post / Light Duty	POL	3.00	0.25
Post / Medium Duty	POM	3.00	0.25
Post / Heavy Duty	POH	4.00	0.25
0	0		
Pan and Tilt Motor Drive	1	2.00	6.00
Control Receivers	RT	2.00	6.00
Specials			
Alarm Input	1	1.00	
Auxiliary Lights	1	3.00	

Cable Estimate		**Feet / Hour**	
Coax		100	
Power and Control Cable		100	
Conduit		20	

Figure 5.9 Table of installation hours for CCTV equipment.

budget for the ongoing maintenance of the system. That expense budget includes an estimate of annual service cost and an estimate of identity card purchase for systems that are card reader based.

Security cards are consumed at a fairly regular rate. Cards are lost or stolen, and in some cases, cards are discarded because employees are terminated. In systems where photo IDs or other unique cosmetic identifiers are imprinted on the card, the turnover rate in the authorized population will have a significant impact on the quantity of cards used. Estimate card cost as an expense item with ongoing system maintenance and include it in the capital budget.

Extending the project costs still further, the security professional may also want to consider recommending that the company stock their own spares for a quicker response time and lower overall costs. The value of this decision can only be measured in light of the annual maintenance costs from the selected vendor (after receipt of bids) and a careful comparison of the options.

Another consideration is planned obsolescence and system replacement. Even if the system is still operational after five years, the state of technology may render the recommended equipment obsolete and some consideration should be given to investment allowance for future replacements. However, looking that far into the future may overstep the point of diminishing returns. That is, the cost of finding the right answer may exceed the savings of early planning. The most prudent choice is to advise the management team that such long range planning requires attention and allow them to decide how far to take the analysis. Sometimes taking such a long-range view in companies that normally see a much shorter forecast can confuse the primary objective of providing for today's needs.

Do not overwhelm the management team with detailed costs for individual components. In most cases, the bottom line is what is most important. Some level of detail is certainly required but all the detail previously described is usually not shared in the primary recommendation. It is usually better to include detail level information on attachments.

HUMAN RESOURCE REQUIREMENTS

A cost estimate would be incomplete without some review of the personnel needed to operate the system. In most circumstances, existing on-site personnel will be used as system operators, but this must be verified.

If it is company management's intention to operate this system with new personnel, there will be hiring and training costs that must also be addressed in the system recommendation. The human resources department is the best place to obtain personnel cost information.

Begin by first estimating how many individuals will be needed to operate and monitor the proposed system. Establish broad definitions of job responsibilities and job titles, then share these expectations with the company's security manager. Develop an outline for the use of existing personnel and help the security manager determine if the current force can do the work.

From these discussions, develop a profile of the force needed to operate and manage the proposed system and the personnel required to supplement the existing force. Conduct an interview with the human resources manager to determine cost for additional resources.

COST ANALYSIS

After compiling the cost data on the preliminary system, further analyze the investment in the project. The anticipated cost for the recommended security system should not exceed the value of the assets being protected. When the best efforts are made to contain costs but the investment exceeds the value of the potential loss of physical assets and there are no human assets to consider, the recommendation will usually be to use insurance or other risk aversion approaches.

The value of the security survey will be the knowledge that the facility has been thoroughly reviewed, and it was determined that the cost of preventing anticipated losses exceed the losses themselves. A valid recommendation in such a circumstance may be to use the security survey and budget as a decision making tool to justify the purchase of additional insurance or duplicate resources to ensure business continuity if the asset being protected is stolen or damaged.

Assistance from company personnel is essential for this step. The security professional must learn which assets are considered critical to the operation and establish a value for those assets. The company accounting can be a useful resource for this information. However, management perception cannot be overemphasized. The raw cost of the asset may not be as significant as the ability to replace the asset if it is lost or the business income loss that will result if the asset is taken out of service.

The preliminary system design should include a cost comparison of potential loss of revenue and the cost of replacing assets if the anticipated threats are realized. This will aid management in making an informed decision to invest in new security measures.

LEGAL ISSUES

A recommendation for security systems can have broad implications for the security professional and the company. In today's litigious society, companies must guard against legal exposure as a result of perceived or implied negligence. One of the frequently used phrases in legal environments with regard to security is the application of "reasonable care."

An excellent example of this perspective can be found in the healthcare industry. In addition to liabilities from medical malpractice, healthcare practitioners also have many of the same exposures as major hotels. Likewise, because of their high visibility, healthcare institutions are often exposed to "slip and fall" claims.

One of the most compelling arguments for investing in security, with regard to litigation in a healthcare institution, is the protection of children and newborn infants. Consider the case of a newborn infant disappearing from a healthcare facility. Juries find it very difficult to place a value on human life and the life of a child is especially significant. Jury awards in such cases are usually extremely high. If the institution that is being protected by the security professional is a healthcare institution that provides care to newborn infants, it follows that a single lawsuit awarded to a claimant can offset the expense of almost any physical security system.

The central question in such cases is usually "Has the institution taken reasonable care to protect the lives and property of their employees, visitors and patrons?" The definition of reasonable care tends to change with each legal jurisdiction and, within those jurisdictions, opinions changes over time. So the security professional and the company must be diligent in their efforts to constantly assess the physical security requirements and, where necessary, improve the devices, procedures and manpower to demonstrate the application of reasonable care.

The security professional must therefore consider the implied potential for loss if reasonable care is not taken and illustrate the comparison of costs for company management.

At the conclusion of this analysis, the security professional must present the assessment to the management team. The next chapter deals with how best to make this presentation.

6

Presenting the Solutions

INTRODUCTION

After completing the Needs Analysis, present it to the management team and bring together the Policy Review, Threat Assessment, Vulnerability Study, and Preliminary System Design so management can make an informed decision to proceed. The management team decides if additional investments are worth improvements in physical security, but it is the security professional's role to present the facts and opinions used to make those decisions.

The goal in presenting the recommendation is to clearly convey the benefits of the security solution and the investment required to obtain those benefits. The recommendation may also conclude that the current level of security measures is adequate and that the company need not take further action. The recommendation may also conclude that the investment to implement the system may exceed the cost of simply replacing the protected assets following an incident. The recommendation will help the management team make the right decision. The company is relying on the security professional to guide them through the decision process.

WHAT MANAGEMENT WANTS TO KNOW

The management team must ensure the successful ongoing operation of the company. To accomplish this, they must provide a safe and secure work environment for their employees, patrons, and visitors. The management team must also protect the assets of a company from individuals with deliberation and intent to cause harm. They are relying on the security professional for answers on how to best to ensure continued operation. Some of the more urgent questions the security profession must answer are:

1. Why would I want to do this?
2. What will happen if I do not do this?
3. Who needs to be involved to implement and operate the system?
4. When should I act?
5. How long will it take to implement the recommended solutions?
6. How much will it cost?

Why Would I Want to do This?

The Physical Threat Assessment and Vulnerability Study explain the most compelling reasons to act. Include a summary of these reports in the system recommendation. These reports identified the threats that the company is (or should be) concerned about and how susceptible the company is to suffer loss from these threats.

The recommendation must make clear the extent to which human lives are at risk and the value of the assets protected by the proposed solutions. A review of the concerns expressed by employees during interviews would also be helpful in creating a well rounded description of the situation. Focus attention on the loss of business income that could result from damage to or loss of the protected assets.

What Will Happen If I Do Not Do What Is Recommended?

Address the consequences of not acting on the recommendation. The Physical Threat Assessment and Vulnerability Survey will provide the basis for the conclusions and the recommendation must remind the management team of what is at risk.

Direct the management team's attention to the loss of protected assets. Help them imagine what the conditions would be like if each of the threats suggested by the Physical Threat Assessment were realized. Emphasize the catastrophic business losses that could result if deaths or serious injury were to occur to key personnel.

Present a review of losses due to indirect cost. Examine the potential for losses due to lawsuits in the recommendation. If a litigant can show an injury resulted because the company failed to take reasonable care in a security matter identified by the Physical Threat Assessment or Vulnerability Study, explain how the company could sustain substantial costs.

Another indirect cost is public image. It is difficult to quantify the losses from negative publicity but easy to imagine. Help the management team envision their company's name on the six o'clock news associated with words like "negligence, apathy, carelessness and mismanagement." These indirect costs can have as much an impact on business results as the loss of a critical asset.

Who Needs to Be Involved to Implement and Operate the System?

Aside from capital investment, the company is also concerned with the human resource investment in implementing any proposed system and the ongoing personnel cost in operating the system. Address the human resources needed initially and what is needed to serve the ongoing operation of the recommended solutions. The most likely candidates are the existing security force. Use the information gathered during the Needs Analysis about force management. Incorporate that data into an outline of the human resource operations plan.

Review the security force utilization by describing what the new post orders for the security officers will be and how the plan will reallocate the force. Assess the savings expected when labor is replaced by automated systems. Those savings can be re-employed in other areas of the company having the effect of "adding security officers to the staff."

For example, when an officer stands an eight hour post at a primary entrance door simply to screen individuals entering and leaving a building, an electronic security system can replace the officer. This substitution can result in a savings of eight man-hours. These savings can also be in dollars but that assumes that the company would dismiss the officer. The more likely (and recommended) outcome is to utilize the officer in other more productive ways.

System implementation will also require the participation of Risk Management, Purchasing, Legal, Facilities, and Information Technology to name a few. Provide an overview of the implementation process and how each of these groups will contribute to the overall success of the implementation in the presentation.

When Should I Act?

If the assets to protect are substantial and the probability of loss is moderate or high, the answer to this question is always "now." Justify the timing of the implementation of the recommended solutions by showing the management team what a delay would mean. If there is a delay in the decision to implement the solutions, illustrate how that delay will affect the recommendation and what additional risks would result. Will equipment or labor prices rise? Will the threat of litigation grow? What are the downside risks of inaction?

In earlier chapters, we discussed a phased approach to implementation. If the company is not ready to move immediately because of budget considerations, have an alternate plan ready for discussion that builds the proposed solutions over time.

How Long Will It Take to Implement?

This is usually a difficult question to answer, especially when multiple disciplines are involved and multiple vendors implement the recommended solutions. The larger the project, the greater the installation time, but installation time is not the only factor. In addition to equipment installation, estimate a time line for the entire process. This time line includes at least the following tasks:

- Final system design
- Preparing the request for proposal (RFP) (followed by an approval process)
- Bid solicitation and vendor response to the RFP
- Evaluating the bid responses
- Examining the equipment (including vendor presentations)
- Visiting installation references
- Final contract negotiations and award
- The equipment delivery interval[i]
- The installation time[i]
- The final hook up time, including testing and troubleshooting
- User training
- Staff announcements
- Issuing credentials (in card based populations)
- Enrollment processes (in biometric applications)

These estimates are generally expressed in months. The recommended solutions may take up to a year to implement.

How Much Will It Cost?

Cost is always an issue for discussion, but there is a relationship between time and budgets. The company may find the cost reasonable but simply cannot assign the capital to the project yet. It is likely that the security professional was called in at this time to help establish a budget.

Display costs as fully and objectively as possible. Usually top management is not interested in the fine details of the cost computation, so omit them from the body of the recommendation. This cost presentation is broad and top level; also have an detailed appendix that will address the most rigorous examination.

---

[i] A good reference source is the local vendors that would ordinarily have an opportunity to serve the company for this project.

METHODS OF PRESENTING THE RECOMMENDATION

There are two components to the security solutions' presentation: a written proposal and an oral/visual presentation. The written proposal outlines in detail the rationale behind the recommendations and describes the proposed solutions. The oral presentation is a less detailed "concept presentation," usually supported by visual aids. In some cases, the management team will simply not have time to read the written recommendations so the oral presentation carries a tremendous responsibility to accurately and briefly convey the entire concept and focus on key issues that will provide sufficient information for a decision.

The Written Presentation

The written presentation contains all of the details necessary for management to make the decision to authorize funding and grant permission to implement the proposed system. Conversely, if the studies conclude that no action is required, clearly describe the justification for these conclusions.

Written proposals usually begin with an "Executive Summary." These opening remarks summarize the main points of the proposal and permit the reader to understand the proposed solutions without having to read all the details. To be effective, the Executive Summary will be well spaced (that is to say, wide margins and ample vertical distance between paragraphs), speak in broad terms and address only key decision points. The details supporting these arguments and conclusions are in the body of the proposal. Assume that the reader will accept the judgment and conclusions in the Executive Summary and do not offer details that prove the point. If details are needed for further justification, the reader can simply read the rest of the written package.

Following the Executive Summary, prepare a table of contents. Numbering the pages is helpful for all written presentations but especially for large ones. Group information together behind tabs to enable the reader to find what they want within a defined section.

If the security professional has not done a written presentation before, obtain copies of other proposals done for other types of projects for the management team. This will provide a good guide as to how management in this company is accustomed to seeing such recommendations. Use this proposal as a guide to the organization and structure of the written package

Section 1 – Project Objectives and Scope of Work

Fully describe the objectives of the study in this section and the benefits expected if the recommendation is accepted. This section is also the appropriate place to limit the Scope of Work addressed by this project. Both definitions are an essential part of the introduction. For example:

Set the Stage

> The company created this project to review the current level security that exists facility wide. The purpose of this project is to establish an improved level of security through a joint effort of all departments by using the combined technical resources and cooperation across departmental lines.

Identify the Goals

> The goal of this project is to create a centralized command and control system with maximum flexibility while permitting individual customization for all users. In conceiving the system, the company intends to take advantage of the most technologically advanced features available in the electronic security industry and integrate the chosen system features into existing communication facilities and data control practices.

Limit the Scope

> The application of this system is limited to the electronic system design to meet the needs identified in the Physical Threat Assessment and Vulnerability Study. The solutions recommended shall also result in a proposed realignment of security watch stations and new procedures for alarm response. It is not the intent of this project to evaluate the existing security force, investigate internal security matters regarding personnel or prepare the company for threats from "natural" catastrophes. This project addresses man-made threats from perpetrators with intention and deliberation to do harm to company personnel or assets.

This definition of Scope of Work also provides management an opportunity to expand the scope of the project in cases where items are not included and are of principal concern. A clear definition of the Scope of Work will ensure that the efforts of the security professional meet the results expected by the company.

Section 2—Threats and Countermeasures

Summarize the Physical Threat Assessment, identifying the key assets and personnel at high risk. Using the data gathered in the Physical Threat Assessment, explain what those threats are and how likely each is to occur.

Define what, if any, systems are presently employed to address the threats identified in the Physical Threat Assessment. The present method of operation includes a detailed list of all existing security systems and resources used to secure the company's facility.

Describe where the company is vulnerable to these threats from information gathered during the Vulnerability Study. Be specific in the description of the areas of exposure; emphasize the reasons for implementing the proposed solutions and the rationale for proceeding with the proposed solutions.

Section 3—Benefits of the Recommended Solution

Explain what the proposed methods of securing operation will do to benefit the company. Emphasize how the proposed systems and other recommendations will satisfy the needs of the Physical Threat Assessment and Vulnerability Study. For example:

> The current method for perimeter access control is to use the security force at the building's reception desk to control visitor access to the facility. However, other doors leading into the facility that are intended for emergency egress only are frequently jammed open to allow convenient access to the parking lot.
>
> As a result, a perpetrator may enter the building through one of these uncontrolled and unmonitored doors, thereby gaining access to the entire facility without the knowledge or permission of the security staff. One of the identified threats in our

Physical Threat Assessment is access to the data center by unauthorized personnel. The failure to prevent unauthorized access may result in sabotage of the data communications network resulting in lost data and delays in the operation that can cost the company $XXX per day.

By comparing each method of operation against the threats identified in the Physical Threat Assessment and Vulnerability Study, the proposed solutions will convey the need for improved security procedures and additional security monitoring equipment.

Section 4—Recommendation

Begin with a description of what the company should do and when they should do it. Specific details of the recommended system such as how many card readers, how many alarm contacts, or the recommendation location for command posts will be listed on attachments. The recommendation section is reserved for summary conclusions giving only as much detail as needed to clearly illustrate what is to be done to solve the identified problems.

Focus attention on the involvement of security personnel in the operation of the new security system. If the plan recommends using existing security personnel to respond to the threats detected by the proposed systems, describe how the system will employ them. For instance, the recommendation may say:

> This system will require the security force to monitor the alarm terminals and CCTV screens 24 hours a day, 7 days a week. This will result in a three shift watch, with each shift standing an eight hour tour. We recommend that the officers in each watch rotate through the command post alternately serving as roving patrol and command center watch station personnel.

By defining the recommendation in this way, the management team will recognize the total investment required in implementing the recommended solutions.

Section 5—Investment Required

Explain the cost of using the recommended systems. Cost details are not an essential part of this section and are to be included on an attachment to the recommendation. The recommendation will provide a cost comparison of all the potential solutions.

To establish these comparisons, begin with the statement of proposed capital investment. Include the investment of labor and material needed to install the recommended systems and the anticipated human resource cost for implementation. Summarize the details of this investment option in a single line item.

The second line item is the anticipated expense for additional personnel to operate or monitor this system.

The third line item is the annual maintenance anticipated for the recommended system. This cost was calculated when the System Design was created. Estimate annual maintenance using approximately 10% of the material cost of all equipment on the project. Estimate annual labor maintenance by using approximately 15% of the final hookup costs established in the system budget.

Next, show the cost of additional personnel, if any, or the resulting savings in redeployment of personnel that will be possible if the recommended solutions are accepted.

Then examine other options to address the identified risks. Compare the cost of these options against the recommended solution. The first comparison is the investment in the recommended solution versus the cost of doing nothing. Assess the potential loss from a perpetrator successfully causing damage to the assets of the company. Add the cost of lost income resulting from damaged property when making this assessment.

Next, compare the cost of using business insurance to offset the loss in income and assets to mitigate the identified risks. Remember that these are "rough order of magnitude" estimates and the substantial investment time to arrive at exact numbers is not necessary.

Examine the phased approach to implementing the recommended solutions. A phased approach will scale back the principle recommendation giving cost containment first priority (see Chapter 5). If the recommendation uses this approach, explain repeatedly and deliberately that this is not the primary recommendation but a "stop gap" measure of only the most critical elements of the recommendation. Always present the best solution to the company first, regardless of the cost.

Type the recommendation on standard 8½ x 11 white paper and bound in some convenient manner so that the reader may examine the proposal quickly and easily. Avoid fancy binders or covers that detract from the content of the presentation.

The Oral Presentation

After the written proposal is finished, prepare an outline for the oral presentation based on the written package. The face-to-face meeting is usually a dialogue, not a monologue, and questions will be raised by the audience. The outline will help to keep the presentation on track and ensure that all of the important elements of the presentation are covered.

Practice the oral presentation before the meeting. Sometimes a passage sounds good when written out but sounds awkward when spoken aloud. This exchange of information should be free and relaxed. Do not "read" from a script. The security professional is there to convey knowledge, not recite a speech. Be intimately familiar with all the details of the recommended solutions.

Prepare visual aids based on the oral presentation. A useful tool for visual aids is a computer program from Microsoft called PowerPoint. PowerPoint allows the user to create a slide show from other programs. This slide show uses a personal computer and a digital projector for the presentation. Ask the company's media center what equipment is available for use in the presentation. One note of caution—computers and other electronic devices can fail. Have a backup! Copy the presentation material to disk so another computer can be used. In complex presentations, create a printed copy of the slide show to distribute to illustrate important points if the electronic devices fail. For mission critical information, one may even prepare easel boards that duplicate the electronic visual aids.

When constructing the visual presentation, it is often helpful to use charts, graphs or other images that do not involve the written word. It is frequently easier to convey a concept with an image than it is to write it on a screen and compel the audience to read the presentation. Remember, you are there to convey concepts, and "a picture is worth a thousand words."

DELIVERING THE PRESENTATION

Here comes the hard part—assembling the right audience. Audience selection for the presentation can be crucial to the acceptance of the recommendation. It is important to obtain support from all members of the staff who will benefit from the successful completion of the security survey. It is also important to include all those who will gain by implementing this project and those that have financial authority over the resources needed to accomplish the mission. Compile the invitation list with the help of the prime contact; she or he will know the audience.

Establish a meeting with the management team. Explain that the purpose of the meeting is to review the system design and to make decisions on the choices offered. Plan the meeting well in advance to ensure attendance. Arrive early for the meeting and test the presentation equipment. Before the audience arrives, dim the lights in the room so it is easier to view the visual presentation. Do not place the written packages on the table for the audience when they enter the room. When you do this, the first inclination of most attendees is to immediately begin reading the proposal and they will be less likely to give the oral presentation their full attention.

Begin the presentation with a brief description of who you are (for those who do not know you) and why this subject has surfaced at this time. Describe the agenda and how long the meeting will last. Note if there will be breaks during the meeting. This will allow the audience to pay more attention to the presentation, knowing that time has been set aside to tend to other company business.

Early in the presentation, be sure to express appreciation for the support of the individuals who have assisted you in the collection of information, and it is always helpful to identify them by name. Restate the objectives of the project. Explain the techniques used to achieve those objectives. It is best to keep the discussions at a relatively high level.

Present the information gathered and the conclusions reached. Answer all questions as quickly as possible. If you do not know an answer, do not guess! It is better to say you do not know and commit to finding the answer after the meeting. Write these questions down and answer by letter after the meeting.

Gaining Acceptance for the Solutions

This step is the most important one in the entire presentation process. It is not difficult to do but anyone who has ever had to convince an audience to take a particular course of action will understand the effort needed to "ask for the decision." After describing the conclusions, what must be done, how to do it, and when to act, a decision is needed to move to the next step. Turn to your audience and ask, "Do I have your support in implementing this recommendation?" You have been doing all the talking up to this point, now it is time for audience feedback.

The presentation builds a business case that helps the company management team decide if improvements needed in company security measures justify the cost. It is the security professional's responsibility to identify and clearly define the options available to the management team and make an appropriate recommendation for the correct course of action. Gaining acceptance means presenting the recommendation in such a way that it is clear and meaningful to the company and can help the company reach a decision.

One of the roles the security professional must play is that of motivator. Large organizations are especially sensitive to major decisions. Managers are reluctant to take chances by making decisions that have a major impact on the company when there are substantial areas of uncertainty. The security professional can help by placing her or his reputation on the line with a solid, well-supported recommendation. The security professional will take the risk of the decision and will guide the management team to the right conclusions that support an informed choice.

Seeking acceptance is an uncomfortable situation for most people; nevertheless, it is an essential step in moving the project forward. It is the moment of rejection and most people have a tough time dealing with rejection. It is helpful to remember that a lack of acceptance simply means that the audience may be rejecting the conclusions, not the work done or the efforts of the security professional. "No" sometimes means they do not know enough and a revision of the presentation is required to make the choices clearer.

Frequently in decisions involving large complex systems, the management team is usually not prepared to make an immediate decision following the presentation. That is one reason why the written package is an essential part of this entire process.

Oftentimes, there is "sticker shock" when the investment cost of the project is revealed. Everything a security professional has presented may be justified and completely logical but the funds are simply not available to act on the proposed recommendation at this time. Do not be discouraged. Make every effort to work with the management team to arrive at an appropriate decision.

In cases where an immediate acceptance is not forthcoming and additional discussions between the decision makers are necessary, the written package will stand in place of the oral presentation. Expect delays. After the oral presentation, distribute the written package so that further review and discussions can take place in light of all the information at hand.

Follow Up

Stay in constant communication with the management team after the presentation. Answer all questions quickly and accurately and help the team arrive at the most useful decision for the situation.

When the management team grants approval for the project, draft a confirming letter. Address this correspondence to all those invited to the presentation. Include a detailed description of the scope of the project, the resources needed, and the schedule for completion with the expected results. Conclude the letter with a brief description of the reports expected regarding the progress of implementing the recommended solutions.

Remember that the role of the security professional is to evaluate, report, and recommend. He or she is there to guide the company to an informed decision. When a decision is made to move forward with the project, begin the system acquisition phase.

7

System Acquisition – Part 1, Technical Specifications

7.1 INTRODUCTION

After approval of the recommended solutions, the security professional must translate the preliminary design into a solicitation describing the products and services needed to meet the design objectives. The solicitation is released to the market to obtain pricing and availability on the specified products and services. The most common way to manage these solicitations is through a competitive bid.

In this chapter, we will examine some of the ways competitive bids are constructed and the reasons for selecting a type of bid for a particular situation. We will review how to create a Request for proposal (RFP) and the benefits of each type of bid process for system bids.

CHOOSE THE BID TYPE

There are several types of bid specifications commonly used to describe a physical security system acquisition. The complexity of the project, the need for specificity in matching the system requirements to the products and services, and the company's purchasing policies determine the type of bid to use. The bid types described below represent some of the more commonly used bid types but by no means represent a comprehensive list of all types of bids. Further, a specification may combine the elements of several types of bids. These bid types are:

- Request for information (RFI)
- Request for quotation (RFQ)
- Request for proposal (RFP)

An RFI is used to gather information to develop an RFP or an RFQ. The RFI usually does not require the vendor to reveal prices but may ask for budget estimates based on the broad parameters of the RFI.

The RFI is a useful tool when the needs defined by the security survey are so unusual that the consultant cannot adequately develop an RFQ or RFP. The RFI will not be specific in what the company wishes to buy but instead will provide a broad definition of the mission and functions that are needed in the system to be acquired. The RFI may address performance requirements to some degree but is usually not specific in the details of how to achieve those requirements. The RFI explains the overall goals of system performance and requires the respondent to describe how to accomplish the mission and the performance results expected.

In this way, the company can gather expertise from throughout the industry and allow the marketplace to share in problem solving. It provides a broad reach of participation and substantial creative input from the manufacturers. Use the RFI for situations where there are unusual environmental circumstances and it is not possible to develop a Preliminary System Design.

Use the RFI sparingly. Because it is non-specific, it opens the design to wide variation and makes competitive comparisons very difficult. The RFI lacks design detail, so the results may not address all of the problems. Vendors will tend to recommend only products that they sell and not necessarily the best fit.

RFIs are usually very good in situations where a completely new product is being engineered, but in most security applications the products already exist to solve the problems. It is the role of the security professional to define the problem and establish the components of the recommended solution.

The Request for Quotation

Use the RFQ to solicit costs from the market when the equipment make and model has been predetermined. It is the most straight-forward method for soliciting competitive offers and comparing bids. Use the RFQ when the security professional does not want to open the bid to a wide variety of alternatives. The RFQ describes the required components, then solicits a price on the equipment and other bid elements needed for delivery. Some of the other elements of the RFQ are:

- Project management
- Scheduling and cost controls
- Project administration
- Fabrication and factory testing
- System demonstration
- Disassembly, storage, freight, and insurance
- Installation
- System testing and start up
- User training
- Warranty
- Post-installation support

Use the RFQ to compare bids when all bidders are making offers on the same products. The RFQ can provide competitive pricing on pre-selected systems. Assuming all bidders meet the bid conditions equally, the company with the lowest overall price generally wins.

Written specifications will often form the basis in constructing RFQs. These written specifications, commonly referred to as boiler-plate specifications are hardware specifications that describe a par-ticular product. Equipment manufacturers that have boilerplate specifications will readily supply them, and the security professional amends these specifications to fit the circumstance. This is a useful approach and saves considerable time in preparing system specifications. In addition, this approach is useful when an internal standard exists for system installations and the intent is to be consistent in acquiring new systems and system additions.

However, when specifying a new system and there is no internal standard established and the products for the system have not been pre-identified, the RFQ can create some unwanted situations. Because the RFQ describes the system in specific product terms, it requires system selection before the bid is released to the market. The catch-22 is that reviewing all available systems before each bid to determine the one best fit is not an economical use of the security professional's time or the company's consulting fees (in the case of a professional consultant). Additionally, if the security professional is not a qualified consultant with years of experience and possessing at minimum a PSP certification from ASIS International, evaluating the market can be arduous and overwhelming. Inexperience in interpreting features and implementation can lead to false conclusions.

A valid argument can be made that the security professional should be an expert in system design and, as such, should specify the exact system components for the proposed solutions. This argument does not consider the commercial aspects of the system acquisition but focuses entirely on the technical capabilities of the equipment under analysis.

There are over 170 access control manufacturers today and over 120 manufacturers of CCTV equipment. (This count was based on the companies listed in the exhibitors' roster for the 2004 ASIS National Seminar.) Having full knowledge of all of the features of all of the manufacturers is a nearly impossible task, even for a trained professional. Further, even if the research identifies the one best system, there is no guarantee that there will be a vendor willing to assume the responsibilities of installation and maintenance on the chosen system. System support is an essential part of the process. In this instance, the definition of support is technical assistance before the sale, qualified installation labor after the sale and user training and system maintenance after implementation. Establishing bona fide offers from interested vendors first reduces the number of systems to review. The RFQ would preclude this advantage.

The RFQ is not a recommended approach for most new installations. The exposure to the company and the security professional is great since the full responsibility of system selection falls on the writer of the RFQ. The vendors have no obligation to perform to specifications but rather must only provide the equipment specified. If the system does not perform as expected, the vendor is not liable. System integrators and engineering firms that have full time technical staff also find it extremely difficult to keep up with product improvements, many of which occur on a monthly basis, particularly in software development.

Complicating the process even more is the variation in network configuration for the various access control and CCTV systems on the market today. The manufacturers of these systems do not use consistent methods for network design or component pricing. The criteria used in system design and included with the RFQ may inadvertently impose mechanical or technical requirements that have little value in system performance. These unintended requirements limit which vendors may participate in the bid process by virtue of the design elements chosen. This artificially reduces competition and may unintentionally exclude a best fit system.

Another consideration to pre-selecting an equipment type is open competition. To obtain the best product for the system design at competitive prices, allow the marketplace to vie for the business on a level playing field. Selecting a manufacturer beforehand removes a large element of competition from the marketplace and restricts bidders to only those products identified by the RFQ. In bids using public funds, such restrictions can open the door for complicated protests that delay system implementation unnecessarily and create a strained relationship between the buyers and the sellers. This also does a disservice to the company by artificially eliminating a competitor that may have a superior system to the one specified in the RFQ.

However, the RFQ should not be dismissed as ineffective. In many cases, there are compelling reasons to specify a unique system type. Some examples of this are system expansions where an existing system is in place and the task is to add to that system. In addition, some companies have set internal standards for their security systems based on technical criteria developed to meet certain compatibility issues or minimum performance standards. Competition in such bids would be legitimately limited to vendors that provide products designed to work within certain technical parameters. In these cases, RFQs are useful and provide an opportunity to obtain competitive prices on products that meet specific compatibility criteria.

If in doubt, add the services of a certified PSP security consultant to the team. To find a qualified consultant, contact the International Association of Professional Security Consultants (IAPSC) at *www.iapsc.org*.

The Request for Proposal

The RFP is the most inclusive method for obtaining costs and establishing project criteria. An RFP contains all the elements of an RFQ but replaces equipment descriptions with performance criteria. This means that the specification describes what the system is supposed to accomplish, not what equipment to use. Performance criteria are based on the needs identified in the Preliminary System Design. There are several forms of RFP, and the most commonly used types for security projects are:

- Firm fixed price
- Fixed price with economic adjustment
- Fixed price with incentive
- Fixed ceiling price with retroactive adjustments
- Cost plus
- Cost sharing
- Cost plus incentive
- Cost plus fixed fee

We will only discuss the firm fixed price option in this book. Many conditions accompany each type of proposal contract. For a comprehensive listing of contract types and conditions usually found in these contracts, please consult the National Contract Management Association. Information about this association is on the worldwide web at *www.ncmahq.org*.

The RFP takes a top down approach to limit the field of possible systems. It begins with a call for all interested vendors, and then examines the broad parameters of system capabilities to exclude the ones that do not meet the stated criteria. By calling for offers instead of specifically asking for certain pieces of equipment, the market defines who is willing to assume the responsibilities for meeting system criteria. A detailed examination of the offers reduces the field further to the most likely candidates that will meet the established needs. The examination process continues until there is only one (or sometimes several) offers that accomplish the required goals. A review of the bidder's business plan rounds out the analysis to focus on the overall best response.

The preceding chapters assumed that we are dealing with a new installation. We will therefore confine our discussions to the RFP and examine the elements of this approach.

PREPARE THE RFP WITH PERFORMANCE SPECIFICATIONS

An RFP with performance specifications does not refer to brand or model for the components required in system acquisition. Requests for proposals with performance specifications tend to be the most difficult and lengthy type of bid to prepare. The performance specifications identify the needs established in the Preliminary System Design then describe specific outcomes expected from the system offered. Use RFPs with performance specifications when developing a new physical security system and there are no established standards for equipment compatibility. RFPs with performance specifications are the best way to obtain a broad reach of competitive bids.

By using an RFP with performance specifications for new installations, the security professional can describe the function that must be performed by the required physical security system and can require the vendors to explain how their systems will meet the performance criteria. Of course, this method requires considerably more time on the part of the security professional in evaluating the vendor bid responses. It also requires the greatest commitment on the part of the vendor. Apply this approach in larger, more complex installations. Vendors will be reluctant to invest this much effort in relatively small projects.

RFPs with performance specifications will allow the security professional to engage the vendors in a discourse about the optimum solutions defined in the Preliminary System Design as compared to the products available from all potential vendors. It is the recommended approach to obtain the broadest response in the marketplace and an examination of all competitive options. This approach also shares the burden of system description and system performance with the vendor, thereby allowing the security professional to evaluate all the company's choices without introducing a bias in the evaluation process.

Using the RFP approach requires the security professional to be intimately familiar with the value and limitations of certain product features to determine if these features may be useful to the company when investing in an electronic physical security system. The security professional conducting this process should be a systems' expert, well qualified in the technical aspects of system design and be certified by ASIS International as a PSP.

A novice should not attempt to use the RFP approach without support and guidance. Evaluating RFPs requires years of experience in system design and a strong background in the nuances of security system installation techniques. If the security professional is not a systems' expert, add the services of a PSP certified consultant to the project team.

Using the RFP approach makes comparing prices on an item-by-item basis very difficult. This is because the manufacturers do not build or price their systems the same way. However, the bottom line is the most important element, regardless of individual component pricing. Even though it is difficult to make price comparisons on individual components, you can compare the total cost of the proposals to determine the best value.

Use major subtotals for additional comparisons to help provide a more detailed analysis of the offers made in RFP responses. For instance, separate labor from material and break down the final hookup and installation. Further, subdivide material into network equipment and field equipment. This subdivision gives a clearer picture of the cost for devices proposed to control openings and the common equipment used to support those devices. These price breakdowns can give an indication of the future costs of system additions.

Regardless of how the analysis subdivides the numbers, the bottom line is what matters in a price comparison. Evaluate the proposals in other areas. Some of these are:

- Product hardware
- Product software
- Installation methods
- Technical skills of the support staff
- Business experience
- Technical experience
- Licensing
- Stability of the firms (both the vendor and the manufacturer)
- Documentation provided with the system
- Training
- User support after the sale

THE SINGLE PHASE RFP

The single phase RFP requires that the bidders supply all the information needed in their response for the final selection process. This means that all the technical and financial considerations will be lumped together in a single response document, thus providing the security professional all the information needed to choose the appropriate vendor. This approach has the advantage of saving time and minimizing the bid cost when soliciting vendors for a new project. A single phase RFP tends to be more useful in situations where the technical aspects of the system design are relatively simple, but use a two phase RFP for more complex installations.

THE TWO PHASE RFP

The two phase RFP approach allows more opportunities to examine product features closely but does not compel vendors to disclose price information and other competitive data early in the process. The two phase RFP begins with a technical evaluation of the offers, then limits the bidders in phase two to only those companies that can meet these criteria.

The two phase RFP process assumes that the bid will occur in two steps or phases. The first phase is discovery and defines the technical parameters of the security needs of the company and other considerations required by the company's management team. In phase one, the vendors have an opportunity to specifically address how they would solve the company's problems using their system. This may reveal new, important features to use in the proposed security solutions. This step brings the vendors in partnership with the security professional and the company. The analysis of phase one will also help identify deal breakers or features that may not be available in some manufacturers' products.

For instance, if the management team determines that the solution must include component communications on the company's local area network (LAN), phase one will eliminate all manufacturers that do not have this capability. This reduces the number of offers to review and only those companies that can meet these criteria will participate in phase two. This saves time, effort and expense for all.

The second phase of a two phase RFP provides the business deal and solicits financial offers and terms from the vendors. The evaluation of both submittals is necessary to arrive at a valid recommendation for the most responsive bidder.

ORGANIZE THE RFP

It is important to organize information in a bid to allow quick and easy comparisons and justify recommendations. This helps the bidders and the security professional focus on the comparison of solutions.

To accomplish this, the RFP must be well organized and indexed. Borrowing from the techniques used in federal government contracting is an organization pattern called the Work Breakdown Structure or WBS. A WBS separates the component parts of the project into clearly definable tasks so that the consultant can verify that all the elements of the work are included and so that bid responses can be easily compared. Anyone who has ever tried to compare two or more reports from vendors with substantially different points of view will be able to appreciate the value of a WBS.

In the case of security system RFPs, the process has been modified somewhat and focuses more on system capabilities than work steps, but the concept is still the same. The WBS separates the features and capabilities identified in the Preliminary System Design. The WBS identifies each feature individually by section, and the vendors are required to respond to each section. It is then easier to compare proposals because all respondents record their answers in the same place.

For instance, if anti-passback is a required feature and the RFP calls for a description of how this feature works in the offered system, the feature question would be labeled with a section number, such as 4.3. All vendors will be required to describe their system's anti-passback capabilities in section 4.3. If this is not done, the description of the feature may be anywhere in the bid and the bid could be many pages long. By using an index, comparing features side-by-side will be much easier. When evaluating the RFP, it will be also be easier to question the vendors by referring to specific sections of their response to ensure complete understanding.

The evaluation can rank RFP responses if using weighted measures, (see the section in this chapter titled "Getting Approval for the RFP"). Ranking allows the evaluator to assess each feature based on the stated outcome as it relates to the specification. Ranking assigns a numeric value to each feature for objective comparisons. It will be easier to support the recommendation using this objective ranking system and will help justify the conclusions reached when selecting the recommended vendor.

PREPARE THE PHASE ONE RFP

The phase one RFP will have a cover page that provides the name of the project, the company soliciting the bid and some unique reference that will permit this project to be clearly distinguished from other bid requests from the company. This is typically a project number consisting of alphanumeric characters. The company will usually have a project numbering plan in place and the security professional should discuss this designation with the company's purchasing office. If the company does not have a project numbering plan, the security professional will use a unique project number based on a list he or she maintains. This will reduce confusion in discussing this project with others. Contact information for the security professional is also required and will include the security professional's name, firm name, address, telephone number, fax number, and e-mail address. The project date and issue number will also be on the cover page.

The issue number (or revision number) is helpful when there are multiple versions of the RFP. The issue number will help distinguish the most current version. Also include the Bid Due Date and Bid Time to ensure that the vendors are fully aware of submittal deadlines. An example of a phase one RFP cover page is on Figure 7.1.

The second page is a Table of Contents to help the reader find information quickly and easily. Each section will be number as described above. The numbering plan is flexible but the recommended approach is to separate the information into top-level numbered sections then indent the subtopics under each section. Within each subtopic, number the individual features or components of

Request For Proposal

By
(Company and Company Address)

For
Project: (Project Number)
Entrance Gate Surveillance System

Prepared by

(Security Professional)

Pre-Bid Conference (Date, Time and Location)

BIDS DUE: (Date and Time)

All bids must be submitted on or before the Bid Date at the time specified in a sealed envelope or package as described in the specifications to:

(Company Purchasing Office Address and Contact Person)

Bids may be hand delivered, or mailed. Early submission is recommended.

(Release Date)
Release (Issue Number)

Figure 7.1   Example of an RFP cover page.

each section. Include the page number beside the description of the topic.

Section 1—Invitation to Bid

Provide the bidders with a general overview of the project. This overview contains the primary objective of the project, where the project is located and the names and contact information of individuals responsible for administering the project. The general project description is an executive summary for the vendors. Reading this section will tell the vendors if this is a bid they wish to pursue and will serve to eliminate vendors who are not interested in the product line sought by this RFP. It is not necessary to provide system specific details in this section.

Primary and Secondary Objectives

The primary and secondary objectives will explain to the vendor what the bid will accomplish. The primary objective may read like this:

> Sealed proposals addressed to (purchasing contact) at the above address will be received until (time/date) for furnishing all necessary materials, supervision, testing, and training for the installation of a state-of-the-art access control network to cover 56 doors in (company location).

> Work for this contract consists of, but is not limited to, providing all network equipment, software, and hardware for the specified system. This contract also includes support during and after the installation of this access control system network.

In addition to this primary objective, explain other goals that help provide a more complete picture of the intention of the RFP. For instance, the secondary objective may be:

> In addition to providing an access control and alarm monitoring system for this facility, it is the intention of the company to integrate this new electronic physical security system into the existing company data network. This system is to make use of the existing LAN network where possible and take full advantage of the security and communication protocols already established for the company's management information system.

The RFP may have as many secondary objectives as needed to fully describe the company's intention in preparing this RFP. Remember that the purpose of the RFP is to establish a complete and comprehensive set of objectives for the bidders.

Scope of Work

The scope of work defines the limits within which this system will be acquired. A phrase that would set the stage for system acquisition is:

> The vendor shall provide a complete and working system in every respect to meet the objectives set forth in this RFP.

But broad, sweeping definitions like this can sometimes be confusing to vendors if the limits of the terms are not fully described. The RFP scope of work will explain how far the vendor must go to make the system complete. For instance, it is usually a better idea to require company personnel to enter cardholder information into new systems. This approach has the benefits of establishing familiarity with the system by in-house personnel and permits the individual doing the data entry to customize system programming to more closely match with internal nomenclature.

An example of this might be how to enter an employee title in the system. Also, vendors are reluctant to assume responsibility for such labor intensive tasks where little technical expertise is required. Vendors will not want to use high cost skill resources for simple data entry functions. This will increase the overall project cost without a corresponding benefit. The scope of work will then continue:

> The vendor shall be required to provide a complete and working system as described in this RFP. The vendor's work shall be limited to providing all locks, card readers, alarm contacts, and other endpoint devices to provide input to the security system network. The vendor shall also be required to provide all labor, tools and material necessary to install, test and fully implement this system except for certain programming features as defined herein. The vendor shall establish all tables, access control parameters, and other system programming features but will not be required to enter the data that establishes the parameters

of these features. The company shall provide the labor resources necessary to enter cardholder information, alarm information, and access control information with the assistance of the vendor. The vendor shall supervise this data input ensuring that company personnel are performing system programming as required.

By clearly delineating responsibilities and scope of work, the RFP shall avoid some potential conflicts during system implementation. This will help to enhance the relationship with the vendor and ensure proper installation and implementation of the acquired system.

Anticipated Future Work

Although this section is not generally required in RFPs, it is usually a good idea to provide the vendors with an expectation of other work that will follow the installation of the proposed system. There are two key reasons for describing the anticipated work to be done at the conclusion of the current project.

The first is to illustrate the potential income for the vendor if awarded the contract for this project. By providing realistic expectations of other work that will follow, the vendor will have an overall appreciation for the revenue potential available. This perspective generally encourages more competitive pricing since there are usually substantially greater profits in a long-term relationship with the company.

The second is to provide the vendors with a forecast of upcoming projects to allow for technical considerations in the initial purchase. There are circumstances where purchasing larger system capacities on the initial order can reduce expenses in future years to expand the proposed system. The vendors know how future equipment additions affect their system price. Providing a forecast of future expectations allows the vendor to assist the company in the planning process.

Design Parameters

Design parameters provide the vendor with unique technical requirements for the systems. This establishes an overview of special technical considerations within which the system must perform. The vendors should be given as much information as possible about all the goals intended for the proposed system so that adequate consideration may be given to all elements of the design criteria.

Section 2—Bidder Qualifications

Bidder qualifications describe the minimum requirements a vendor must meet to be able to compete for this business. This also limits the number of competitors that may bid on the proposed system. Some of the most frequently used qualifications are:

1. Minimum years in business
2. Minimum years as a dealer for the system proposed
3. Number of technicians trained to install and service the proposed system
4. Authorized dealer for the proposed system
5. Minimum number of installations of the proposed system done
6. Location of a service office within "X" miles from the company location
7. Service operations available 24/365
8. Centralized service dispatch

This list by no means comprises all of the bidder qualifications. Determine bidder qualifications by the task and the circumstance for the acquisition of the new or upgraded system.

For instance, in installations where there is an existing electronic physical security system, add other criteria requiring the vendor to be an authorized dealer and service company for the existing electronic physical security system. Obviously, this is true only in cases where the RFP intends to add components to the existing system and not replace it.

Section 3—Performance Specifications

Performance specifications are usually the lengthiest section in the RFP. This section describes in complete detail the performance expected from the devices to be purchased under the RFP for the electronic physical security system. Performance specifications describe the function of each operating component.

For example, a typical RFP for an access control system begins with a description of the identity card carried by system users. A description of the card reader follows, then a description of the access point manager or electronic control device to which the card reader is connected. Indicate any preferences required for the manner in which card readers are associated with access point managers.

An example of this might be to distinguish between systems that require an interface installed at control points for managing the devices at that location. Some equipment manufacturers will require that their card readers be connected directly to the access point manager while other manufacturers will require an intermediate device that transmits card information and lock control decisions to the door with all of the endpoint devices being connected to the intermediate panel. There are limitations and benefits of each approach so the system designer must consider if either of these approaches would result in benefits to the system user and include those requirements in the performance specification.

After describing the performance requirements of the access point manager it may also be necessary to describe the manner in which these devices are connected to the host computer. In some cases, manufacturers will permit communications over LANs. Some of the benefits of this design approach include using existing facilities for multi-building communication.

Finally, the performance specifications describe the software features needed in the new access control system. The security professional may use software feature names designated by certain manufacturers but must make a full description of how this feature should work. In so doing, it will become clear to the bidders why this feature is being requested since each manufacturer uses their own nomenclature for software feature.

Software features provide the greatest area for definition. There are simply too many variations of features to examine them all in this book but certain feature areas are important to all systems. A list of these areas follows:

1. In access control systems:
    *   How data is entered into the system
    *   What fields are available

- How the fields can be sorted
- What data is recorded by the system
- How data can be reported
- How the product governs who goes where and when
2. In CCTV systems:
   - How camera images can be selected
   - How the system searches for specific images
   - What automated features are available for monitoring scenes
   - What the playback characteristics are
3. In alarm monitoring systems:
   - How alarms are displayed and announced
   - How the user responds to alarms
   - What alarm information the system records
   - How recorded alarm information is reported

Remember that these are performance specifications and the elements contained in the description relate to the benefits desired by that characteristic. A description of a product's physical characteristics is not necessary unless there is compelling reason to include physical properties in the device description. For instance, some access control systems require that card readers be small enough to mount on narrow aluminum mullions for glass store front doors.

Specify the electrical characteristics of access point managers to ensure that there is adequate protection against damage due to lightning or power surges. A good example of a characteristic that is not necessary for performance specification is the physical size of the housing in which the access point manager electronics are mounted. Conversely, it may be acceptable to say access point manager housings may not exceed a certain set of dimensions when space in the equipment mounting location is limited.

Consider minimum quality certifications. One widely recognized certification is Underwriters Laboratories Inc. (UL) approval. Not all systems from all manufacturers meet UL criteria. However, such approvals are not always mandatory. Add these approval certifications to the RFP requirement if it will enhance the quality of the products received.

Door Detail Schedule (DDS) and Command Center Alarm and Access Control Equipment List

The DDS is the primary resource for access control and alarm monitoring end-point information. The Command Center Alarm and Access Control Equipment Lists are the primary resource for common equipment information. These documents may be included either in the body of the RFP or as an attachment. Since these documents tends to change based on shifting user priorities and the discovery of other information regarding product capabilities in the market, including the documents as an attachment is usually the preferred approach.

However, it is important to communicate in the body of the RFP the existence of these schedules and what information may be found on it. For example, under this section the RFP may say:

> Attached to this RFP is a Door Detail Schedule and Command Center Alarm and Access Control Equipment List, which provides a list of all openings included in this system, the proposed field devices, and the common control and display equipment.

The DDS also contains references to the equipment location on company floor plans and references the appropriate illustrations for elevation drawings of each type of door. The vendor will also find remarks associated with certain doors that will be helpful in pricing and planning the installation of the proposed system. By including these descriptions there can be little misunderstanding that another document exists that provides the necessary details that are included in the DDS.

Camera Detail Schedule (CDS) and Command Center CCTV Equipment List

The CDS is the primary resource for video end-point information. The Command Center CCTV Equipment Lists are the primary resource for display and signal processing equipment. These documents may also be included in the body of the work or as an attachment. Since the CDS also tends to change based on shifting user priorities and the discovery of other information regarding product capabilities in the market, also including it as an attachment is usually the preferred approach.

However, like the DDS, it is important to communicate in the body of the RFP the existence of the CDS and what information may be found on it. For example, under the section of CDS the RFP may say:

> Attached to this RFP is a Camera Detail Schedule, which provides a listing of all the camera views that are to be included in this system, an example of the images expected, and a list of display and signal processing devices.

The CDS also contains references to the location on company floor plans and references elevation drawings for each camera location. The vendor will also find remarks associated with certain cameras that will be helpful in pricing and planning the installation of the proposed system.

Door Elevation Drawings

The marked blueprints will provide the vendors with a reference to the physical location of the field equipment. However, not all vendors are fully aware of the life safety considerations and general conventions used in placing equipment. Oftentimes, manufacturers provide drawings showing how equipment is mounted. This is not true in all cases, and there are frequent variations on standard arrangements that are necessary for unique situations. Equipment placement needs to be consistent for all components of a physical security system. This will increase the professional appearance of the installation and ensure compliance with all requirements. Include door elevation drawings with the RFP to describe what is expected for the physical installation of each device.

Figure 7.2 provides an illustration of a standard single leaf door with a door status switch, a card reader, a request to exit button and a power magnet lock. The security professional will maintain a library of such drawings and provide a sample of these drawings for each equipment location in the system. In special circumstances where companies have unique requirements for equipment placement, make variations on these standard drawings when creating new system installations and system additions.

For instance, Figure 7.2, shows the card reader and exit button at door handle height. Placing these devices above door handle

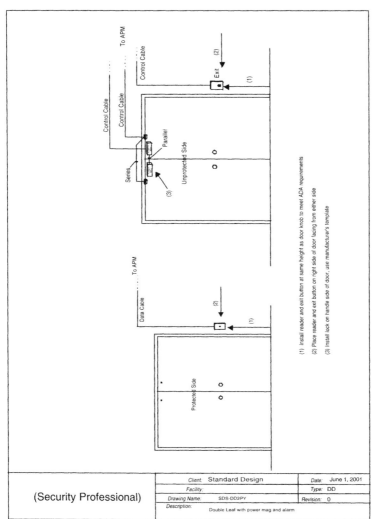

Figure 7.2 Door elevation drawing.

height may be a violation of the Americans with Disabilities Act (ADA) and expose the company to code violations or other statutory constraints. It is important for security professionals to familiarize themselves with the applicable codes and standards regarding device placement. Further, while it may not violate an existing safety standard, incorrect placement of a lock or alarm contact may inadvertently defeat or diminish anticipated security benefits. Be aware of the manufacturer's recommended placement of products and indicate these placements on the drawing. Sample drawings of additional door configurations are in Appendix 1.

Camera Elevation Drawings

As in the case of door detail drawings, Camera Detail Drawings are an essential element of the security survey documentation. Although life safety constraints are usually not an issue with regard to camera equipment placement, there are a number of other factors in camera placement that affects the overall effectiveness of the video system.

An example of placement issue that may affect camera system performance is a camera viewing an object with backlighting. Without drawings to describe specific placement, vendors may opt for a more convenient installation than is optimally required for good camera views. In such cases, backlighting may hinder the view, and the observer will frequently see silhouettes instead of a clear, identifiable image. Additionally, a fixed position camera installed within easy reach of a pedestrian can be either intentionally or inadvertently moved, changing the camera angle to an unwanted view. Be aware of the correct placement of each camera and indicate that placement on the drawing. An illustration of a Camera Elevation Drawing is in Figure 7.3.

Network Drawing

The network drawing serves to illustrate the connections between the communication devices of the electronic physical security system. The network drawing is most important when the security professional is designing large complex systems with multiple floors or multiple buildings. Figure 7.4 provides a sample of a network

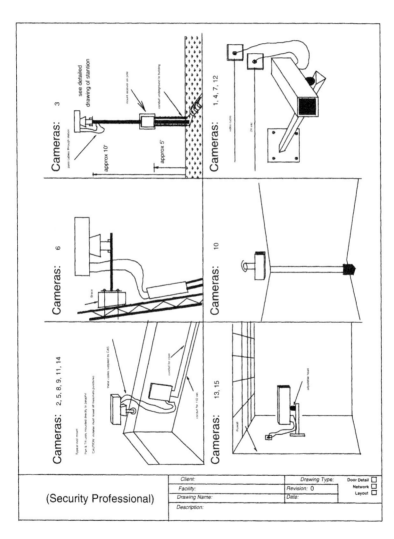

Figure 7.3 Camera elevation drawing.

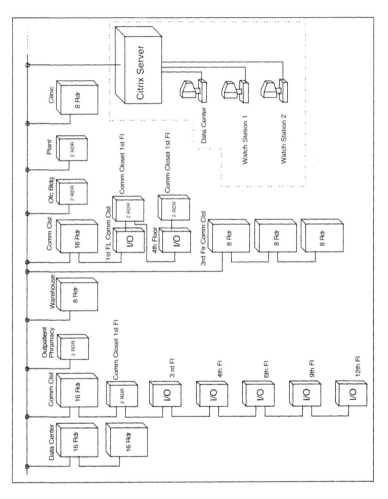

Figure 7.4 Network drawing.

drawing. Although not essential, the network drawing is especially helpful in illustrating the interrelationship between systems or when device communications is complex.

Network drawings provide a comprehensive illustration of the desired interconnection between devices in the electronic physical security system. However, exercise caution in preparing a network drawing for open bids. These configurations are sometimes unique to manufacturers' systems. When special applications exist, such as multi-building environments, a network drawing clearly indicating the use of a company provided LAN would help the bidder understand that a LAN requirement is an integral part of the system specifications.

Network drawings include electronic communication devices but usually exclude low voltage electrical connections such as cabling to door status switches, exit buttons, and other similar devices. These illustrations are usually included in the Door Elevation Drawing. Add comments to network drawings that provide bidders with the opportunity to provide modified versions of these configurations. Doing so removes artificial limitations from the specification where no direct tangible benefit results from this unique wiring approach.

Command Center Drawing

The Command Center Drawing illustrates the physical layout of the equipment (including special security furniture) to achieve the identified objectives. This drawing should clearly indicate how to arrange the proposed equipment to provide optimum performance for the user. An example of a Command Center Drawing is shown in Figure 7.5.

Common Equipment Elevation Drawings

Common Equipment Elevation Drawings are an illustration of how to arrange the equipment in the equipment locker rooms. In small systems, this illustration is usually not required but is helpful if special circumstances exist. It is an essential part of the equipment specification in larger systems. An example of a Common Equipment Elevation Drawing is in Figure 7.6. Some of the more useful considerations for the Common Equipment Elevation Drawing are to (see list after page spread):

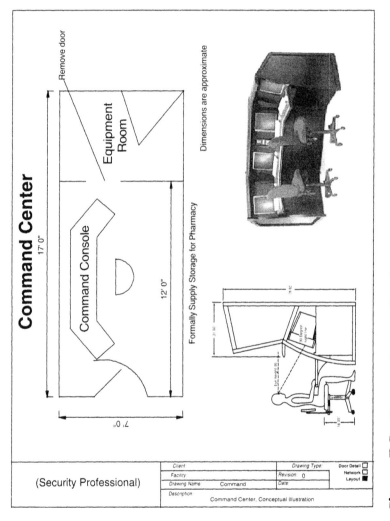

Figure 7.5 Command center drawing.

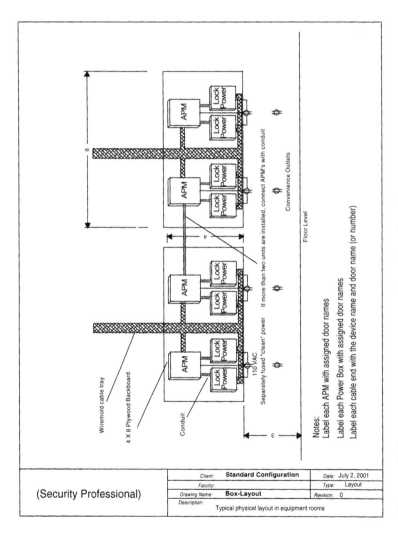

Figure 7.6 Common equipment elevation drawing.

- Mount equipment not more than 6 feet from the floor.
- Use conduit or similar cosmetically acceptable cable race-ways to interconnect devices.
- Allow space between the cabinets for access and system additions.
- Label all cabinets.

Custom Circuit Drawings

In some instances, the system can only achieve the desired performance by a unique non-standard wiring arrangement of certain components. An example of such a circumstance may be a "mantrap." A mantrap is an arrangement of two locked doors connected by a vestibule. In this application, both doors may not be unlocked at the same time.

Most manufacturers can accommodate this by interconnecting the control and sensor ports in the access point manager (network panel). However, to illustrate this fully, it will be necessary to provide a custom circuit drawing to show how the mantrap will work. Providing this level of detail helps to achieve the expected results when implementing the system.

In the case of CCTV applications, a custom circuit drawing may be needed when pan, tilt and zoom features are used in the CCTV system. In this application, the security professional may wish to have a camera automatically pan, tilt, and zoom to a particular image when an alarm is registered. The custom circuit drawing will illustrate which alarm contacts or access control system output signals will trigger the preset image.

Marked Blueprints with Equipment Location

Blueprints are usually too large to be included in the body of the RFP. Blueprints are usually attachments to the RFP; however, in the age of sophisticated CAD programs, blueprints can often be reproduced on standard 8½ × 11 or legal size pages. Under such circumstances, floor plans may be included in the body of the RFP. If the floor plans are an attachment, remarks are required in the RFP that refers to these attachments:

Accompanying this RFP are floor plans, which describe the location of equipment for the proposed system. Please note the reference numbers used on the Door Detail Schedule as they relate to the symbolic references on the floor plans.

Be consistent when marking blueprints with the symbolic references to indicate security system devices. Figure 7.7 provides an example of a symbol set that is gaining increased acceptance among security professionals. It is also important to provide a key or symbol reference on the drawings to aid in understanding the symbols.

Split Contracts

A split contract is a circumstance in which the company elects to provide some portion of the labor or material themselves while requiring the vendor to provide the remainder for a complete and working system. Cost containment is the usual motive or to take advantage of existing facilities or personnel that are available to the company and not utilized for other functions. Although there is a certain value to the cost savings in this approach, it is fraught with problems and even under the best circumstances can result in conflicts between the vendor and the company and a potentially dysfunctional system.

For example, the company may have a staff of electricians who routinely work in the facility. In an effort to fully employ these electricians and to reduce the cost of the security system installation, the management team may suggest that company personnel provide the cabling and equipment mounting portion of the work.

On the surface, this sounds like a desirable outcome but the results are usually not as beneficial as it would initially seem. This is especially true if the personnel elected to do the installation have never performed this type of work before. If in-house personnel install devices improperly and damage occurs, serious equipment liability issues can arise. This can lead to contract disputes and ill will between the company and the vendor.

Avoid split contracts whenever possible to minimize company and vendor frustration. Coordination in these situations is often difficult, and it can be nearly impossible to clearly delineate lines of responsibility for correcting system anomalies. The savings in dollars does not always warrant the risks associated with split contracts.

SIA/IAPSC CAD Security Symbols					RELEASE: 1 PAGE 1 OF 5
SYMBOL #	ASTM 967 1994 SUBMITTAL	ASTM 967 1995 SUBMITTAL	BLOCK NAME 1995 SUBMITTAL	DESCRIPTION M = MOUNT T = TECHNOLOGY/TYPE (SPECIFIC TO DEVICE) M: P = PEDESTAL T = TURNSTILE S = SURFACE F = FLUSH R = RACK M = MULLION D = DESK W = WALL C = CEILING H = HIDDEN	SUGGESTED LAYER / COLOR
	1. ANNOTATION				
1.01	NUM	A B C	REF	DEVICE REFERENCE A: DRAWING SHEET B: DETAIL C: DEVICE/ZONE NUMBER	170 / BLOCK
	2. ACCESS CONTROL				
2.01	P	M T	CR	CARD ACCESS READER T: B = BARCODE W = WEIGAND P = PROXIMITY M = MAG STRIPE F = ELEVATOR FLOOR CALL H = ELEVATOR HALL CALL T = TOKEN S = SMART CARD	173 / GREEN
2.02		M T	BIO	BIOMETRIC ACCESS CONTROL DEVICE T: H = HAND GEOMETRY F = FINGER PRINT V = VOICE R = EYE RETINA I = EYE IRIS	173 / GREEN
2.03		M	KPD	KEYPAD DEVICE	173 / GREEN
2.04		M	CR-KPD	CARD READER WITH KEYPAD	173 / GREEN
2.05		M	CR-TA	CARD READER WITH TIME AND ATTENDANCE	173 / GREEN
2.06		####	DET	DETAIL SYMBOL	/
2.07		P M T	JBOX	JUNCTION BOX	/
2.08		M	STROBE	STROBE LIGHT	/

Figure 7.7 Security symbols, page 1.

SYMBOL #	ASTM 967		BLOCK NAME	DESCRIPTION	M : P = PEDESTAL M = MULLION	SUGGESTED LAYER / COLOR
	1994 SUBMITTAL	1995 SUBMITTAL	1995 SUBMITTAL	☐ M = MOUNT ☐ T = TECHNOLOGY/TYPE (SPECIFIC TO DEVICE)	T = TURNSTILE D = DESK S = SURFACE W = WALL F = FLUSH C = CEILING R = RACK H = HIDDEN	

SIA/IAPSC CAD Security Symbols RELEASE: 1 PAGE 2 OF 5

3. ANNUNCIATION: CONSOLE/PANEL

3.01		M / T	MUX	MULTIPLEX PANEL T: V = VIDEO A = ALARM C = CARD READER	176 / BLUE
3.02		M / T	C-PANEL	CONTROL PANEL T: B = BURGLAR F = FIRE P = PERIMETER D = DOOR	176 / BLUE
3.03			CPU	CENTRAL PROCESSING UNIT	173 / GREEN
3.04			KBD	KEYBOARD	173 / GREEN
3.05			PRNT	PRINTER	173 / GREEN

4. ANNUNCIATION: DEVICES

4.01		M / T	AUDIO	AUDIO DEVICE T: Z = BUZZER L = LISTEN-IN B = BELL K = KLAXON C = CHIME M = MICROPHONE H = HORN S = SOUNDER S = SPEAKER	177 / PURPLE

5. BARRIERS AND VEHICLE CONTROLS

5.01			TRNSTL	TURNSTILE	170 / BLACK
5.02			REVDOOR	REVOLVING DOOR	170 / BLACK
5.03			TR-ARM	TRAFIC ARM	/
5.04			TR-LOOP	VEHICLE LOOP DETECTOR	175 / ORANGE
5.05		T	WIN-SCR	SECURITY WINDOW SCREEN T: S = SHADE (SEE 10.04 FOR B = BLIND ALARMED SCREEN)	/

Figure 7.8 Security symbols, page 2.

	ASTM 967		BLOCK NAME	SIA/IAPSC CAD Security Symbols		SUGGESTED LAYER / COLOR

SYMBOL #	1994 SUBMITTAL	1995 SUBMITTAL	1995 SUBMITTAL	DESCRIPTION M = MOUNT T = TECHNOLOGY/TYPE (SPECIFIC TO DEVICE)	M: P = PEDESTAL M = MULLION T = TURNSTILE D = DESK S = SURFACE W = WALL F = FLUSH C = CEILING R = RACK H = HIDDEN	SUGGESTED LAYER / COLOR
6. COMMUNICATIONS						
6.01			IC	INTERCOM T: M = MASTER S = SUB-STATION		178 / LT-GREEN
6.02			RADIO	TWO WAY RADIO		177 / PURPLE
7. ELECTRICAL						
8. LIGHTING						
9. MISCELLANEOUS						
9.01			SCHRED	DOCUMENT DESTROYER		170 / BLACK
10. SENSORS						
10.01			MD	MOTION DETECTOR T: M = MICROWAVE I = INFRARED U = ULTRASONIC X = EXIT		175 / ORANGE
10.02			360 PIR	360 PIR MOTION DETECTOR T: X = PIR F= Y = 360		175 / ORANGE
10.03			GBS	GLASS BREAK SENSOR T: S = SHOCK A = AUDIO		175 / ORANGE
10.04			WIN-SCRA	SECURITY WINDOW SCREEN WITH ALARM T: S = SHADE B = BLIND (SEE 5.05 FOR NON ALARMED SCREEN)		/
10.05			SD	SCREENING DEVICE T: M = METAL DETECTOR E = EXPLOSIVES DETECTOR X = X-RAY T = TAG DETECTOR (EAS) A = ACCESS		/

Figure 7.9 Security symbols, page 3.

SYMBOL #	ASTM 967		BLOCK NAME	DESCRIPTION	M : P = PEDESTAL M = MULLION T = TURNSTILE D = DESK S = SURFACE W = WALL F = FLUSH C = CEILING R = RACK H = HIDDEN	SUGGESTED LAYER / COLOR
	1994 SUBMITTAL	1995 SUBMITTAL	1995 SUBMITTAL	☐ M = MOUNT ☐ T = TECHNOLOGY/TYPE (SPECIFIC TO DEVICE)		

SIA/IAPSC CAD Security Symbols — RELEASE: 1, PAGE 4 OF 5

11. SURVEILLANCE

11.01	[CRT]	▨ M ▢ T	MON	MONITOR T: V = VIDEO D = DATA G = GRAPHIC M = MULTISCREEN	176 / BLUE
11.02	☐ x ☐	☐ M T	CAM	CAMERA	176 / BLUE
11.03	☐ x ☐	☐ M T	CAM-PTZ	CAMERA WITH PAN / TILT / ZOOM	176 / BLUE
11.04	▦	▦➔	VKBD	VIDEO CONTROL KEYBOARD	176 / BLUE
11.05	▦	▦	VMUX	VIDEO MULTIPLEXER	176 / BLUE
A.05		▤	MPBL	MECHANICAL PUSH BUTTON LOCK	/
11.07		◌◌ M T	REC	RECORDER T: V = VIDEO A = AUDIO	176 / BLUE
12.01	⊘ x ⦵	⊘ M T	SW-A	AUTOMATIC MONITORING SWITCH T: T = TEMP G = GATE B = BAL. MAG H = HUMIDITY W = WATER L = LATCH	174 / RED
12.02		☐ M T	SW-M	MANUALLY OPERATED SWITCH T: E = EMERGENCY L = LOCK F = FOOT M = MAT H = HOLDUP	174 / RED
12.03	⊙ ▫	☐ M T	BUTTON	PUSH BUTTON T: P = PANIC D = DURESS R = DOOR RELEASE B = BELL PUSH	174 / RED

Figure 7.10 Security symbols, page 4.

SYMBOL #	ASTM 967 1994 SUBMITTAL	ASTM 967 1995 SUBMITTAL	BLOCK NAME 1995 SUBMITTAL	DESCRIPTION M = MOUNT T = TECHNOLOGY TYPE (SPECIFIC TO DEVICE)	M P = PEDESTAL T = TURNSTILE S = SURFACE F = FLUSH R = RACK M = MULLION D = DESK W = WALL C = CEILING H = HIDDEN	SUGGESTED LAYER / COLOR
			SIA/IAPSC CAD Security Symbols		RELEASE: 1 PAGE 5 OF 5	
		13. DOOR AND LOCKING HARDWARE				
13.01			EL	ELECTRONIC LOCK T: M = MAGNETIC S = STRIKE L = LATCH SET H = HYBRID		173 / GREEN
13.02			EX-DEV	EXIT DEVICE T: E = ELECTRIFIED M = MECHANICAL D = DELAYED EGRESS X = HIGH SECURITY		/
		APPENDIX A: SAMPLE COMBINATION DEVICES				
A.01			VID-IC	CAMERA WITH INTERCOM		/
A.02			VID-CR	CAMERA WITH CARD READER		/
A.03			VID-KPD	CAMERA WITH KEYPAD		/
A.04			CB	CALL BOX W/ INTERCOM & STROBE		/

Figure 7.11 Security symbols, page 5.

Section 4—Submittals

Requests for proposals for large, complex projects usually result in requirements for extensive vendor information submittals. The amount of information required can be confusing to vendors and omissions may occur. Include a submittal page with each RFP to provide a simple comprehensive list of items that the vendor must supply.

The Proposal Submittal page is a valuable tool that helps the vendor understand what is required in a proposal response and avoid omissions that can disqualify them from the bidding process. It provides a clear and unambiguous list of documents that are required from the vendor to bid on the project. Include in the submittal page:

1. Bidder qualifications:
   The bidder shall provide a complete response to each item listed in the Bidder Qualification section of this RFP.
2. Materials list to meet system design specifications, including:
   a. Description and quantity of products proposed
   b. Names of manufacturers and model numbers
3. Technical specifications and sales literature on each product proposed
4. A complete operations manual for the primary systems proposed
5. One line block diagram of proposed system
6. A copy of the RFQ, signed by an officer of the bidder's company indicating acknowledgment of the RFP and all subsequent amendments. List amendments by number on the signature page

Require the vendor to submit all documents described with one original and "X" copies. (The number of copies should include one for each member of the system selection committee and one for the security professional. The purchasing manager will hold the original.)

Require the vendor to submit the bid typewritten on 8½ x 11 plain white paper using a font not smaller than 10 points nor larger than 14 points. Specify that the bid must have a cover page showing the project description as provided on the cover of the RFP, and the cover page must list the vendor's company name, address, telephone and fax numbers (and website, if applicable). Require the cover page to indicate the name and telephone number (if different) of the contact person and his or her e-mail address.

The RFP requires the vendor to assemble the entire package in a suitable binder (the exact type of binding is not important) and stipulate that the binder include an index as the first page with tabs or similar stationary supplies showing the start of each indexed section.

If the RFP requires electronic submittals, state that they must be complete and contain an index file page (called Index). Require electronic submittals to be in PDF, MS Excel, or MS Word format and require all electronic submittals on a 3.5 floppy or data CD or DVD to be submitted with one original printed copy.

GET APPROVAL FOR THE SPECIFICATIONS

When the RFP is finished, seek the approval of the management team before proceeding to the next step. This approval process is crucial in this stage of bid development. Call for a meeting of the management team to review the RFP. Provide all members of the committee with a copy of the finished bid before the meeting, then allow sufficient time for a review of the document.

When presenting the RFP, promote an open debate on the validity of all assumptions and specifications listed. The security professional's role is to explain what the recommended system will do and to guide the committee to an informed decision. It would help to remember that while selection committee input is valuable, it is also uninformed. Explain the consequences of each choice and ensure that the company is well acquainted with the benefits and limitations of the proposed solutions.

This is also the best time to establish the criteria for bid evaluation. The preliminary design step established the capabilities needed to achieve the design objectives but meaningful objective measurements are needed to evaluate the proposed systems.

For example, the Physical Threat Assessment may have discovered that a disgruntled ex-employee attempted to sabotage the company's billing records by accessing the facility's main computer library and tampering with devices or records. Further, during the Vulnerability Study, it was determined that a single card reader now controls the entry door to the computer library but there is free egress and the door status is not monitored.

Additional door security equipment and an egress card reader are included in the recommendation for this situation. One of the recommended software features in this circumstance might also be anti-passback. This feature gives the System Administrator the ability to help enforce a rule that cardholders must badge in and out in alternating sequence for proper passage through the controlled door. The security professional included the anti-passback system feature and must now describe how and where it will be used.

After presenting this recommendation, solicit feedback from the management team. Have the management team weight the feature to establish relative importance in system operation. Weighting a feature means assigning a numeric value to the feature to describe its importance, relative to other features. This weight will help the security professional judge the significance of a particular feature in the vendor responses and lead to a more objective evaluation of all offers. Doing this for all proposed system features, the security professional will learn which features are most important to the company.

If a system lacks certain features in the bid description and, based on this lack of capabilities, it is necessary to reject the system, the weighted value for those features must be high. A threshold can be set that equals the sum of all mandatory features, and vendor response scores with less than the threshold are disqualified. This level comparison provides an objective and fair evaluation process for all bids. Objectivity helps to make vendor selection "bulletproof" and provides substantial justification for recommending a vendor or system.

Issue minutes of the meeting. Note any major changes made by the committee that differ from the original design in the RFP. Provide the evaluation weights for the selected features in the minutes. When the management team approves the RFP, release it to the company's purchasing department to begin the bid process.

SOLICIT BIDDERS

In most cases, the security professional will be representing major corporations or government entities. Of high importance to such organizations is the potential liability for improperly managed bids for major purchases. Given the complex nature and probable size of the security systems specified, it is likely that the systems under bid will be a major purchase. As a result, the rules of fair play are an essential part of the bid process. Fair play is generally interpreted to mean that all bidders have an equal opportunity to vie for the company's business.

In some cases, there are circumstances that compel the company to have a particular preference for or against a vendor. The basis for these preferences may be previous experience with the vendor or other conditions not immediately apparent. Solicit comments on any biases during the bid review process. Document these biases in the meeting minutes and provide the rationale. Suggest methods for excluding undesirable vendors.

An example of this may be a company that has had prior experience with a vendor and this vendor has failed to perform as expected. An examination of the circumstances may reveal that the performance failure is a result of inadequate labor. In such cases, add a vendor qualification or performance criteria to the RFP that provides a rigorous requirement for personnel to handle the installation. The criteria for vendor qualification would include a requirement that no less than three technicians are available for service on the proposed system. Such criteria will exclude all vendors with insufficient labor to serve the company's needs.

With full approval of the selection committee on the proposed bid, the security professional will then work with the purchasing department of the company to release the RFP to the market. In some companies, there are strict guidelines for vendor selection and bid notification. In all cases, follow the company's purchasing policies. Before compiling a bidders' list or releasing notification of the bid opportunity, discuss the plans for the bid with the company's purchasing agent. The purchasing agent will have the final word on how to conduct the bid.

Identify Bidders

An effective bid release will have as many participants as possible. Planning a bid advertisement is the first step used to notify a broad range of bidders. Advertisements in local and national media will provide open public solicitation to all vendors of the upcoming bid.

However, the intended audience does not always read the advertisements.

Compile a list of selected bidders for this project. The first candidates for this list are the vendors that currently provide services to the company. Before bid development, it is likely that local vendors have solicited, and in some cases been awarded, contracts for providing or maintaining existing security systems. Identify these companies through conversations with company employees.

In developing the preliminary system design, the security professional determined what types of vendors could best meet the system requirements. The ASIS Buyer's Guide from ASIS International will provide a good resource for identifying companies that manufacture products to meet the needs described in the RFP. Using the ASIS Buyer's Guide, the security professional can compile a list of potential manufacturers for this project.

The security professional should know the market and maintain a bidders' list. This list will include remarks about each bidder and how they performed on prior contracts. Look for other publications to expand this list of potential bidders. Explore all reasonable sources of information and include as many potential candidates as possible.

Greater participation by the market results in more options for the company. The vendor qualification list and performance criteria in the RFP will serve to cull this list to a manageable size. It is not necessary to artificially limit the number of bidders on a project except as the company directs.

The company's purchasing agent will do the bid release and will be responsible for documenting bid mailings and receipt of responses. This again serves to reinforce the unbiased nature of the bid and avoids putting the security professional in a compromising position.

Bid Notification

After identifying potential bidders, advise the purchasing agent to release the bid advertisement. Coincident with that release, contact each of the bidders and inform them of the bid opportunity. Exercise caution when making these contacts and treat all vendors equally. Avoid any hint of bias.

A good resource for identifying local vendors is to contact the manufacturers of the most likely systems to satisfy the needs of the RFP. Telephone the head of the sales department and ask a key question during the conversation:

> Do you wish to bid this project directly or do you have dealers in this area that will want to participate in our bid process?

Usually, the manufacturers will have a ready answer and can identify the dealers that will want to participate in this bid. Then contact all the vendors on the bid list to ensure that they are aware of the opportunity.

THE PRE-BID MEETING

Conduct a mandatory pre-bid meeting prior to the bid submittal date. The purpose of this meeting is to present the system bid opportunity to the marketplace and to answer questions about the RFP or the bid process from the interested vendors. Invite the following company personnel to the pre-bid meeting:

- At least two members of the management team
- The company's purchasing agent
- At least one representative of the company's maintenance department
- At least one representative of the company's security department

The security professional and the purchasing manager will moderate the pre-bid meeting jointly. Usually, the security professional takes the lead role in this moderation and the purchasing agent answers questions about the bid process and verifies that the process follows the company's purchasing guidelines.

Require the vendors to sign a sheet confirming their attendance. Review the entire RFP in an orderly fashion and answer questions from the vendors fully during the meeting. Questions given verbally in an open forum may be answered verbally, providing a full and complete answer is rendered. Since all vendors are present, there is little need to document every question and every response. However, in some cases the answers are not readily available and unanswered questions are to be recorded and responded to in a written addendum that will be attached to the RFP. The security professional may find that bidders do not understand some items. Document the question and answer in the RFP addendums in cases where these issues are complex or the question and response may have a significant bearing on the outcome of the award of the contract.

At the conclusion of the pre-bid meeting, remind vendors that additional questions must be in writing. The deadline for questions must allow sufficient time to respond before bid opening. Respond to these questions as quickly as possible by RFP addendum and provide a copy of all questions and answers to all vendors participating in the process. Since the pre-bid meeting is mandatory, send the responses only to those bidders attending the pre-bid meeting.

BID ACCEPTANCE AND BID OPENING

The company purchasing office will receive the RFP responses from the vendors. The RFP has a specific bid date and time and some companies have stringent policies that prohibit the acceptance of bids beyond the allotted time. The security professional must be aware of and honor these constraints. There have been many situations where such rigorous constraints were imposed and bidders presented their bid response only a few minutes late. Those responses were rejected and the bidder's offer was not considered. If the security professional's company has such rigorous constraints, emphasize these constraints at the pre-bid meeting.

Most companies have policies with regard to bid openings. Some bid openings are public while others are private. In a public opening, bids are submitted by potential vendors and must be examined in part at the instant of opening. An example of this might be a government institution with strict public bid rules that require full disclosure in a public forum. Bidders may witness that their bid remained sealed until the bid date. Public bid openings serve to assure the bidders that their bid is given a fair and equal opportunity for consideration and that competing vendors are likewise excluded if they do not meet the minimum criteria. Learn the company's bid policies and follow them closely.

However, if there are no compelling reasons for a public bid opening, a private bid opening is usually preferred. It is less involved, simpler and allows the security professional more time to examine bids before commenting. When conducting a private bid opening, sealed bids are not accessible until the close of bidding at the appropriate date and time. Sealed bids are to be opened in the presence of witnesses usually consisting of selection committee members and a representative of the company's purchasing department. This means that the company's purchasing agent will accept and hold all bids as received from the vendors. At bid opening, the seal is the broken in the presence of these witnesses demonstrating that the bid information remained confidential until bid opening.

TECHNICAL EVALUATION

The Work Breakdown Structure (WBS) was referred to as a tool for organizing information throughout the system development and bid management processes. The evaluation process makes use of the WBS. Figure 7.12 provides an illustration of this evaluation method.

The desired system features are listed by WBS number in the left hand column followed by a description of the desired product or feature. Also in Figure 7.12, a weighted measure has been established to assign a numeric value to the importance of each feature described.

Review each vendor's bid in light of the required features and determine if the vendor submittal falls below, meets or exceeds the criteria established for the desired feature. Assign a point value to determine how well the bid met the requirement. Responses that simply say, "Our system can do this" are unacceptable and require further clarification.

Provide a fair and equal opportunity to all bidders. Remove as much subjectivity in the evaluation process as possible. Obtain clarification for responses that appear to be inadequate or result in a negative conclusion based on the information provided. Give the bidder an opportunity to correct misunderstandings or misapprehensions about the submittal so that a more objective evaluation is possible.

Upon receipt of the vendor's reply to these queries, either amend or confirm the initial conclusions reached about the vendor's

Client and Project Description

1 = Full Credit for Feature

Paragraph	Specification	Feature Value	Vendor	Vendor 1	Vendor 2	Vendor 3	Vendor 4	Vendor 5	Vendor 6
2	Infant Tags								
2.1.1	The infant identity tag must be lightweight and durable. The desired badge size is no greater than 1" x 1" X 0.5" thick. The desired weight is less than 3 oz. Vendors should stipulate the dimensions and weight of the tags being offered.	5		1	1	1	1	1	1
2.1.2	The infant identity tag must and have a battery capacity for a minimum of 1 year. Vendor shall state the tag capacity.	1		1		1	1	1	1
2.1.3	The tag should provide a system alarm for low battery conditions. Vendor shall state the nature of the alarm and describe it fully.	5		1	1	1	1	1	1
2.1.4	The infant identity tag must be able to operate in a temperature range at least between 45 degrees and 150 degrees Fahrenheit. Vendor shall acknowledge this requirement and state the limits of the product offered.	2		1	1	1	1	1	1
2.4.1	An enrollment process must precede the use of each infant and escort tag. That enrollment process should require an authorized system user with a proper password or other positive identification method to add a tag to the system or modify the authorized association of an infant tag with an escort tag. Vendor shall state how this is done.	5		1	1	1	1	1	1
3.1.4	Vendor shall state the size, weight and material construction of the system antennas and how the antennas shall be mounted. This criterion shall apply to antennas at the door openings and the alarm receiver antennas located throughout	3		1	1	1	1	1	1
3.1.6	All antenna panels must be lockable and provide safeguards against vandalism and tampering, including tamper switches and "off line" alarms. Vendor shall acknowledge this requirement.	2		1	1	1	1	1	1
3.2.3	It shall also be possible to locate an infant by a system poll of all antennas that will respond by providing an antenna area where the subject infant can be found.	100		1			1		
3.2.4	When in an alarm state, the system shall continuously and automatically poll all antennas and display the location of the alarm at selected display stations.	50		1		1	1	1	
4.1.4	The door controller shall buffer transaction data while simultaneously communicating those transactions to the subsystem processor for logging on the	2		1	1	1	1	1	
4.1.5	The door controller shall also include a real time clock giving it the ability to record date and time for all transactions independent of the system central	2		1	1	1	1	1	
4.1.7	The design of the door controller shall employ a variety of electrical and electronic filters that shall inhibit power surges and damage from static discharges	1		1	1	1	1	1	
4.1.8	The door controller shall be enclosed in a metal or fiberglass enclosure that shall include a tamper switch and security lock.	1		1	1				
4.4.1	The system shall be capable of announcing alarms with both lamps and audible signals and with data as described in 1.5.3 at the following locations and the user shall be able to select which alarms are announced in each location. The violated door . Selected nurse stations (up to a maximum of 10), MCLNO Police via an alarm interface.	10		1	1				1
4.5.1	Normal conditions shall result in the system permitting anyone with or without an escort tag, not accompanied by an infant tag to exit any door in the facility. Normal conditions shall also permit anyone to access the facility with or without an identity tag.	10		1	1	1	1	1	1

	Summary	Point Value		Vendor 1	Vendor 2	Vendor 3	Vendor 4	Vendor 5	Vendor 6
	Total All Points	2341		2,339	2,131	1,976	2,196	1,923	1,755
90	Minimum Criteria: Total all MANDATORY features (100+ points)	1,400		Deal Breakers					
				1,400	1,300	1,200	1,300	1,200	1,200
80	Total of all OTHER features (less than 100 points)	941		Pass / Fail					
				Pass	Pass	Fail	Pass	Fail	Fail
	Threshold for Selection 90% of Minimum Criteria Plus 80% of OTHER	2,013		Rank, Highlight Top 3					
				1	3	4	2	5	6

Figure 7.12 Bid evaluation.

willingness and ability to respond adequately to the RFP requirements. When the tabulation is complete, calculate a score for each vendor by multiplying the weighted value of the desired feature against the weighted measure of the vendor's response.

At the conclusion of this evaluation, prepare a report to the management team that clearly illustrates the results of the bid process, the method used to evaluate data and the conclusions arrived at to make the appropriate system or vendor recommendation. End the report with a description of the follow-up action required and how the next step in the process will be handled. At this point, the one best offer might not be evident. The recommendation may consist of three or more vendors, who all meet the minimum criteria for the desired system. This step is a "pass/fail" criterion and does not seek to select the one best system.

In summary, the security professional began with the broadest possible bidders' list. The number of bidders was (potentially) reduced when the Vendor Criteria in the RFP was applied. Only bids from qualified candidates were accepted. The number of bidders was again (potentially) reduced when the technical offers were reviewed. Only bids with system that met the RFP objective were accepted. This resulted in a short list of potential vendors for detailed examination. This technique will save time for the security professional and expense for the company. It permits the broadest possible participation and then filters the results to closely scrutinize only the most likely candidates.

However, be cautious and do not disclose the results of the evaluation to the vendors at this time. There may still be unrevealed differences in the vendors' offers and the selection list may change as further examinations take place. Vendors that did not make the initial cut may be added to the list if there are adjustments in the evaluation process.

VENDOR PRESENTATIONS

After evaluating the written proposals, request a product demonstration from the vendors identified as the most likely candidates to meet the requirements of the RFP. Develop a presentation agenda that focuses on the features that are most valuable to the company. Based on that agenda, create an evaluation form that the selection committee will use to review the vendor's presentation. This helps to guide the selection committee in the presentation process. The agenda will allow for breaks at 90-minute intervals and permit the vendor approximately 30 to 60 minutes at the end of the presentation to discuss features not shown on the agenda. Vendors may also use this time to sum up their presentation.

When scheduling meetings with the vendors, set no more than two presentations each day and limit the vendors to a maximum of three hours for the entire presentation. This will reduce "buffer overload" and permit the management team to attend to other duties between presentations.

Begin the presentation with an introduction of the selection committee by name and title but remind the vendor that the security professional is the prime contact for all follow up calls pertaining to this bid. Allow the vendor to take charge of the presentation process but moderate the proceedings to ensure that the agenda is followed.

FINAL EVALUATION AND RECOMMENDATION

At the end of the presentation, collect the evaluation forms and tabulate the results. Prepare a final report on the comparison of the systems presented, incorporating the evaluation of the written proposals and the product demonstration. The report will amplify, confirm or amend the initial evaluations (from the written responses) and conclude with a final recommendation for the most responsive bidders. Please note that a single best system recommendation is not required at this point, only a general recommendation of the most suitable candidates with the benefits and limitations of each system. The evaluation of the business plans will provide the final answer.

The phase two RFP will examine the business plan available from this short list of vendors and will consider price (and other business offerings), and service as the acceptance criteria. The results of phase one identified the vendors that meet the technical criteria and only those vendors will participate in phase two. When the management team accepts the phase one recommendation, prepare a letter that acknowledges acceptance and begin preparing the phase two RFP.

8

**System Acquisition—
Part 2, The Business Plan**

INTRODUCTION

In phase one of the bid process, we identified and documented the system requirements, released the bid to the market and analyzed the responses. The analysis of the bids provided a recommendation to select certain bidders to participate in phase two of the bid process because their offer met the minimum technical criteria set by the system design and specifications.

In phase two, the selected bidders from phase one are required to respond to the administrative requirements for bidder selection. They will respond with a business plan for the purchase of equipment and labor needed to install and support the system offered. The security professional's goal in phase two is to identify the offer that provides the best overall value to the company.

Please note that the measurement is value, not just price. Certainly, price is a big component of value but the distinction is that value gives a much broader perspective in making a buying decision. Value requires examination of the quality of the offer and the reliability of the vendor. A cheap bargain is rarely a bargain at all. When price receives too much attention, and quality and reliability are in the background, the investment is often wasted.

When this happens, the company is actually worse off than when the project started. The installed system may not meet expectations, the budget is spent and the opportunity to do the job properly has passed. Company management rarely looks favorably on doing the same job over, at twice the price. A favorite phrase is, "If you're going to spend money, spend money, don't fool around." This means that if you try to do a job cheaply, you spend more money in the end than if you simply took the time to properly determine needs and then bought based on performance. This is the definition of value.

In this chapter, we will develop and examine each section of the phase two RFP. Phase one identified the bidders for phase two, so there will only be a general review of the solicitation process in this chapter. The chapter ends with a discussion and techniques on bringing the two bid results together to form a complete recommendation.

Identify Participants for the Phase Two Bid Process

After the management team approved the recommendations in phase one, prepare the bid for phase two. Request the company's purchasing agent to inform the phase one bidders that have been selected for phase two of the evaluation results. (The terms "bidder" and "vendor" are used interchangeably in this book. Vendor normally refers to the company that will deliver the specified systems while bidder refers to those same companies before the bidding process results in an award.)

First, notify the bidders recommended for participation in phase two and verify that these vendors are still interested in continuing the bid process. Then notify the unsuccessful bidders that their offer in phase one did not meet the project objectives. Changing business conditions may compel a bidder to withdraw from competition, and the goal is full participation of all bidders that passed the phase one test. By verifying acceptance of the selected group first, the opportunity remains open to adjust the acceptance criteria to increase the field of competition.

A formal rejection letter to the unsuccessful bidders is a simple business courtesy. Although the bidder will not win the contract, the formal rejection helps them know where to end their efforts and expectations. A formal notice of rejection, if properly written, will also encourage the rejected bidder to participate in future bid opportunities.

THE PHASE TWO BID

Many of the principles that apply to the phase one bid also apply in phase two. Phase one focused on the technical aspects of the proposed system, phase two will examine the business offer. The objective of phase two is to help the company build a good business relationship with the bidder that will provide and service the proposed solutions.

Two of the cornerstones of a solid business relationship are communication and agreement. The phase two bid is more than a simple price request; it is the "contract" between the company and the bidder. Constructing a good contract means considering all the aspects of a business relationship and making provisions for each aspect that is fair and reasonable. The security professional represents the company in this transaction and must first endeavor to provide for the company's needs at the lowest overall cost. However, a one sided business deal is not the bargain it may seem. Bidders who become trapped into delivering products and services at a price below fair market value or who are compelled to render unreasonable levels of service without adequate compensation will not approach the project with enthusiasm.

Sometimes, the bidder makes an error in price calculations or the true nature of the obligation is not clear before the agreement is accepted. There exists a legal obligation to fulfill the contract so the bidder will make efforts to comply. However, one may expect the bidder in such circumstances to take every avenue allowed to reduce cost and minimize labor effort. Thus the focus of the project, from the bidder's perspective, changes from doing the best job possible to doing a job that meets minimal acceptance standards so they may be discharged from the obligation.

The security professional can help avoid such difficult situations by making the business plan as clear and forthright as possible. If the phase two RFP fully explains all of the expectations and limitations of the agreement, bidders will have a greater opportunity to understand what is expected of them and what constitutes outstanding performance.

The phase two bid establishes the agreement for the initial installation and sets the stage for the subsequent agreements for system additions and maintenance. Construct each section of the agreement with the understanding that this document will endure far beyond the initial installation.

The phase two bid represents a bilateral agreement between the company and the bidder. The purchase order resulting from the bid will most likely refer to the bid document as the basis for agreement. It is important that this document be complete and accurate. The subsections below provide examples for constructing the phase two bid. Include a cover page with phase two using the same methods suggested for phase one.

SECTION 1—INVITATION TO BID

The invitation to bid describes the intent of the offer. Some of the usual and customary paragraphs included in this section make these points:

1. State that this is a request for bid "by invitation only" and describe the criteria for participation.
2. State the security professional's name, firm name, and contact information.
3. Show the company's name, purchasing department, purchasing contact, and bid address for receipt of bid.
4. Provide the date and time the bid is due.
5. State that this is a sealed bid.
6. Provide an overall description of the system and where the system will be located.
7. Refer to the phase one bid for the equipment descriptions and quantities. This section may also contain amendments or adjustments to the initial system configuration that alter the original scope of work or technical parameters.

8. Require the bidders to submit prices on the same systems offered to the company in the phase one bid.
9. If this is to be a "turnkey" installation, state so in the RFP. Use the phrase, "a working system, complete in every way" to make clear that the bidders must supply all the labor and material required for full functionality.

    Turnkey is a common term used in various technology industries. As the name implies, the buyer simply has to "turn the key" to make the system work.
10. Provide a general statement that describes default conditions when elements of this RFP conflict with any of the general terms and conditions of the company or applicable laws. The possibility for conflict exists even in carefully written documents. Most RFP writers are not both security professionals and lawyers so provisions should be made when the RFP conflicts with previously established rules. State that where conflicts exist between the vendor and the general terms and conditions of the company's purchasing policies, the company's rules will apply. Make the same declaration regarding any applicable federal, state, or local laws.
11. State that any or all bids may be rejected without cause and include a statement that informality or irregularity in bids may be waived at the owner's discretion.

SECTION 2—ADDITIONAL BIDDER QUALIFICATIONS

Since this is a pre-selected group of bidders, new qualifications are not necessary. There are circumstances where it will be necessary to amend the qualification list from the phase one RFP. The evaluation of bids in phase one will reveal if the RFP requires more qualifications to improve the standards used for vendor selection. For instance, if the phase one analysis reveals that it is desirable to use the company's LAN for system communications and that was not part of the original design, the selected vendor should also be LAN certified.

Do not change the vendor qualifications indiscriminately. If such changes do not appear to have a legitimate basis or seem designed to exclude one or more of the bidders without good cause, there will be protests. In extreme cases, lawsuits could be filed that could delay, and may even cause cancellation of, the project.

SECTION 3—BID REQUIREMENTS

Bid requirements provide boundaries for the bid process. Sometimes there are unique aspects to an environment or installation that require clarification. In other cases, clarity is not the issue for the bidder, but rather latitude. Well written RFPs will help produce good purchase agreements, minimize contract disputes and increase mutual understanding. Add terms and conditions in the RFP that clarify vendor performance and expectations.

The rule of thumb is that if you do not specify something, bidders are open to select the option that suits them best. There is nothing wrong with giving bidders some leeway, as long as it does not affect the quality of the product or service delivered. Each case is different, but some of the more frequently used elements of this section are:

Basic Definitions

Explain terms used in the RFP that may cause confusion to the bidders. This section is not essential unless certain nonstandard terms are used.

Specific Performance

1. Require the bidders to attend a mandatory pre-bid conference and include the date and time of that meeting. As in phase one, this is a face-to-face meeting to clarify requirements.
2. In cases where the installation requires turnkey performance, state that this is an "all or none" opportunity. This indicates that labor is an integral part of this offer and that the company will not accept "material only" bids. Add "this does not preclude bidders from subcontracting some portion of the work to others but overall project responsibility must be borne by the bidder."

Verify Conditions

State that there may be certain pre-existing conditions that could have a bearing on the price quoted. Advise the bidders that they are responsible for informing themselves of any pre-existing condition. Make clear that the bidder shall be responsible for any additional costs for system modifications resulting from pre-existing conditions after award of contract.

Owner Requirements

Require the bidder to specify facilities or services required by the owner to provide a complete and working system. An example: The RFP requires the bidder to use the company's LAN for system communication. This interface requires communications devices that are compatible with the LAN. Company network managers usually want full control over any devices connected to their network. The bidder would require the company to furnish these devices.

Require the bidder to clearly describe all devices or services the company must furnish. If the requirement contains technical devices to work with bidder provided equipment, like personal computers, the bidder must provide a full technical description of the required equipment. Also state in this section that if the bidder fails to describe these devices, the bidder will be responsible for providing these products or services at their expense.

Life Safety Considerations

In some installations, the state fire marshal's approval is required for the interface of any locking system to a fire alarm system. State that the bidder must make these submittals to the state fire marshal (unless the fire alarm service company wants or needs to do this in your area) and obtain approval before making connections to the fire alarm panel.

A catchall phrase also helps to include the bidder in the burden of compliance, for instance:

> "The bidder shall comply with all applicable local, state, and federal regulations concerning life safety. Failure to comply will be at the bidder's peril. Costs associated with compliance after system installation will be borne by the bidder."

The company cannot relieve themselves of life safety responsibilities in this way, but including the vendor's responsibility in the RFP adds bidder liability and provides the company with recourse if the bidder violates life safety rules.

Prior Approvals

The RFP requires the bidders to offer in phase two the same system described in their bid for phase one. However, since the bid process may take several months and system manufacturers change or substitute system components, such changes place bidders in technical violation of the RFP.

Describe the conditions under which a bidder may receive prior approval in the RFP. State the timeframes allotted for substituting or changing system components and the terms and conditions for changes. Describe the submittals required for making a technical comparison. If the substitute products have equal or greater capabilities, grant prior approvals to the bidders.

Bid Bond and Performance Bond

Bid bonds are usually required on construction jobs to ensure that that bidder will honor the bid price submitted. The bid bond provides this guarantee by allowing the bondholder to file a claim against the bid bond if the bidder fails to honor the price offered in the bid. The claim permits the bondholder to recover the difference between the bid price and the price paid by the bondholder to engage another contractor if the bidder defaults on delivery.

Bid bonds help to establish the financial stability of bidders. In order to obtain a bid bond, a company must also be able to obtain performance bonds. Financial companies issue performance bonds after a review of a bidder's business. They must fund the completion of work should the bidder fail to finish the project. Therefore, requesting a bid bond ensures that the bidder has the wherewithal to obtain a performance bond. Bid bonds are a good indication of a bidder's financial stability.

In most situations involving the installation of a new electronic physical security system, a performance bond does not substantially enhance the company's position in the award of contract. Usually, withholding payments will serve as sufficient motivation to guaranty that the bidder finishes what they start. Moreover, a well crafted payment schedule (earned value schedule) will encourage quick substantial completion. Performance bonds serve little purpose in these circumstances and usually are not recommended. This item was included so that the reader would be aware of the tool.

There are costs associated with bid and performance bonds, but these costs provide certain benefits to the outcome of the project. Use bid bonds on all major installations to confirm that a financial professional reviewed the bidder's performance history and found them a capable provider. Performance bonds are substantially more expensive that bid bonds and, as explained above, do not usually provide additional value in these installations. Do not plan to use performance bonds but discuss the option with the company's purchasing agent. There is often a standing policy in most company purchasing offices on the use of these financial instruments.

Insurance

Most state laws require companies to provide workmen's compensation insurance. Require these certificates in the RFP.

To protect the company from liability exposure, require the bidders to provide proof of liability insurance in the RFP. Discuss this requirement with company purchasing; there may be pre-established limits for this insurance. If such limits exist, add them to the RFP.

In either case, add to the RFP a "Hold Harmless Clause." This requires the bidder to relieve the company of any liability burden for faults created by the bidder in the course of fulfilling the contract. These protection clauses provide another modest layer of protection for the company.

SECTION 4—PRICING REQUIREMENTS

In most cases, the bid process results in a turnkey installation by the selected bidder. There are several ways to arrange these contracts but the one used most often in these situations is the firm fixed price agreement (see Chapter 7, Choose the Bid Type).

Firm Fixed Price

Firm fixed price agreements require the bidder to submit a single price that includes all of the labor and material necessary to complete the work. Other information required in the RFP, such as material inventory and block diagrams, serve to confirm that the firm fixed price quoted covers all of the areas that are to be included in the system design.

Recommended Spares

In addition to the firm fixed price, ask the bidder to provide a list of recommended spare parts. The company will maintain these parts for use with the installed system. This approach helps to guarantee that parts are readily available for service calls. Require the bidder to include unit prices for each part.

Projected Costs for Major System Components

In addition to the list of recommended spares, request the bidder to submit a price schedule that illustrates the unit cost of each of the major system components. Require this schedule to be valid for at least one year. This will permit the security professional to establish a cost forecast for system additions and assist in determining the system with the best value. This approach also places a ceiling on prices for the period chosen. Extend this forecast and price ceiling in large installations to three years. The intent of these requirements is to prevent a bidder from offering a low initial price to receive the contract then substantially increasing the price for system additions.

Annual Hardware Maintenance

Require the bidder to state the anticipated annual hardware maintenance cost for the proposed system and state when the maintenance contract begins and ends.

Maintenance Forecast

Require maintenance costs for three years following the expiration of the system warranty. This forward looking cost projection prevents the bidder from providing an initial low price only to recover these lost profits at the conclusion of the initial contract. Bidders do not want to be in a money losing or break-even position for three years. This forecast will provide clues about the bidder's pricing strategy.

Annual Software Maintenance

Software is the fastest changing item in most manufacturers' catalog. Be sure that software maintenance is included in the offer. This may be a separate contract with the system manufacturer but the bidder will administer it. Request the bidder to provide software license and maintenance fees for a period of three years following expiration of the system warranty.

System Addition Forecast

If the company expects security needs to grow rapidly in the first few years, request a long term price forecast from the bidders. Provide the bidders with a purchase forecast of system additions and require that they submit price projections for known system elements. This could be tedious if taken to extremes. Limit these long-range projections to the provision of major equipment components and technical labor. Exclude installation and end piece devices such as locks, alarm contacts and exit push bottoms to make bidding and evaluation easier.

SECTION 5—EXECUTION OF CONTRACT

The execution of contract section provides general terms and conditions under which the work shall take place. In this section, explain how the bidder is to perform while on-site and add any unique conditions to avoid or give special attention.

Requirements After Acceptance of Bid

Determine if there are special conditions that require the bidder's attention or action before starting the work. Add such actions to the RFP. Always include a requirement for the following:

1. Completions schedule (firm installation schedule)
2. Schedule of earned values (when will payments be requested for each billable item)

   An example of another requirement is registering the contract with local authorities. Contract registration simply means that the agreement between the company and the bidder becomes a matter of public record and follows certain rules and guidelines. The company's purchasing office will usually have a policy regarding contract registration and the RFP should reflect that policy.

Equipment Substitutions

Stipulate in the RFP that written prior approval is required for equipment substitutions (see Prior Approvals).

Scheduling

Require the bidders to submit a commitment for the earliest installation start date. In some cases, the ability to start a project quickly will have a bearing on the award of contract. In those cases, advise the bidder of the desired installation interval.

Require the bidder to provide an installation schedule expressed in "man days" for each set of tasks. This completion schedule is the man-days needed for the installation, not calendar dates for completion of work. In comparing offers, there may be situations where several bidders are proposing the same equipment and have near identical prices. Completion time may be a deciding factor in these circumstances.

Equipment Storage

Define in the RFP how to store the equipment before the installation. This can vary in importance based on where and when delivery will actually take place. Said another way, define the point in the process at which the company owns the equipment. This is not a minor detail. It is important to specify the point of ownership because equipment may be lost or damaged before installation due to unforeseen events. Contract disputes may arise regarding the replacement of this equipment if the point of ownership is not clearly established.

The term Freight On Board (FOB) is generally used to indicate the place for accepting equipment. The FOB point is usually the company's receiving area. However, the RFP must define what constitutes delivery. What complicates the issue is equipment staging and testing. The RFP will require the vendor to stage the system (see below) but the vendor will want to effect delivery so they may bill for the hardware.

Equally important is when the system equipment is accepted. Regardless of the physical location of the equipment acceptance, the RFP must define the point in the process where the company will accept ownership of the system equipment. Stipulate in the RFP that the company will accept equipment at the vendor's place of business, under the following conditions:

1. All equipment for the entire system installation is on hand (minus cable and connectors).
2. The vendor must provide an inventory of the equipment delivered before the inventory inspection (matching the equipment list required in bid submittal, see Bid Submittal later in this chapter). The inventory must include the serial numbers of all major items of equipment.
3. The vendor will submit to a physical inspection of the equipment and verification of the inventory by the security professional. (The RFP will permit the vendor to bill for the equipment after this initial inventory.)
4. The vendor will provide adequate insurance to protect the equipment against all forms of loss until the system is installed on the company's premises. Insurance certificates may be required in the RFP but are not essential.
5. At physical delivery (FOB), the vendor will again allow a physical inventory of the equipment for verification. A clerk in the receiving department usually does this. The clerk will verify that the equipment arrived at the company's loading dock and the serial numbers of that equipment. This requirement allows a cross check against the inventory at the vendor's place of business versus the inventory of delivered goods. This second inventory is important because some of the equipment will be installed above ceilings or in other areas that are difficult to access for verification.

System Staging

One of the most troubling aspects of a new installation is "infant mortality." This term refers to the failure of a system device shortly after installation. To minimize these failings, require the bidder to "stage" the system before installation. Staging means to connect all major system devices together in the vendor's workshop and test the system for at least 72 hours. This burn-in period can usually identify borderline components that the vendor must replace before system delivery.

Usually, end-point devices such as locks or alarm contacts are not subject to staging. This test identifies critical components that require data communication to operate properly. Require the bidder to assemble the major component parts, power up those parts then demonstrate the use of the entire system

Require the vendor to electrically test the end-point devices in the RFP. Require the vendor to power up electrical devices and verify operation. Require the vendor to meter non-power devices (e.g., door status switches) for proper signaling operation.

Job Site Rules and Regulations for Vendors

Describe the conduct expected of the vendor's employees in this section of the RFP. In some cases, there are time constraints that prohibit the bidder from working after normal business hours. Describe the times of day and days of the week the bidder may perform work on the premises and any special access permissions the workmen need.

An example of this may be requiring the bidder's workmen to wear identification badges and to check in with the company's security force upon arrival at the job site. Also, include general conditions for workmen conduct. For instance, prohibit the use of profane language or loud speech. Also, prohibit the workmen from playing music or any other conduct that is disruptive to company employees.

Include in this section of the RFP a description of clean up responsibilities. Most electronic systems have protective packaging for shipment to job sites. Make it clear that the vendor is to dispose of this material and any recommended methods for that disposal.

Supervision of Work (Project Management)

Require the vendor to provide a project manager to interface with the security professional and supervise the vendor's employees while on the company's premises. Direct the vendor to channel all questions that arise during the installation through the project manager to the security professional. This will reduce confusion and foster good communications.

The security professional will act as the company's representative in all circumstances. This does not mean that the security professional must have all the answers but must be the first person to receive the question. The security professional will direct the vendor's project manager to the company employee who can properly answer the question.

Require the vendor to hold periodic meetings to review the progress of the installation. On very large, complex installations, hold these meetings weekly. For smaller installations, require these meetings at installation milestones. Those milestones are:

1. All equipment on site
2. Completion of cabling
3. Completion of equipment mounting
4. Completion of final hook up
5. Preliminary test
6. Final test

Invite selected company employees to coordination meetings when there are issues concerning their department. The information technology department plays a growing role in the implementation of security systems and is usually involved early in the process.

Power Quality and Reliability

Explain any unusual power conditions that may exist and advise the vendor of their responsibility to notify the company about power quality requirements of the system. Do this to avoid situations where the company has large power consuming devices connected to the same power feed as the vendor equipment. These devices cause variance in power quality that the system equipment finds intolerable. Require the vendor to specify the power tolerances and where power is required. Establish these requirements before the award of contract to avoid undisclosed additional costs to the company for providing power at these locations.

Specify backup power in the RFP for system critical components. State the time expected for back up power to engage when commercial power is lost and the amount of time the backup power will allow the system to continue to operate.

Be aware that backup power is not always required for locking systems. In cases where life safety issues apply, the fire code may require locks to unlock in the event of a commercial power loss. The RFP must stipulate where to furnish backup power.

Cabling

System cabling is a critical element in the installation of low voltage security products. If the vendor uses poor quality cable or the cable is installed improperly, the system will not communicate effectively and the installation will be plagued by numerous service calls.

Provide conditions in the RFP for cable routes. For most electronic systems, the current carried on these cables is miniscule and measured in milliamps. These circuits carry digital information and a variety of outside influences can degrade the data.

The National Electrical Code provides guidance on the installation of "low voltage and cabling." Require the vendor to follow these guidelines in the RFP. Some additional guidelines are:

1. Low voltage cable should not be strapped to or run parallel with high voltage cable.
2. Do not place low voltage cable in the same conduit with high voltage cable.
3. Do not run low voltage cable over fluorescent ballast.
4. Always use the manufacturer's recommended cable size and cable type for the system.
5. Follow the manufacturer's recommended suggestions for grounding cable shields.
6. Use spade tips when terminating cables on screw terminals.
7. Use cable studs when terminating cables on push in connectors.

Cable Labeling

Require the vendor to provide a cable-labeling scheme for all cables to be marked using that scheme. During the installation process, the vendor's installers usually become very familiar with the cabling between devices. That familiarity leaves with the installers.

Cable labeling assists the installers in doing the installation but is more important when used after the installation for system additions and repairs. The security professional may insist on a particular scheme to be followed but vendors generally have their own labeling methodology and as long as that methodology is clear, there is little reason to demand a another method.

Component Installation Criteria

Each manufacturer will usually publish installation criteria for their system. However, some general rules for installing devices are:

1. Install card readers on the door handle side of the door at door handle height. There are cases where such reader placement is impractical or impossible. A good example is double leaf doors. To place the reader on the door handle side of the door would require a set of posts between the door leafs. Since none is available, the most acceptable alternative is to place the card reader on the right side of the double door adjacent to the doorframe.

   However, there are still other circumstances where this is not possible because the door is at the end of a corridor with an adjacent wall on the right side. In these cases, require placement of the card reader as close to the door as possible but outside the "door swing" of the door leaf. This is a life safety consideration. Such placement will help to avoid injury to the users (see Appendix 1 for some examples of Door Detail Elevations).

2. Install door status switches on the door handle side of the door as close to the end of the door as possible. The reason for selecting this location is that this edge of the door is farthest away from the hinge point and a small opening in the door will result in a perceptible opening between the magnet and reed switch. This is an important technique since it provides the earliest possible detection.

   Although doors are the most common barricades, some do not lend themselves well to the installation of standard door status switches. An example is chain link gate monitors. These devices consist of armored cables mounted to chain link openings. Two "pigtails" are connected across the opening and must be disconnected to open the gate. Stipulate any mounting methods in the RFP that would affect the operation of these devices.

3. Many of the advanced security alarm monitoring systems prevent tampering with alarm monitoring circuits by using "supervised" alarm ports. Supervised circuits prevent a perpetrator from defeating an alarm system by placing bare end wires across the monitoring point as a shunt to prevent detection of an opening.

    A supervised alarm port does not simply measure whether or not a circuit is present but the resistance value on that circuit. A resistor is installed at a predetermined location and has a specific value. This resistor is an electrical device that provides impedance to the current used to monitor the status of the reed switch. If a shunt is placed across the alarm contact or across the alarm cable at any point, it changes the resistance value of the circuit. This change is detected and an alarm is registered.

    In high security applications using supervised alarm ports, require the vendor to install appropriate resistors at points recommended by the system manufacturer.

4. CCTV cameras should be placed out of reach of pedestrians to prevent tampering.

5. Avoid installing cameras in areas where backlighting is present.

Startup Responsibility

Specify startup responsibilities in the RFP and describe in clear specific terms what the vendor is required to do to make the system active. This may include programming card data and card readers, camera alignment and the adjustment of preset points on pan tilt zoom devices.

Startup responsibility should also include a definition of those preparations necessary for acceptance of the system installation. This could mean documenting and programming the system for alarm messages and alarm map displays in access control systems. Indicate all the elements necessary for system turn on.

Card Testing

In some instances, the company has acquired other types of systems that use identity card credentials for a variety of purposes. In those cases, the RFP stipulates that the new system must work with the existing cards. This is particularly important in systems where the population is very large (1000 cards or more) and replacing all cards may be expensive and cumbersome.

If the system must work with existing cards, include a statement regarding testing the existing cards in the new system before installation.

"As Built" Project Drawings

The security professional will document special circumstances as part of the RFP development, but changes may take place in the system design during the installation. Require the vendor to update the system plans after the project is finished. These updates are referred to as "as-built" drawings.

Require the bidder to provide as-built drawings when the work is finished. Also, include a requirement for a narrative that describes unique aspects of the wiring. These notes will be helpful when making additions or changes after the initial installation.

Test Criteria

Some manufacturers provide specific written tests for components after installation. Require the bidder to provide a copy of all manufacturers' test instructions with their bid. In the absence of manufacturers' recommended tests, require the bidder to supply the test criteria they will use to certify system acceptance. Amend these criteria if they do not appear to be adequate. Adequate acceptance testing can be a condition of contract award.

System Acceptance

Another area that frequently leads to contract disputes is what constitutes a "finished" job. To prevent misunderstandings, state in the RFP what constitutes system acceptance. This is the best indicator of a system installation being finished. System acceptance should include at least the following elements:

1. Demonstration of the completed product installation
2. Successful completion of an acceptance test
3. Delivery of the required manuals
4. Delivery of specified training

Describe the steps taken when evaluating the system at final delivery. Include the following steps in the RFP:

1. Deliver all the documentation specified in the RFP.
2. Conduct a pre-acceptance test. Conduct this test without company personnel. This will prevent embarrassing situations involving overlooked items in the installation. Correct these anomalies before company representatives witness the final acceptance test.

   For card readers (and other access control devices) the test includes presenting a valid and void card to all card readers to ensure that doors unlock when a valid card is presented and do not unlock when a void card is presented.

   Test alarm monitoring points by deliberately violating protected openings throughout the system. Verify that the system senses the violation and displays it at the system consoles. In the case of multiple watch stations, several individuals may be required to observe system performance.

   Have the vendor demonstrate CCTV systems to show the observation, recording and playback of recorded scenes.

   If life safety systems are included in the system installation, test and certify these devices. Specifically, locking systems interfaced to the company's building fire alarm system should unlock when the fire alarm panel is in an alarm condition. Alarm conditions can be simulated without actually triggering the alarm. The fire alarm service company can create this simulation. Observe that all locks that are so connected automatically unlock.

   Require the vendor to demonstrate software features of the new system. For access control systems, this includes the addition of new cards, assigning reader groups and time periods and how the user responds to alarms.

To test CCTV systems, observe all views, the recording and playback of all views and the movement of remotely controlled equipment. Also include a test of pre-sets for video alarm responses.

3. Conduct a Final Acceptance Test with the vendor and company representatives. Perform the same tests as described in the Pre-acceptance Test and demonstrate system operation for the company's approval.

4. At the conclusion of final acceptance testing, prepare a report to describe the results of the test. Record in the report any non-working device or failure of the system to perform as expected. Add the follow up steps needed to complete the installation. Identify the parties responsible for making the corrections and the timeframe expected for those corrections to occur. Issue the report to the company and provide a copy to the vendor for action is required.

Change Orders

Although the security professional will endeavor to be thorough and accurate in the creation of system performance specifications, company circumstances may change or the environment may change thereby requiring alternative approaches.

In such cases, the RFP must provide for ways to change the existing plan. Those changes may also cause changes in the price quoted. Explain in detail the conditions for a change order. Describe how to document and submit these changes and who will receive these change orders (almost always the security professional).

Default Considerations

Indicate in the RFP what constitutes default of the agreement and what action will result if the vendor is in default. Define the conditions for default. This includes the inability of the system to perform as promised, the failure of the vendor to deliver in a timely manner and other conditions the company finds unacceptable.

Promised delivery intervals are part of the decision in awarding contracts. The vendor must be permitted time to correct system anomalies but if the system fails to perform as expected in a reasonable period of time, the RFP must provide recourse for the company.

The RFP will detail what actions the company will take if the vendor is in default. This could include a demand for a full refund of all monies paid, the substitution of another system at the vendor's expense or on-site correction of anomalies by the system manufacturer.

This section will also describe the "escalation" procedures taken in the event of potential default conditions. For example, the first recourse would not be demanding a full refund. State the steps taken, in the order taken, to correct the problems. The progressive order provides the vendor with a specific interval to bring the system up to expected standards. Failure to do so requires the next step of escalation. Then require the manufacturer of the system to participate in the correction process. State a specific interval for the manufacturer to correct system deficiencies. If they cannot correct the system deficiencies, then the bidder is in default of the agreement. The vendor is then required to remove the non-compliant parts of the installed system and refund payments for labor and material used for that part of the installation.

Proper planning and thorough investigations will prevent installations from arriving at this point. The security professional is responsible for the success of the installation.

This section should also deal with the company's obligation for default. The purchasing department will be a good guide for these terms. A suggested approach is:

> The (company) has the right to cancel this agreement at any time, without cause. Said cancellation shall obligate the company to pay for all labor and material, calculated at cost, expended for the installation of this system up to the stop work notification. The company shall not be required to provide a profit to the vendor but only make the vendor whole with regard to expenditures for this project.

Basis of Payment

The RFP must stipulate how and when the vendor will be paid. Contract disputes occur when payment terms are not clear. Avoid such disputes by clearly describing when the vendor should invoice for payments, where to send the invoices, and what can be included in each payment request.

Instruct the vendor how to request payments. Vendors have invoicing procedures and the company has payment procedures. The RFP establishes the payment terms so these two methods merge successfully. Discuss payment terms with the company's purchasing manager. They will describe considerations expected before releasing funds. Add these considerations to the RFP. In some cases, waivers against liens are required with each invoice or the use of special payment request forms.

Work closely with the company's purchasing manager to ensure that payment demands are properly structured and submitted in a timely manner for prompt payment. Require the vendor to submit a duplicate copy of all invoices to the security professional for approval. This will permit the security professional to verify delivery before payment is authorized.

SECTION 7—POST INSTALLATION SUPPORT

Personnel Training

In addition to the delivery of the installed system, the bidder must provide training for system administrators and system operators. The RFP establishes the criteria for training.

System training is a small part of the overall training the users need to fully implement the recommended solutions (see Chapter 9 for additional requirements). Specify the vendor's portion of user training.

Require the vendor to describe in detail what system training will be provided. The extent of vendor training provides another comparison of the offers. Training is an essential part of system performance and vendor participation is essential to a successful installation.

Warranty and Service Agreements

Require the bidder to provide a complete statement of warranty terms including a detailed description of the milestone that signals the start of this warranty and the period for which the warranty will be valid.

Warranties usually begin at system acceptance and last for 12 months. However, in business negotiations such as these, assume nothing. If the company has pre-established criteria for warranty, state these requirements for the bidders and add that these conditions nullify any contrary terms in the bidder's offer. However, it is usually prudent to simply require the bidder to state the conditions of their warranty so as not to provide too many barriers to bidder participation. Warranty descriptions include:

1. Which components are covered
2. The length of time the coverage will exist
3. What elements are included in the warranty (labor or material)
4. The milestone at which the warranty shall commence
5. Any special conditions which may adversely affect the warranty

Require the vendor to state the milestone for starting the warranty. Warranties sometimes begin upon deliver of equipment and sometimes when the equipment is turned on. The RFP will require the warranty to start when the System Acceptance Test is finished and when all parts of the system work as expected.

The RFP will also state the duration of the warranty. Manufacturers usually provide a 12-month warranty on hardware and installing dealers offer a corresponding 12-month warranty on installation work. Do not leave the warranty term to chance. State that the warranty should apply to all devices for 12 months.

Also state that the warranty must include all devices provided by the vendor (in some cases the company provides a portion of the equipment). Stipulate the time expected for device replacement when reported to the vendor.

Require the vendor to state how company representatives place a warranty service call. The vendor must include the contact number and, if applicable, the person to contact when placing service calls.

Add the expected response time to the RFP. Usually a 24-hour response is satisfactory but certain portions of the system may require shorter intervals. State all intervals expected.

Sometimes, warranties are "at factory," meaning that the vendor is not responsible for the expense of removing the defective equipment and sending that equipment in for repair. The RFP will require "in-field" service that sets the service point at the company's premises.

SECTION 8—SUBMITTALS

Describe the submittals required for a complete bid. In complex systems with lengthy submittals, it is easy to overlook a required document. The submittal section of the RFP provides a checklist for bidders to help them assemble all of the required information for their offer.

Document Submittals

The same rationale for RFP organization in phase one applies to phase two. Each bid is unique and not all of the items described below are essential for every bid. Select the items that are right for this RFP. Examples of submittal requirements:

1. Submit a complete response to all item listed in Additional Vendor Qualifications.
2. Submit a list of products or services (except commercial power) that the company must furnish to make this a complete and working system.
3. Submit a bid bond equal to X% of the purchase price of the contract (this is usually 5%). See the section titled Bid Bond and Performance Bond.
4. A X% (usually 100%) performance bond will be required with this contract. See the section titled Bid Bond and Performance Bond.
5. Submit the following insurance certificates:
    *   Workmen's compensation
    *   Liability
    *   Material loss (see Equipment Storage)
6. Submit a revised material list that shows the quantity of each product proposed, the manufacturer's name and the model number.
7. Submit an updated block diagram of the proposed system. Include in the diagram an illustration of each communications device in the system and the interconnecting cable that provides communication pathways. The block

diagram should also illustrate where commercial power is required for each component.

8. Submit prices for the proposed system that include all the elements in the block diagram (in accordance with the Pricing Requirements section of the RFP).

9. Submit the installation schedules described under Execution of Contract.

10. Submit a letter from the manufacturer of the proposed system stating that the bidder is an authorized distributor or dealer and the length of time that dealer has represented that manufacturer.

11. Submit the manufacturer's test criteria and any other criteria used for system acceptance.

12. Submit a copy of the RFP signature page (usually the last page of the RFP), signed by an officer of the bidder's company indicating acknowledgement of the terms and conditions contained in the RFP and an acknowledgement of all addendums described by addendum number.

13. Submit a training syllabus as required in Post Installation Support.

14. Submit the warranty description required in Post Installation Support.

15. Submit a Dun and Bradstreet identification number for the bidder and the primary equipment manufacturer.

16. Submit a list of at least five other similar systems sold and installed by the bidder. Include in this list the name and address of the company, the contact person and her or his title and her or his telephone number.

    (Add a phrase: This submittal authorizes [company name] or their agents, to contact the representatives of these systems to discuss the bidders capabilities and past performance.)

Describe how the bidder should present the bid. General criteria include:

• Require the bidder to prepare the bid typewritten on 8½ x 11 plain white paper using a font no smaller than 10 points nor larger than 14 points. (This simply makes reading and reviewing the document easier.)

- Required the bidder to provide a cover page with the bid that includes all the information on the cover page of the RFP. Require the bidder to include the name and telephone number of the contact person for this bid with their telephone number and e-mail address. Have the bidder indicate if this individual represents the manufacturer or the dealer.

Allow the bidder to include other documents at the bidder's discretion that would clarify their bid. But add:

The indexing and sections described in the RFP should be strictly adhered to and other documents that are not called for in the RFP are to be added at the end of the bidder's submittal package.

Instruct the bidder on how to package the bid.

- Place the bid in a three ring binder or similar cover with an index page immediately following the cover page. Provide tabs in this binder and indicate which elements of the submittal are behind which tab.

  (The purpose of this regimented organization is to make reviewing and evaluating the bidder's submittal easier for the company and the security professional. This is more than just a matter of convenience—if bid information is difficult to find, the review may miss important details).

The more the bidder knows about the bid review process, the more likely they will be to follow those instructions.

Electronic Submittal

Most federal government contracts require electronic submittals for large RFPs. The RFPs separate bid responses into technical descriptions and cost volumes. Phase two requires an in depth examination of costs, and electronic submittals makes this comparison much easier.

Electronic submittals usually mean submitting offers in Microsoft Excel format. In large committee buying decisions, the management team will require multiple copies of the bid so that all members of the committee can view bid results. They will rely on the security professional for analysis but everyone wants to see the offers.

Request (though not require) the bidders to submit other documents in electronic format. Specify the acceptable programs and use common software such as MS Word and Adobe Acrobat (see Document Submittals section). This will help when sharing and discussing the bids. This will also reduce the paper burden in the process. If the bidder can submit all parts of the bid electronically, allow the bidder to submit only one paper copy (for legal reasons) and a data CD, DVD, or floppy disk containing the electronic submittal.

Phase one allowed an option for electronic submittals; phase two should require it for the pricing portion of the bid. Consider the process used for bid evaluation when deciding if electronic submittals should be an integral part of the RFP response. If an electronic submittal is used, it can save considerable time and effort.

A requirement for electronic submittal should include a pre-formatted Excel worksheet with clear indications of where the bidders should place the requested prices. All price submittals will look the same, and it will be easy to combine, compare, and analyze bid worksheets.

If electronic submittals are required in the RFP, also require one hard copy of any electronic submittal with the written bid. An accidental keystroke can alter electronic copies unintentionally. This could result in incorrect conclusions during bid evaluation. A hard copy submittal helps to confirm the offer and avoids misrepresenting a bidder's submittal.

GET APPROVAL FOR THE SPECIFICATIONS

Call for a meeting of the System Selection Committee and present the RFP Business Plan for approval. Provide all members of the committee with a copy of the finished phase two RFP before it is released to the marketplace, then allow sufficient time for review before the meeting.

During the meeting, promote an open debate on the conditions listed. The security professional's role in the debate is to ensure that the RFP addresses all committee members' concerns and to guide the committee to an informed decision. Explain the consequences of choices suggested by committee members and acquaint them with the benefits and limitations of alternate solutions.

After the meeting, adjust the RFP as required. Release the RFP to the marketplace. Confirm approval of the RFP in the minutes of the committee meeting. The minutes should reflect major changes by the committee that may differ from the security professional's recommendation.

SOLICIT BIDDERS

The opportunity to submit a bid for the Phase Two Business Plan should be limited to those companies that successfully completed the phase one RFP.

As in phase one, the company purchasing personnel should manage the documents for bid mailings and receipt of responses. This serves to reinforce the unbiased nature of the bid process and avoids putting the security professional in a compromising position.

THE PRE-BID MEETING

Before the bid submittal date, there should be a mandatory pre-bid meeting. The purpose of this meeting is to present the system bid opportunity to the marketplace and to answer questions about the phase two RFP or the bid process.

Invite at least two members of the system selection committee to the pre-bid meeting. The company's purchasing representative is also required and representatives of the company's facility and security departments. The security professional and the purchasing manager should moderate the pre-bid meeting jointly. Usually, the security professional takes the lead role in this moderation and the primary purpose of the purchasing manager is to answer questions about the bid process.

Require the bidders to sign an attendance sheet, confirming their presence. Review the entire phase two RFP in an orderly fashion and fully answer questions from the bidders during the meeting. Answer verbal questions with verbal responses. If a complete answer is not possible at the meeting, prepare a written response following the meeting in an RFP addendum.

In cases where the issues are complex or the question and response may have a significant bearing on the outcome of the award of this contract, document the question and answer in an RFP addendum.

At the conclusion of the pre-bid meeting state that additional questions may be submitted but these questions must be in writing and submitted no later than a date designated in the meeting that is appropriate to allow sufficient time to respond prior to bid opening. Respond to these questions as quickly as possible, also in writing, and send a copy of all questions and answers to all bidders participating in the process.

BID ACCEPTANCE AND BID OPENING

The company purchasing office will receive the RFP responses from the bidders. The RFP has a specific bid date and time and some companies have stringent policies that prohibit the acceptance of bids beyond the allotted time. The security professional must be aware of and honor these constraints.

There are situations where such rigorous constraints exist and bidders presented their response only a few minutes late. The company rejected the bidder's offer. If these constraints exist in your company, emphasize these constraints at the pre-bid meeting.

Most companies have established policies with regard to bid openings. Discuss the company's policies with the purchasing manager before deciding on the method to use. Some bid openings are public while others are private. Public openings require some examination of the bid when the seal is broken. The opener verifies that the bid includes certain mandatory documents and usually reads the firm fixed price aloud. Such public bid openings serve to assure the bidders that their bid remained confidential prior to the bid opening.

However, if there are no compelling reasons for a public bid opening, a private bid opening is usually preferred. It is less involved, simpler, and allows the security professional more time to examine bids before commenting.

Even in private openings, sealed bids are not accessible until the close of bidding at the appropriate date and time. In private openings, open sealed bids in the presence of members of the system selection committee and a representative of the company's purchasing department. Purchasing will accept and hold all bids as received from the bidders.

BUSINESS PLAN EVALUATION

A Business Plan Evaluation is usually more straightforward than a technical review. The bid elements are more objective and quantifiable. Make a side-by-side comparison of each offer and, where appropriate, comment on the bidder's submittal.

Subjectivity is usually not an issue in this evaluation but variations in bidder responses may introduce variations that cannot be easily reconciled. To ensure that all bidders are provided with a fair and equal opportunity to bid on the RFP, bidder responses that appear to be inadequate or appear to result in a negative conclusion based on the information provided in the bid response should be communicated back to the bidder before making a final evaluation.

Prepare written comments for the bidder on each point in the Business Plan where it appears that the bidder has not met the requirements. Send the letter to the respective bidder. This gives the bidder an opportunity to correct misunderstandings about the submittal and reinforce the desirability of their offer.

Upon receipt of the bidder's reply, amend, or confirm the conclusions reached about the bidder's willingness and ability to respond adequately to the RFP requirements. The principal objective in doing this detail level comparison is to ensure that the process is as objective, fair, and even as possible for all prospective bidders.

After evaluating the bids, check the bidder's references. Contact the previous buyers listed by the vendor and discuss the vendor's performance during the installation and, if applicable, the performance of the installed system. Create a form for this investigation similar to the example in Figure 8.1 through 8.2.

At the conclusion of the evaluation, combine the comparison summary of the phase one RFP with the conclusions reached in the evaluation of phase two bids. Prepare a written report for the management team identifying the most responsive bidder, how they rank against each other and the benefits of selecting one over another.

Interview Guide Physical Security System Selection Process Vendor Questions

(Consultant)
(Date)

Questions are to be address to the service manager who will handle the system:

<u>Administrative:</u>

1. What is the address and telephone number of the primary service contact office?
2. Who is the top management person at this office and how long have they held that position?
3. What is the address and telephone number of other offices in the state of Louisiana that could service our facilities?
4. Who are the top management persons at each subordinate office and how long have they held that position?
5. What are the hours of operation of each service office?
6. Do service calls come directly to the field offices or are they channeled through a dispatch center?
7. What is your average response time for a routine service call (document studies would be helpful) for a Maintenance Contract customer?
8. What is your "guaranteed" response time for a service call for a MC customer?
9. What is your response time for a major system outage for a MC customer?
10. What is your average recorded time from initial call to "problem cleared"?
11. Is there a charge for after hours service calls for a MC customer?
12. Will it make a difference in service response if (The Company) provides the installation?
13. If you perform the system installation, what documentation do you produce prior to the installation?
14. If you perform the system installation and follow up maintenance, do you maintain and update your system documentation (show examples)?
15. Your bid included a price for system maintenance, is that price negotiable if (The Company) assumes some of the maintenance responsibilities?

<u>Labor:</u>

1. How many technicians are at the primary service office?
2. What is the training history of each technician with regard to the system you are proposing?
3. How many technicians are at the subordinate offices?
4. What is the training history of each technician at the subordinate office with regard to the system you are proposing?
5. What continuing education program do you have for technicians?
6. Do you assign technicians on a first come basis or are technicians assigned specific accounts?

Figure 8.1 Sample contact form, page 1.

7. What duties other than "maintaining access control systems" are your technicians required to do?

8. Approximately how many accounts does each technician handle?

9. What is your performance measurement index for a technician?

10. What is the average employment length "on the job" for your technicians?

11. If your service office is not open 24/7, how do you handle after hours service calls?

12. Who are your top 3 MC service customers in each office that will serve an (The Company) facility and what is there approximate MC value?

Material:

1. Where do you stock spare equipment for the system you are proposing (address or address(es))?

2. How many spare readers (of the type you are proposing) do you stock?

3. How many network panels (of the type you are proposing) do you stock?

4. If you perform a service call for a MC customer, and use a spare from your stock is there a charge for material?

5. If a MC customer receives a spare from your stock, is it a new product or refurbished?

6. If a MC customer receives a new or refurbished spare from your stock, is the original product repaired and returned or is there simply a "swap" of possession?

7. What is the warranty on a replaced product?

END OF INTERVIEW

Figure 8.1 cont'd

Interview Guide Access Control System Selection Process
Referred Customer Questions
(The Company) Vendor Selection Committee

(Consultant)
(Date)

Questions are to be address to the System Administrator (users):

1. When was your system installed?

2. How did you select this vendor for your system?

3. Why did you select this vendor?

4. What features were you most interested in when selecting your system?

5. Did the vendor do your installation or did you contract with others?

6. Do you use your access cards as ID cards?

7. Do your ID cards have photos and does the vendor supply this photo system?

8. Approximately how many card readers are in your system?

Figure 8.2 Sample contact form, page 2.

9. Which card reader technology are you using?
10. Are all the card readers located in the same building?
11. How did you handle inter-building communications (if applicable)?
12. How many workstations do you have?
13. Are there any off-site workstations?
14. Do you use your system for alarm monitoring?
15. Do you use your system for CCTV control?
16. Do you use your system for elevator control?
17. What is the model name of your system software?
18. What version of the vendor's software are you using?
19. How long does it take for the vendor to deliver additions to your system?
20. Generally, has the system met your expectations?
21. How often does the vendor communications system fail?
22. What system limitations have you found that you cannot overcome?
23. How difficult is the system to learn to use?
24. How would you rate the vendor's user training program (1 – 10, 10 being the best)?
25. How would you rate the vendor's telephone support for user problems (1 – 10, 10 being the best)?
26. Do you have a maintenance contract with the vendor?
27. Where is the vendor service office that maintains your system?
28. What are their hours of operation?
29. Who do you call to place a service request?
30. What is your average response time for a routine service call?
31. What is your response time for a major system outage?
32. How many visits does it take the vendor to clear a problem?
33. About how many service calls do you have in an average month?
34. Do the technicians seem knowledgeable about the system?
35. Has the vendor ever charged your for items you felt should have been covered by your MC?
36. Does the vendor have adequate records on your system installation (cable runs, interconnections etc.)?
37. Do you generally get the same technician for each service call or are they randomly assigned?
38. Have you ever had to place an after hours service call, and what was the response time?
39. Have parts been readily available for your system?
40. Would you make the same decision again to use this vendor?

END OF INTERVIEW

Figure 8.2 cont'd

Illustrate the method used to evaluate the bids. Conclude with the follow-up action is required and how to handle the next step in the process. Remember that the recommendation may have more than one bidder if all comparison elements are equal. The recommendation may also conclude that the benefits do not justify the cost of the project and the recommendation may suggest another approach. The security professional's job is to help the management team make the best decision based on the information available.

Call for a meeting of the system selection committee, present the evaluation and the final recommendation. At the conclusion of the meeting, ask the committee if they are ready to decide to proceed. As with the decision to conduct the bid process, expect delays in the final choice. Usually by this time, there are no big surprises and the choice is "who to buy from" not "should we buy."

Prepare minutes of the meeting and follow up the selection committee at reasonable intervals to determine acceptance of the final recommendation if they do not make a decision at the meeting. After receiving final approval, release a recommendation to purchase the system to the company's purchasing office with full instructions on how to establish the contract with the selected bidder.

The next step is system implementation.

System Implementation

9

INTRODUCTION

Even when an electronic physical security system is properly designed and successfully acquired, the security system has failed to achieve the desired results because the implementation was poorly carried out. The preceding chapters were dedicated to the identification of the right system components and the professional delivery of those devices. Now the security professional must focus attention on project management and implementation to ensure proper delivery and professional installation of this new security tool.

AWARDING THE CONTRACT

Review the RFP; this forms the basis of the agreement between the company and the vendor. Prepare the procurement recommendation for the company's purchasing manager and request that the purchasing manager issue a "Letter of Intent" to purchase the system from the selected vendor. This will provide the vendor with notification to proceed with pre-award submittals. Refrain from notifying the unsuccessful bidders of the results of the contract award until the successful bidder accepts the order.

If the RFP requires pre-installation submittals, follow up receipt of those submittals before awarding the contract. Inspect the submittals for conformity to the requirements of the RFP and require the vendor to correct any errors or deficiencies. The mandatory submittals described in Chapter 8 are:

1. Completions schedule (firm installation schedule)
2. Schedule of earned values (when payments will be requested for each billable item)

Notify the company's purchasing department when the submittals are in order and request preparation of the purchase order with instructions to the vendor "not to proceed until after attending an initial walkdown meeting and receiving a Notice to Proceed."

Now recommend that the purchasing manager notify the unsuccessful bidders of the contract award in a letter. It is helpful, though not imperative, for the security professional to also telephone the prime contact of each bidder and thank them for their efforts.

GET STARTED

The most important aspect of system implementation is communication between the company, the security professional and the vendor. Good communications ensure that changes in the design and unforeseen problems can be quickly and easily resolved. The relationship is not adversarial but cooperative. All parties want a smooth successful installation and one of the primary duties of the security professional is to facilitate that process. The company wants a useful, effective system and the vendor needs to make a reasonable profit.

To begin the communication process, convene an Initial Walkdown meeting with vendor and select members of the company's system selection committee. Begin with a review of the terms and conditions of the RFP. Confirm that everyone understands what is expected of them to successfully implement the security solutions.

At the conclusion of the meeting, visit all equipment locations and discuss how to carry out the installation and the concerns for operational aspects of the installation. This process is called the Initial Walkdown.

Prepare a report on the Initial Walkdown for the management team and enumerate all the concerns expressed by the meeting attendees. If additional information or decisions are required before proceeding, document the responses in follow up letters to the vendor and the company.

Prepare a request to the purchasing manager to release a Notice to Proceed to the vendor. This signals the vendor that their proposals are acceptable, and they may begin the investments needed to deliver the proposed systems.

MILESTONE REVIEWS

There are no rigid rules that apply for every installation; each installation requires individual review planning. The vendor's work schedule is a good resource for this coordination planning; this was part of the submittal after award of contract. The RFP also required periodic meetings with the vendor's on-site project manager; they probably have a plan in mind already for project coordination. Discuss the best times for coordination meetings with the vendor. Establish a firm meeting schedule coordinated with anticipated work completion milestones.

In addition to the milestone inspections, plan to perform periodic spot inspections to confirm progress. These are informal walkdowns to review the work. Exercise caution during these inspections. Remember that the workmen report to the vendor and should always be given instructions from the vendor's project manager. If an installation error is discovered, that error should be reported immediately to the vendor's project manager and not directly to the workmen. An exception to this might be if a workman is about to cut a doorframe to install a lock on the wrong door. Direct communication with the workman would save everyone concerned time and money but report the error to the vendor's project manager for verification.

The inspection process described below is the customary and usual method for installation of most types of electronic physical security systems. After inspecting the installation for each milestone, create a punch list of unfinished items or items that require correction. A punch list is a term used to identify incomplete or defective items discovered during an inspection of an installation. By addressing these items early in the installation process, confusion is reduced and errors are eliminated more easily.

After each milestone inspection, conduct a meeting with the vendor's project manager and representatives from the company's selection committee. This will aid in the communication process and keep the company informed about the progress of the installation.

Milestone Meeting 1—Cabling Complete

The project usually begins with cabling. When the vendor announces that cabling is complete, inspect the cable installation paying particular attention to the following items:

1. Is the cable type that was proposed by the vendor (or recommended by the manufacturer) the cable that was used?
2. Is each cable labeled so that it can be easily identified at both ends?
3. Has the installer allowed enough slack in selected cables for future additions?
4. Is there excess cable (coils of communications cable in ceilings can act like antennas for attracting stray signals and interfering with the proper communications between the devices)?
5. Is the cable properly suspended in ceiling areas?
6. Has cabling been provided to all equipment locations?

After completing the inspection and coordination meeting, report the progress of Milestone 1 to the management team and plan to follow up on any action required.

Milestone Meeting 2—Equipment Staging Complete

If the RFP required bench testing and staging of the system before installation, follow up with the vendor to determine when the equipment is in hand. Require the vendor to provide an inventory by serial number of each major piece of equipment.

When the vendor is ready for a staging inspection, visit the vendor's place of business and observe that all devices are working properly. Allow for the absence of software set up, but all major components should be test and confirmed operational. At the conclusion of the test, record the names of the individuals performing the test and the results of the test. Note any system defects and the vendor's commitment to replace defective equipment. Prepare a report on the progress of Milestone 2 to the management team. Provide the results of the test and plan to follow up on any action required.

Milestone Meeting 3—Equipment Mounting Complete

When the vendor announces that the equipment is mounted, conduct the Milestone 3 inspection and coordination meeting. Some areas of concern are:

1. Is the mounting cosmetically acceptable?
2. Are all components securely mounted?
3. Does equipment mounting interfere with the operation or access to other devices?
4. Is the installed equipment the same product demonstrated during staging process?

After completing the equipment mounting inspection and coordination meeting, report the progress of Milestone 3 to management team and plan to follow up on any action required.

Milestone Meeting 4—Final Termination Complete

When the vendor announces that the final termination (connecting the low voltage cabling to the equipment) is complete, conduct the Milestone 4 inspection and coordination meeting. Some areas of concern are:

1. Are all cables terminated at each device?
2. Is each cable labeled so that future system expansion is easy to do?

3.   Do the termination areas appear neat and orderly?
4.   Are the control boxes clearly labeled identifying the purpose of each box?
5.   Is there a chart in each control box indicating the end devices connected to it?
6.   If tamper alarms were specified on the control boxes, are they installed?
7.   Are there locks on the control boxes?

Please note that at this point, power should not be applied to the devices. The vendor will be permitted to connect to commercial power when all devices are wired and ready for use.

When Milestone 4 is finished and the coordination team has agreed in the follow up meeting that the system is ready to be "turned on," the vendor should give permission to power up the system and begin the testing and troubleshooting phase. Report the results of Milestone 4 to management team and plan to follow up on any action required.

Unscheduled Visits

Periodically visit the job site to determine progress and inspect the work. A good rule of thumb is to do an unescorted inspection on a weekly basis. Much can be learned by a simple visit, and it will be relatively easy to gauge the progress of the work by seeing what has been accomplished since the last visit. Report problems found to the vendor to aid in the installation process but remember that these are unscheduled visits outside regular milestones. In managing labor resources, a vendor may allow intermediate progress to lapse on one project while emphasizing another more urgent project. There is no reason for recrimination if milestone deadlines are met. Your project may be the next one to get special attention to meet the milestone dates.

FINAL INSPECTION

When the vendor has announced that the system is ready for final inspection, call for a pre-test of system operation. The pre-test saves time and trouble for all concerned by ensuring that the final acceptance test will be conducted without incident. Conduct all of the steps of final testing (see System Acceptance in Chapter 8). Develop a final punch list that describes items requiring attention before final delivery.

When the vendor announces that the Final Punch List is finished, convene Milestone Meeting 5.

Who Should Attend

Invite the vendor's sales representative, project manager and support personnel to the final test. Invite members from the selection committee who were assigned the duties of monitoring the system installation. Arrange to have two-way communications between the groups doing the tests. Most large companies and many vendors have radio/telephone systems that can be used for this purpose.

When Should the Test Be Conducted

It is best to conduct the test on a Tuesday, during a week that does not have company holidays. This will allow the vendor a day for last minute preparation and time to correct any anomalies discovered during the final acceptance test before a weekend. Start the test early; it may take all day in large systems.

What Should Be Covered

Test all operational aspects of the system. The phase two RFP provides for test criteria from the system manufacturer and the vendor. Some recommended test criteria are listed below to help determine if the tests submitted are adequate. For access control systems, the tests should include at least the following:

1. System sign-on and verification of date and time.
2. The basic software capabilities of the system such as adding a card to the system, responding to alarms and controlling field devices from the system's consoles.
3. Give two access cards to each technician conducting the test, one valid card and one invalid card. Test each access

control point to demonstrate that a valid card is accepted and the invalid card rejected. In addition to observing the system's reaction at the control point, the testers should also observe that card transactions are displayed at each system console.

For alarm monitoring systems, the tests should include at least the following:

1. Controlled openings should be deliberately violated to ensure that the alarms are properly registered at the system consoles.
2. Monitored areas should be deliberately intruded upon to ensure that the alarms are properly registered at the system consoles.

For CCTV systems, the tests should include at least the following:

1. Observe the views from all cameras and all monitors.
2. Test the limits of pan/tilt/zoom for all cameras so equipped.
3. Record from all cameras.
4. Playback from all cameras.
5. On more sophisticated systems, test the basic software capabilities such as search, motion sensor, and hard copy printout.

After the tests are complete, prepare a final system acceptance letter and transmit it to the vendor. This establishes the date that the system was accepted. The final acceptance letter should include a final punch list for the vendor. Follow up that list to completion. Report the results of Milestone 5 to management team

POST INSTALLATION SUBMITTALS

Based on the requirements of the RFP, vendors will provide additional documentation at the end of the installation. In this example, the vendor was required to provide an as-built drawing. This is a modification of the original wiring arrangement and reflects the changes from the original design resulting from unforeseen installation conditions. The as-built drawings will be invaluable when modifying or adding to the system later.

Confirm the vendor training arrangements and discuss training commitment dates with the company's security managers. Verify that the vendor and security staff set class dates.

The system is now operational but should remain turned off following the acceptance test. Turn the system on when the training is complete and the security staff is ready to place the system into service.

SECURITY SYSTEM PERSONNEL

In past chapters, the term the system referred to the electronic devices the company needed to purchase to provide the recommended security solutions. To implement the proposed solutions, the system also needs people. People manage the electronic systems. People determine the most appropriate constraints to program into the system to meet security objectives. People respond to alarm conditions perceived by the system.

The system is the combination of the devices and the people that work with them. The security professional's role does not end with the successful implementation of devices; that is just one step in the process. The security professional must also address the human side of the equation.

Identify the System Administrator (SA)

The SA serves as the central point for all decisions concerning system operation. The SA may seek advice and counsel from various department managers where system components are; however, the SA is responsible for implementing the decisions. The SA reports to the Chief of Security or Risk Management Manager and sometimes is the manager of the department.

The security professional should work with the management team to identify the SA. Advise the company that the responsibilities of SA are not casual and will demand considerable effort from the designated person. In other words, the SA, especially for larger systems, should not be a human resources clerk assigned this role as a sideline project to their other duties. The SA is a dedicated individual, usually in the company's security department, who is prepared to devote at least 50% of their work time to managing the electronic physical security system.

Identify the Help Desk

In complex systems with multiple work stations and especially in systems that provide work stations to departments (in some cases department heads control their own card authorization) identify a Help Desk. The Help Desk works with the SA and provides software support and guidance to other participating departments. In some cases, the Help Desk is actually the SA since that person is the most familiar with system operation in the company.

System User Training

The company relies on the security professional to guide the implementation of the new electronic physical security system. The security professional must rely on the system vendor to teach the software programming steps and mechanical details of the selected system to the users.

There is simply too much information available for all such systems for the security professional to be a knowledgeable expert in the intricate details of the ever-changing software world of electronic physical security. Make sure that the company receives full user training from the vendor or the manufacturer of the system and provide oversight to that training.

There are two levels of user training, SA and Operator. The names of these levels may differ from company to company but the concept is essentially the same. A SA manages all the functions of the electronic physical security system and has the top-level password that will permit them to change all system user functions.

An Operator is usually an officer standing a post watch who must respond to alarms in the system and requests from authorized employees to alter the system's performance. For instance, a controlled door that normally requires an access credential must remain opened for an extended period to permit moving large or heavy objects in and out of the facility. To prevent company security from responding to repeated alarms from this door, the employee would request that security disable the alarms and hold the doors unlocked while the opening is used. The post officer usually has the authority to decide to unlock the door and operator training should include instructions to do this.

Discuss these procedures with the SA. Alter the vendor's training agenda before delivery of the training class if it does not appear to address all users' needs. This modified agenda will help the training technician focus attention on the most needed procedures.

Attend a portion of each level of training class provided. Conduct exit interviews with the attendees to determine their satisfaction with the training. When the system is in service, some spot testing will help determine if the product training was effective. If the users cannot use the system tools effectively, request additional product training from the vendor.

CREATE USER DOCUMENTATION FOR SYSTEM MANAGEMENT

Personnel in all companies—especially in large companies—tend to move between jobs. As a result, knowledge gained in the procedures and use of company tools can be lost when employees transfer or leave the company. This is especially important when the lost employee is the SA or Help Desk Technician.

System documentation is an important part of the security professional's job. An adequate structure is essential to the proper management of any complex electronic physical security system, and having a carefully documented structure will help orient new employees.

IDENTIFY THE AUTHORIZED POPULATION

To identify the authorized population, start with organizing cardholder access control data. Note that this technique applies regardless of the technology used (keypad, biometrics, card reader). For this example, we will assume that the system selected is a card reader based product.

Many of the sophisticated electronic physical security systems available today provide a substantial database for collecting and displaying a variety of information about cardholders. Designate the information needed for the security system database carefully. Just because you "can have" 50 items of information on every employee in the new security tool, it does not follow that you "must have" that much information on everyone.

Certain pieces of information are essential in the proper handling of any security system database. This would include:

1. The name of the cardholder
2. The company department affiliation
3. An internal identifier used to designate the employee (usually an employee number)
4. The authorized access constraints for each employee

Some companies use Social Security numbers as employee numbers. In those cases, seek the advice of the company's human resources department to minimize liability and exposure for using employee Social Security numbers in the security database. Some other recommended fields for the security system database are:

1. Items used to identify an unconscious employee discovered on
   - company grounds
   - Gender
   - Height
   Complexion light, medium, dark
2. For situations involving vehicles, include:
   - Vehicle make, model, and color
   - Vehicle license plate number
   - Parking sticker ID number

Maintaining vehicle data can be troublesome. Use vehicle data only if employees park their vehicle on company premises and the company is responsible for the security of the parking area. Along with this requirement, recommend that the company employ a vehicle parking sticker system to recognize authorized vehicles in the employee parking area.

Omit non-essential information that has limited value to the security function. Be especially careful about personal information to which the company has access and is available to security. Examples include:

- Date of birth
- Wage data
- Home address
- Home telephone number

Good arguments can be made for using information like this for identification during a crisis but it is a slippery slope. If someone with access to this database discloses personal information to unauthorized personnel, the company has significant liability exposure. Help the SA develop a list of information types, otherwise know as "fields," that the SA considers valuable in assessing identification in a crisis. Discuss this list with human resources before committing to a plan of action.

Identify cardholders and then segment them into like groups. The groupings usually reflect departments or job functions. Cluster the groups based on the anticipated access permissions, that is, deciding where they can go. It is not necessary to make the door access decision at this step, only to group similar cardholders together. By assigning individuals to groups, it will be easier to manage and make decisions on large populations of cardholders.

Organize Card Reader Data

The primary purpose of an access control system is to help the company control who goes where when within their facility. Card data provides the answer to "who" was assigned the card. (Remember, in a card based access control system, the card represents the employee. The system can certify the card but not the individual carrying it. Higher forms of access permissions can help achieve user recognition, see Chapter 4.)

Organize reader data to establish "where" a card may go within the facility. All sophisticated access control systems in the market today provide opening control by requiring that authorized individuals present a valid credential (including biometric measurements) to the device controlling the opening. Construct a matrix for access decisions by using a copy of the Door Detail Schedule (DDS) developed during the system design phase of this installation. Please see Figure 9.2 for an example of this Door Group Schedule.

In Figure 9.2, the doors are listed in the left-hand margin as they are in the DDS. However, the columns across the top now bear a different nomenclature. The decision matrix columns include the group names of authorized groups within the system. Request the SA make decisions on which groups access each control area.

Work with department heads and other company employees to verify the access decisions. In Figure 9.2, a "1" is used to denote

Women's Services Department

NAME LAST	NAME FIRST	Title	Department	Nursery Staff	Pediatrics	GYN	OB	Neo Nat	Labor and Delivery	Emergency	Clinic
				1	2	3	4	5	6	7	8
	Alma	Nursing Asst 2	Nursery	1							
	Kristen	Rn 2	Nursery	1							
	Lynn	Rn/McIno Section Mgr	Nursery	1							
	Madelena	Clerk Chief 1	Nursery	1							
	Elimaris	Rn 3	Transitional Nursery	1							
	Shannon	Rn 2	Transitional Nursery	1							
	Portia	Rn 1	Transitional Nursery	1							
	Christine	Nursing Unit Aide	Transitional Nursery	1							
	Cecilia	Clerk Chief 1	Pediatrics		1						
	Bridgette	Nurse Registered	Pediatrics		1						
	Marleen	Rn/McIno Asst Sect Mgr	Pediatrics		1						
	Sandra	Rn 2	Pediatrics		1						
	Meagan	Rn 2	Pediatrics		1						
	Brenda	Practical Nurse–Licensed, 3	Pediatrics		1						
	Beverly	Rn 2	Pediatrics		1						
	Mary	Nursing Asst 2	Pediatrics		1						
	Angela	Rn/McIno Asst Sect Mgr	Gyn-Inpatient			1					
	Natasha	Psychiatric Aide 3	Gyn-Inpatient			1					
	Leslie	Practical Nurse–Licensed, 1	Gyn-Inpatient			1					
	Geraldine	Nursing Asst 2	Gyn-Inpatient				1				
	Sharon	Clerk Chief 1	3 West Ob				1				
	Wanda	Rn 3	3 West Ob				1				
	Dianne	Practical Nurse–Licensed, 2	3 West Ob				1				
	Theresa	Rn/McIno Asst Sect Mgr	3 West Ob					1			
	Michelle	Rn 2	Neo-Natal Icu					1			
	Cecille	Clerk Chief 1	Neo-Natal Icu					1			
	Mitzi	Rn 2	Labor And Delivery						1		
	Lethia	Clerk Chief 1	Labor And Delivery						1		
	Denise	Rn-Clinical Nurse Spec	Labor And Delivery						1		
	Glenda	Rn-Supervisor 2	Emergency Medicine-Peds							1	
	Kim	Nurse Registered	Emergency Medicine-Peds							1	
	Sheena	Clerk Chief 1	Emergency Medicine-Peds							1	
	Brenda	Nursing Asst 2	Ob-Gyn Clinic								1
	Gustavia	Clerk 4	Ob-Gyn Clinic								1
	Gralina	Clerk 4	Ob-Gyn Clinic								1
	Julie	Rn-Supervisor 2	Pediatric Clinics								1
	Brenda	Rn-Clinical Coordinator	Pediatric Clinics								1
	Colette	Rn 2	Pediatric Clinics								1

Figure 9.1   Cardholder matrix.

Door Group Schedule

By: (Consultant Name)
Revision: 0
Date: (Date)

Client: (Company Name)
Work Location: (Area)

Project: (Project Designation)

Door Description	Group 1	Group 2	Group 3	Group 4	Group 5	Group 6	Group 7	Group 8	Notes
First Floor:									
old pediatrics	1	1							
old pediatrics	1	1							
morgue ramp exit	1		1						
east entrance	1	1	1	1	1	1	1	1	
front entrance	1	1	1	1	1	1	1	1	
west entrance	1	1	1	1	1	1	1	1	
admitting	1								
medical records_admin	1								
walk-in clinic	1		1	1					
family doctor	1			1					
walk-in clinic 2	1			1					
east entrance to oncology	1				1				
west entrance to oncology	1				1				
Radiology Oncology	1				1				
fire stair -	1	1		1	1	1	1	1	
walkway	1	1		1	1	1	1	1	
psyc triage	1								
west rear stair	1					1			
loading dock	1					1			
ER Admit	1					1			
Triage Station	1						1		
Admitting	1						1		

Figure 9.2　Door group schedule.

permission is granted and a blank field is used to denote permission not granted. The choice of symbols is arbitrary but creating these tables in a Microsoft Excel worksheet allows easy manipulation and data sorting with numerals versus alpha characters. Any set of symbolic references can represent a yes or a no.

Time Zones

Time zones define "when" an authorized credential has permission to access (or egress) an opening. Exercise caution when establishing time zones; do not be overly restrictive. The following example may be helpful in understanding what overly restrictive means.

Assume that the company is a manufacturing facility with 24 hour operations, manned by three 8-hour shifts. Also assume that the first shift begins at 8:00 a.m. and concludes at 4:00 p.m. Monday through Friday. In an overly restrictive environment, the individuals authorized to work during shift one will be given a time zone assignment of 8:00 a.m. to 4:00 p.m., Monday through Friday. Such restriction does not allow for employees who work odd shifts when it is convenient for the company or the employee. This also does not allow for employees arriving and departing at mid-shift.

As a result, departments must report all changes in shift assignment to company security to change access permissions. The resulting flood of shift change information can easily overwhelm a SA. Further, department managers who authorize shift changes may neglect to inform security that a change has taken place. This will delay workers from reporting to their assigned location at the proper time.

A more acceptable approach to assigning time zones is to determine if significant breaches in security will occur if an employee accesses the facility at times other than their normal working hours. If there are no compelling reasons to restrict the hours an employee may enter a facility then assign the employee or group 24-hour access permission.

Conversely, many companies operate on a standard business hour schedule, 7:00 a.m. to 6:00 p.m. It would be unusual for employees to access the facility after hours and on weekends. In such cases, assigning most employees to a normal working hour time period is the most acceptable means of restriction.

Some exceptions may be made for managerial personnel and others who have frequent need to access the facility after normal working hours and, since most sophisticated systems today permit multiple time periods, one time period may be assigned for after hours employees while another is assigned to regular hours employees.

There are no hard and fast rules; it is a question of practical judgment. What the reader should take away from the foregoing is that you may restrict access based on time when it is apparent and necessary, but you should not arbitrarily restrict access based on time when there are no good reasons to do so.

The security professional can assist company personnel in making time zone decisions by providing a data entry tool or form for compiling the data. See Figure 9.3 for an example of a Time Zone form.

Assigning Access Permissions

Use a top down approach when designating authorized access permissions. Work with members of the system selection committee to determine how to handle access permissions. In some cases, conflicts arise between department managers regarding access to their assigned areas. The system selection committee sets the policy for these decisions.

Following the guidelines established by the committee, determine the controlled areas each cardholder group may access. Assist the department managers in establishing these permissions. Resolve conflicts between departments and document the decisions. To help with the documentation, refer to Figure 9.4 for an example of a permission form.

Avoid unduly restrictive access permission tables and counsel the department managers against overcomplicating the permission tables. Frequently, company managers will request highly specific access constraints that unnecessarily limit the times and locations that an authorized employee may be granted access. Their lack of experience in establishing these controls coupled with the zeal to support the company's new approach to security is often one of the contributing causes. The rule of thumb in making these decisions is to restrict an employee from accessing the facility only during those times when their presence might provide an unwarranted security risk.

Security System Procedures
Department Submittal, Security Control Time Zones

		Revised:	11/17/03
		Version:	2-4
		Submitted:	04/19/05

Department: (Department Name)

Time Zone	Description	Start Time	End Time	M	T	W	T	F	S	S
1	Normal Working Hours (NWH)									
2	Alarm Only Door Monitoring 2									
3	Auto Door Unlock Times 1									
4	Auto Door Unlock Times 2									
5	Auto Door Unlock Times 3									
6	Cardholder 24 / 7 hour Access	0:01	24:00:00	X	X	X	X	X	X	X
7	Cardholder Limited Access NWH									
8	Cardholder Limited Access 1									
9	Cardholder Limited Access 2									
10	Cardholder Limited Access 3									

Figure 9.3 Time Zone form.

(Client Name)		Revised:	11/17/03
Department Submittal, Access Privilege Request		Version:	2-4
		Submitted:	04/19/05

Department:

Please list the security privileges all of the cardholders:

(1) If a card was previously issued

Card Holder Name	ID Number (1)	Time Zone	Reader Group

"Add lines as required"

Figure 9.4   Access permission table.

Video Observation and Recording

If a CCTV system was included in the system recommendation, watch officers require instructions on what to observe and how to manage the recording devices. Help the SA prepare a set of instructions on how to observe and categorize incidents.

For example, the SA may want to pay special attention to a vulnerable area along a fence line. The post orders will include a requirement to view an area several times a day and note suspicious activity. This observation is required in the absence of alarms and intended to categorize conduct or activity in these areas for later investigations.

Provide a plot plan showing the location of each camera within or around clearly identified structures. Make the perspective of each camera clear to the watch officer.

Image recording accompanies most CCTV applications. Some system maintenance is required at the user level such as archiving image files on a routine basis. Help the SA develop a process for managing the recorded images. This process depends on the type of system implemented. Images are transferred to compact disks (CD) or Digital Versatile Disc (DVD) or copied to other media as required by the system. The user training classes teach the techniques available on the installed system but the SA and the security professional must decide on how best to use those capabilities.

Alarm Response

In the planning and implementation process, the system design recommended devices to monitor and control openings. Openings were monitored to ensure that they were not opened during periods when the facility should be secured. However, simply monitoring the doors and recording when unauthorized openings were made will not fully address most security situations.

Alarm recognition is an integral part of the overall physical security system. The electronic physical security system will provide information regarding unauthorized use of controlled openings. It is essential to recognize these breaches in security and clearly identify the area to take appropriate action.

During the design phase, the DDS established the identity for each opening. The identity given to each opening included the common name used by employees for that opening. Some new members of the security force monitoring the system may not be familiar with all the names used to describe openings. A clear description of each secure point helps the watch officer dispatch a roving patrol to the area in question.

Electronic security systems provide alarm messages in response to the violation of a secured opening. These alarm messages begin with a text description of the alarm point. If the company is located on a campus with multiple buildings, a building name or number is usually associated with each building.

The first element of the description is the building name or number (in multiple building sites). Next, indicate the floor number and if the door is internal or external. If the door is external, indicate the side of the building (by compass point) where the door is located. Even without specific recognition of the violated door, knowing the building and facing side where the opening is located will be helpful in initially dispatching the patrol officer to investigate. Designations can continue with floor number and subject area. For example:

Admin Building, first floor, external door, southeast corner

Again, the level of description is a matter of judgment. The SA will know the level of familiarity of the facility by the company security staff. Anticipate some employee turnover in the security staff. At any time, a new employee who is unfamiliar with the internal names may be the watch officer on duty during an alarm event. The description should be clear enough so that a person who is not familiar with all aspects of the facility could find the violated door with relative ease.

In addition to a text description of the violated door, integrate floor plans or facility maps that provide a graphic representation of the alarm location. Most of the sophisticated electronic security systems available today provide a means to link an alarm event to an embedded floor plan or facility map. Work with company departments to create the necessary images for linkage to the new electronic physical security system. In these cases, the vendor can usually assist the company in establishing this graphic link.

Responding to Alarm Events

After identifying the alarms, the security staff must respond to the incident. Work with the SA to describe in detail what response should occur when an alarm event takes place. Usually, these instructions are limited to a few short sentences, for example: "Unauthorized access building 127, first floor north, main entrance. Officer to investigate immediately and report findings to the command post."

Help the SA write procedures such as these for each alarm event that could occur in the system. Once written, seek concurrence of the department manager in charge of the area where the security opening is located. See Figure 9.5 for an example of an Alarm Message Submittal form.

The message may include contact information for department employees. In the case of highly toxic or dangerous biological agents inside a protected area, the procedures may also include contacting the department manager, the police or the fire department. When layering these additional contact requirements on an alarm response, remember that contact individuals might not be available during an alarm event. Use a descending list of contact personnel and have several contacts for the watch officer.

In addition to the personnel response during alarm events, many of the electronic physical security systems can automatically trigger devices that will help to detect, deter, and delay a perpetrator. For instance, systems can automatically turn on lights, sound sirens, or trigger CCTV systems to focus in on the area of incident as soon as the incident occurs.

The mandate for private security is substantially different from the mandate for publicly funded police officers. Private security endeavors to protect the people and property of the companies for whom they work. Apprehending criminals is not the primary concern. The goal of private security is preventing criminals from

Security System Procedures			Revised:	11/17/03
Department Submittal, Security Control Alarm Messages			Version:	2-4
			Submitted:	04/19/05

Department: (Department Name)

Message Number	Alarm Message
1	
2	
3	
4	
5	
6	
7	
8	
9	
10	
11	
12	

Figure 9.5 Alarm message form.

perpetrating their crimes on the employer. It follows then that an immediate response by some device that will cause the perpetrator to flee a scene before a crime is committed may be preferable to having a patrol officer catch them in the act. Work with the SA to determine the means needed to detect, deter, delay and respond to criminal activity.

System Reporting

After the security system devices are in service, software management is essential to a successful operation. Most of the sophisticated electronic physical security systems provide a set of system reports that identify system programming decisions.

The first set of system reports describe how the readers are grouped together and how time zones are arranged. The second set identifies the credentials used in the system and the authorized access permissions. Other system reports include alarm descriptions and the timing of automatic events based on alarm information or time of the day. These are the standard system reports. Help the SA select a list of standard reports and develop a schedule for periodically re-printing these reports. Base the frequency of reprints on the expected number of changes in system programming over a given time.

Obtain a ringed binder and create an index to store the reports. Help the SA prepare a copy of each report for the binder. This will be a useful tool when discussing system arrangements during company meetings.

In addition to programming reports, activity reports are also a part of system management. In most systems, when an alarm event occurs, the system records the date, time and location of the alarm. When company security acknowledges that alarm, they are required to make an entry in the system and describe the action taken before clearing the alarm. Use alarm event reports when evaluating facility-wide security violations and security force responses.

Additionally, all systems on the market provide some form of transaction history. This transaction history is a database of events that occurred during system operation. The most useful reports from transaction history are "exception reports."

An exception report focuses on those transactions that occurred outside of the normal range of business activity. For instance, if an employee attempts to use their credential to enter an opening without permission, the system will record that attempt. In most cases, security officers do not investigate such incidents since it is often user error. However, the exception report will reveal trends in employee activity. The report filter will isolate unauthorized attempts to gain access to restricted areas and identify employees repeatedly attempting to violate access restrictions. This could indicate that security must conduct an investigation.

In some situations the electronic physical security systems monitor other systems, thereby centralizing information for all safety and security matters on the company's premises. For instance, the electronic physical security system can monitor the status of alarm and trouble indicators of building fire alarm systems. The security system can produce a report showing the behavior of these systems over time. Fire alarm systems that are not physically inspected on a frequent basis may show repeated troubles before actually going into alarm or failing. By running periodic reports on these other systems, company security can focus the attention of the facilities department on systems that may be on the brink of failure. By addressing such concerns early, the company can avoid false alarms and reduce potential disruption of work.

Programming

Work with the SA to supervise the programming of all the decisions into the system. Remember that training alone will not guarantee good results, and the SA needs support and guidance from an experienced professional.

SYSTEM MANAGEMENT PROCEDURES

The preceding sections have addressed how the electronic physical security system is to be implemented from a logistical point of view. However, even projects that are implemented exceedingly well can fail if the appropriate management procedures are not in place to work with the new system. It is essential to have management controls for all elements of the new physical security system to prevent unauthorized persons from having access to critical control processes.

Establish Procedures to Issue Credentials

The security credential that is most widely used today for system identification is the access card. There are a variety of other access devices as described earlier in this book that do not require the physical presence of a card but instead are authorization numbers or biometric measuring. The same rules apply for each of these other access credentials that apply to access cards. For this discussion, we shall confine our remarks solely to card based systems.

In most sophisticated electronic physical security systems, a user must enter information about the credential into the system for the credential to work properly. Although it seems that an unprogrammed card is useless, it is not. Advise the SA to handle new access cards carefully.

Some electronic physical security systems have a default mode when communication is lost. In default mode, the higher level qualifications for access permissions are ignored. Under these circumstances, any access card sold to the facility will automatically have access permission in all doors. Some companies use security credentials without photos as a form of physical identification. If a perpetrator wishing access to a facility steals a security card, the perpetrator may approach an unwary employee and suggest that their card is not functioning today and would like the employee to help them gain access to the facility. This is an employee training issue but is also a credential safeguard issue.

The physical security system may have substantial safeguards, but a perpetrator with deliberation and intent can circumvent those safeguards more easily with a stolen card. Keeping an accurate inventory of available identity credentials is an important part of safeguarding system operation.

As part of the SA's record keeping process, instruct them to keep a complete and accurate list of all orders placed and received for security credentials. The SA should note the order information that requested the security cards and indicate the starting and ending number of the card sequence. Match that inventory to the system card report described earlier and maintain a list of lost or destroyed cards. The SA will then be able to identify every card that was acquired for the system, its current condition, and final disposition.

Assist the SA in preparing a set of procedures that describes how and when to issue a new security credential. Require departments that hire new employees to complete a Card Request Form. Include in this form the signature of the department manager authorized to grant access to their area, and what access permissions are available for the employee (see Figure 9.6). Require the new employee to present this document to company security for a security credential.

The procedure should include how to maintain the authorization form after issuing the security credential. A card form file or binder is the simplest choice. File the form alphabetically for quick and easy recalls during updates and replacements.

Procedures for Lost or Replaced Security Credentials

Anticipate that cards will be lost or destroyed. Include in the procedures the steps needed to replace a lost or damaged card. Use the card request form for card replacement. In most cases, the employee's department manager should be required to sign this document authorizing card issuance or replacement for their subordinate. Such procedures provide department managers with additional information regarding the security awareness of their employees. An employee who constantly loses or destroys identity cards may be subject to disciplinary action.

A technique used successfully is to require an employee wishing a replacement card to pay a fee for the new card. Although these fees help recover some of the cost incurred in this card replacement, the primary purpose is to deter negligent employees. Seek broad acceptance to this policy before recommending that the SA implement it.

Include disabling the lost or damaged card in the replacement card procedure. Even in cases where card damage is minimal (my dog chewed it, I left it in my pants and the dryer warped it, I used it as an ice scraper last week and it split) disable that card number in the electronic physical security system. It is to the company's

(Client Name) Department Submittal, Security Card Request	Revised:	11/17/03
	Version:	2-4

1. Department Requesting Card:

Date Card Requested

Department

Employee Name

Employee Title

Employee ID Number

Type of Card Request:

New

Replacement

Old Card Number:

Security Assignment:

(See departmental records for Codes)

Reader Group

Time Period

Authorization:

Supervisor Name (print)

Supervisor's Signature _____

2. Human Resources Card Assignment:

Date Assigned

Card Number Assigned

Picture Used:

From File

New

HR Representative Assigning

Print Name

Initial _____

3. Security Department:

Date Security Privilege Assigned

Security Representative:

Print Name

Initial _____

Security Department Emergency Call Log:

Telephone requests from other departments to change the security status of this card:

Date	Caller	Department	Request	Responding Officer

Figure 9.6 Card request form.

advantage to have only one legitimate credential recognized for each employee of the company.

Procedures for Dismissed Employees

Employee turnover is an unpleasant fact in companies today. Sometimes an employee leaves a company voluntarily and is ready, willing, and able to return all company property, including security credentials. At other times, a dismissal occurs that is contrary to the employee's wishes and that employee is less agreeable to these requirements. Under such circumstances, employees often fail to return their security credentials. Moreover, in situations where the termination results in hostility from the terminated employee, a level of threat exists. In these cases, securing the facility specifically against that employee is prudent.

In most cases, access to a facility may be denied by a simple set of commands entered at a workstation of the electronic physical security system. However, those commands are always based on instructions from company managers, and in a situation like the one previously described, those managers may not be aware of the urgency needed for such a request.

Assist the SA in establishing firm access denial procedures with the human resources department of the company. Encourage the SA to repeatedly inform company managers of the importance of notifying company security quickly when such a termination takes place.

Changes in card authorizations (including removing access privileges) should be communicated to company security in written form. This is a form identifying the credential to be removed from the system. However, in situations like the one described above, time is of the essence. Part of the procedures should require the terminated employee's department to contact security by telephone and immediately initiate a removal of access permissions for the subject employee. Require a confirming form from the department but deny access based on verbal instructions.

In addition to procedures for denying access, a portion of that procedure should deal with retrieval of the physical credential from a dismissed employee who has failed to surrender it upon dismissal. Much like a perpetrator whose falsified credential may be used for dishonest purposes, a dismissed employee with intent to do harm is familiar with the policies and procedures of the company and can be a far more damaging opponent than an outsider with criminal intent.

Assist the SA and human resources department and, if necessary, the company's legal department in effectively handling security during terminations. Assist the SA in preparing written procedures based on these discussions.

Procedures for Changes in Access Permissions

We have thus far dealt with the possession of the credential but it is also important to deal with the authority level assigned to that credential to fully implement company policy. In addition to employee turnover, employees move around a company (especially in large organizations) through promotions and transfers and these changes may have a significant impact on their access permissions. Written permission for changes in an employee's access privilege is as important as providing an employee with an appropriate credential.

Require department signatures when defining changes in access permissions. Permission changes and new card authorizations can easily be included on the same form to minimize paperwork.

SYSTEM TURN ON

After all processes are in place, training is complete for the staff and the written procedures finished, schedule a visit with the vendor to turn the system on. In companies with fewer than 100 employees, it may be helpful to call a brief company-wide meeting to allow the security professional to introduce the new system to all employees. This introduction should include some discussion of security procedures and the means and methods for using the various credential identification devices located throughout the facility. This meeting should emphasize the company's desire to provide a safe and secure work environment for the employees and the security of company property.

In larger companies, such meetings may not be possible but a written notification of these same concepts is appropriate. The formal introduction of this system should come from the highest level possible within the company to reinforce the company's commitment to the new security processes.

EVALUATE THE IMPLEMENTATION

Perform weekly reviews of system operations for approximately one month after system implementation. These reviews should include sampling and reading system reports to identify potential problems with system performance and discussions with employees to identify system anomalies. Recall the system vendor to perform changes or corrections to system programming and equipment installation where needed to more closely meet company objectives.

Review the performance of individuals managing and operating the system. Meetings with the SA can often reveal concerns or confusions about the installation.

Construct a practical application test for the system operator. Each operator should be tested in the early weeks to ensure that they understand the training they received. Specifically, certain aspects of system use such as opening doors from a keyboard or the meaning of certain alarm messages should be included in a quiz for each officer on an individual basis. The purpose of these exercises is not to evaluate the employee but rather to evaluate the employee's need for additional training. At the conclusion of each examination, prepare a report to the SA for handling knowledge deficiencies found in their subordinates.

Confirm the system's acceptance by department managers and other employees. Conduct at least one interview with all of the company managers involved in the selection and acquisition process for this electronic physical security system. Also, meet with the managers in key departments to determine the level of satisfaction with and acceptance of the delivered system.

Prepare a final report to the management team regarding the success of the implemented solutions. If appropriate, identify new ways to use the system to satisfy additional company needs revealed in the implementation process.

FOLLOW-UP EVALUATION AND TRAINING

When the new electronic physical security system is fully implemented and all the procedures and personnel training are in place for the system to operate as expected, the job of the security professional is essentially finished. However, the astute security professional knows that circumstances change over time and certain adjustments in system performance may be required. Revisit the company on a periodic basis to test the satisfaction with the installed system. Determine if the system requires changes or improvements to meet the ever-changing demands for security requirements.

Review the selected vendor's performance with regard to corrective and preventive maintenance. Frequently, promises made during bid submittals are not always remembered in exactly the same way presented by the vendor. For the first year of the system installation, plan on quarterly reviews to determine service satisfaction. Determine the company's level of satisfaction with the vendor's current level of service and whether competing offers may be required for future system additions and maintenance.

THE LAST WORD

The professional security consultant provides a way to bring together needs and solutions. To the company, the consultant represents the marketplace. They want the right products that will provide a safe and secure environment for their employees and their possessions without excess costs. To the marketplace, the consultant represents the business opportunity to sell their products. They want a fair opportunity to show what they can do to meet the needs of the company. The professional security consultant has a fiduciary responsibility to select the most appropriate products and services in an unbiased manner that offers the best value for the company.

The techniques in this book help the security professional reach those goals. A good business deal is one where all parties leave the table feeling that they have gained something. As a security professional, you should always strive for a win–win situation. Above all, a security professional must have integrity, honesty and a sense of fair play.

Technical skills and the knowledge and experience gained in physical security are an essential part of the job. However, ethics are paramount in any business arrangement. Even the best designed system will fail if the business arrangements are not equitable. Be forthright in dealing with the company and the vendors and remember that you are a business consultant as well as a security expert.

Appendix

Appendix 1 contains additional sample drawings for Door Detail Elevations.

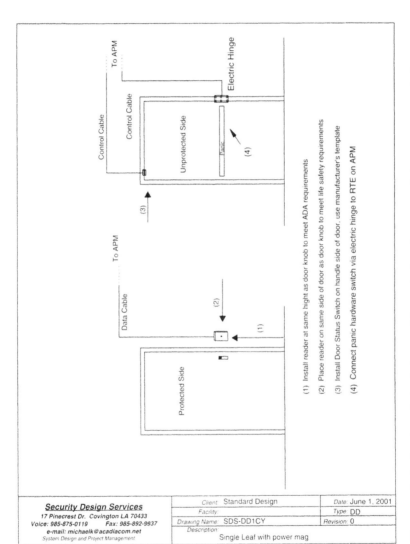

To APM

Control Cable

Control Cable

Electric Hinge

Unprotected Side

Panic

(4)

(3)

To APM

Data Cable

(2)

(1)

Protected Side

(1) Install reader at same hight as door knob to meet ADA requirements
(2) Place reader on same side of door as door knob to meet life safety requirements
(3) Install Door Status Switch on handle side of door, use manufacturer's template
(4) Connect panic hardware switch via electric hinge to RTE on APM

Security Design Services
17 Pinecrest Dr. Covington LA 70433
Voice: 985-875-0119   Fax: 985-892-9937
e-mail: michaelk@acadiacom.net
System Design and Project Management

Client: Standard Design	Date: June 1, 2001
Facility:	Type: DD
Drawing Name: SDS-DD1CY	Revision: 0
Description: Single Leaf with power mag	

Figure A-1-1 Single leaf door with panic hardware and door status switch.

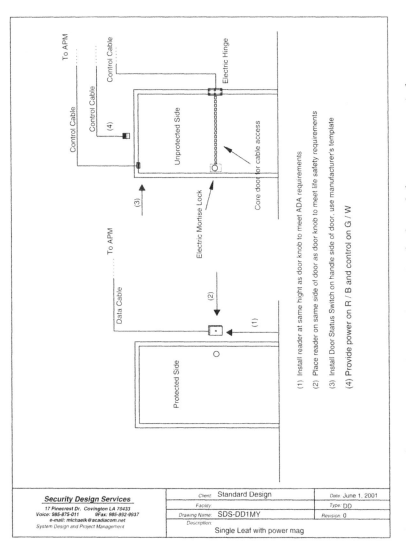

(1) Install reader at same hight as door knob to meet ADA requirements
(2) Place reader on same side of door as door knob to meet life safety requirements
(3) Install Door Status Switch on handle side of door, use manufacturer's template
(4) Provide power on R / B and control on G / W

Security Design Services
17 Pinecrest Dr. Covington LA 70433
Voice: 985-875-011   9Fax: 985-892-9937
e-mail: michaelk@acadiacom.net
System Design and Project Management

Client: Standard Design	Date: June 1, 2001
Facility:	Type: DD
Drawing Name: SDS-DD1MY	Revision: 0
Description: Single Leaf with power mag	

Figure A-1-2 Single leaf door with mortise lock and door status switch.

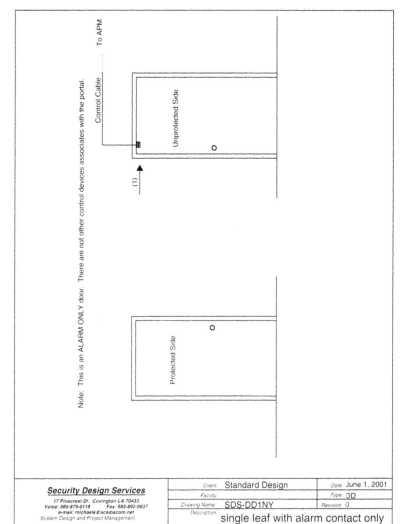

Figure A-1-3 Single leaf door with no lock and door status switch.

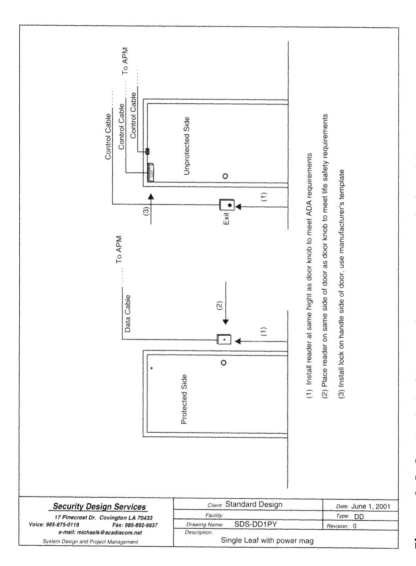

Figure A-1-4 Single leaf door with power magnet lock and door status switch.

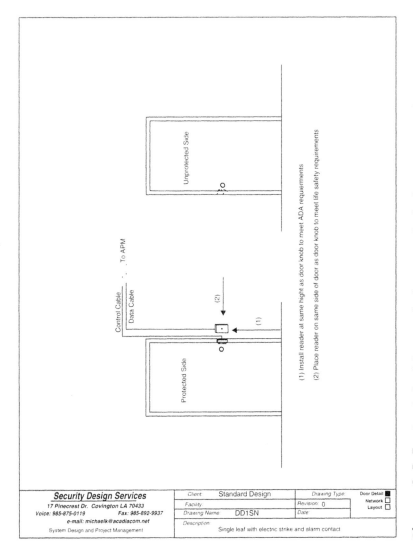

Figure A-1-5 Single leaf door with electric strike lock unmonitored.

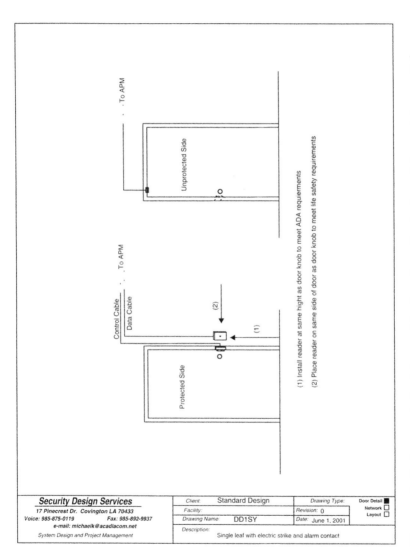

Figure A-1-6 Single leaf door with electric strike lock and door status switch.

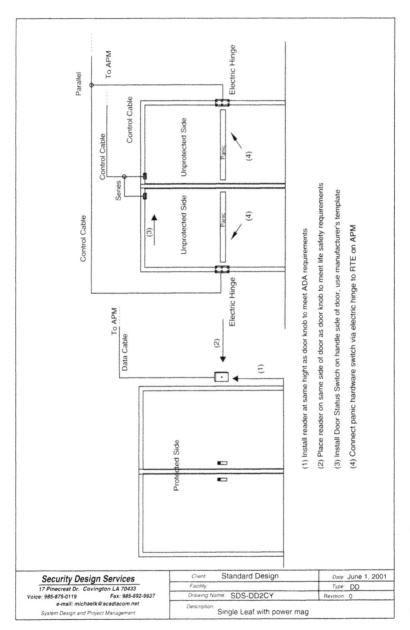

(1) Install reader at same hight as door knob to meet ADA requirements

(2) Place reader on same side of door as door knob to meet life safety requirements

(3) Install Door Status Switch on handle side of door, use manufacturer's template

(4) Connect panic hardware switch via electric hinge to RTE on APM

Security Design Services	*Client:* Standard Design	*Date:* June 1, 2001
17 Pinecrest Dr. Covington LA 70433	*Facility:*	*Type:* DD
Voice: 985-875-0119 Fax: 985-892-9937	*Drawing Name:* SDS-DD2CY	*Revision:* 0
e-mail: michaelk@acadiacom.net	*Description:*	
System Design and Project Management	Single Leaf with power mag	

Figure A-1-7 Double leaf door with panic hardware and door status switch.

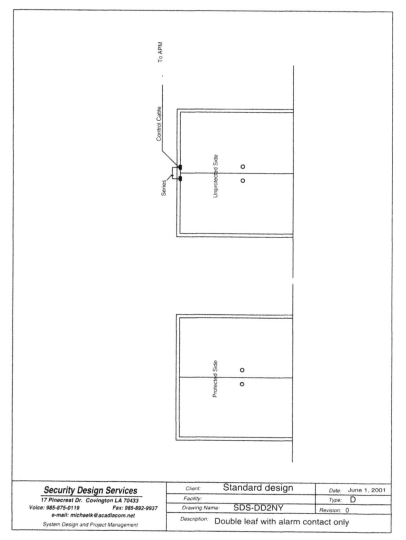

Figure A-1-8 Double leaf door with no lock and door status switch.

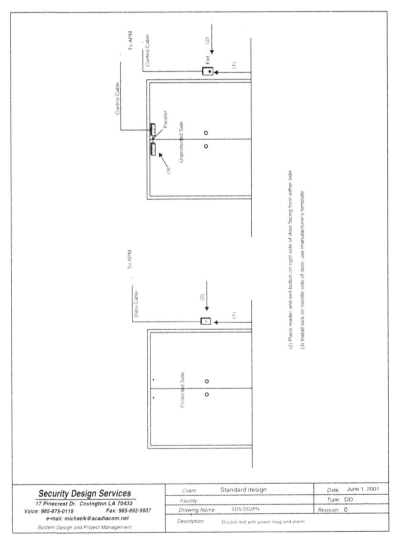

Figure A-1-9   Double leaf door with two power magnet locks, unmonitored.

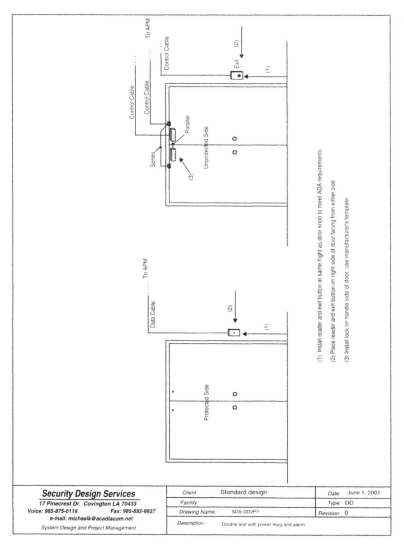

Figure A-1-10 Double leaf door with power magnet lock and door status switch.

Index

Printed and bound by CPI Group (UK) Ltd, Croydon, CR0 4YY

03/10/2024

01040433-0004